VAGABONDS ALL

"BARONET OR BUTCHER"

*A Caricature by "Ape" of Arthur Orton, the Claimant
From "Vanity Fair," June 10, 1871.*

VAGABONDS ALL

BY

SIR EDWARD ABBOTT PARRY

WITH EIGHT PLATES

Essay Index Reprint Series

 BOOKS FOR LIBRARIES PRESS
FREEPORT, NEW YORK

First Published 1926
Reprinted 1969

STANDARD BOOK NUMBER:
8369-1425-2

LIBRARY OF CONGRESS CATALOG CARD NUMBER:
73-93370

PRINTED IN THE UNITED STATES OF AMERICA

" This is your charge : you shall comprehend
all vagrom men."

Much Ado About Nothing.   Act III, Scene 3

CONTENTS

LIST OF PLATES

INTRODUCTION

I F we are to follow Dogberry's maxim and " comprehend all vagrom men " we must study the stories of their lives with the enthusiasm of an entomologist. And here Dogberry cannot assist us, for he, good easy man, was not a scientist but a much more useful human personality, namely a constable, and his comrade Verges was a head-borough.

It is one of the charms of our language that in many of its names for things we may read the history of our country. The constable is an ancient survival of the Roman occupation, being a poor relation of the *comes stabuli* or head groom of the imperial stable. The head-borough was a Saxon official, being the head of the tithing.

The Parish Constable in Dogberry's day was appointed by the Lord of the Hundred and was bound by statute to carry out the cruel laws passed by Parliament. Providentially most constables and head-boroughs were like Dogberry, inefficient, indolent, and good-natured. " I would not hang a dog by my will," he says to Verges. It was this spirit of humanity in its officers that tempered the cruelty of the laws of olden days. The Parish Constable was Nature's remedy for oppressive legislation.

Dogberry and Verges remained with us until 1872, and their departure was a sad break in a long and honourable legal tradition. Their efficient modern representatives, however, often exhibit some of Dogberry's best instincts and sound common sense. The police are, as a race, merciful men and full of forbearance towards wrong-doers.

Now when Dogberry spoke of vagrom men he was merely using a short title for the statutory phrase " rogues and vagabonds." These poor creatures in Shakespeare's time were no doubt a great social pest, but the cruelty of the laws against them did little to stop their activities. The Home Counties probably suffered more than the provinces from the depredations of Elizabethan rogues and vagabonds. Rufflers and Priggers, and Doxies and Delles, were apprenticed to crime in the great city then, exactly as they were in the days of Oliver Twist. Mr. Thomas Harman of Crayford in his *Caveat* gives a vivid picture of the Elizabethan rogues that carried on their business in Kent in 1567, and describes the laws that were then in force to put them down. A first offender was " grievously whipped and burned through the gristle of the right ear with an hot iron of the compass of an inch about, as a manifestation of his wicked life and due punishment received for the same." A second offence received a similar punishment with the addition that the misdemeanant was " set to service ; from whence, if he depart before a year be expired, and happen afterward to be attached again," he was condemned to suffer death as a felon without benefit of clergy or sanctuary.

But all this chapter of horrors had little or no effect on the daily life of Autolycus. Harman being a typical county magistrate, with an intense desire to put down these pestilent vagabonds, notes that " the punishment that is ordained for this kind of people is very sharp, and yet it cannot restrain them from that gadding, wherefore the end must needs be martial law."

How very modern in sentiment is this phrase. Each generation has had a few reformers with sufficient insight to understand that force, though necessary to restrain, is no remedy for crime. But the great bulk of the well-to-do classes still hold by capital punishment, and clamour for more corporal punishment, under the impression that these exhibitions of cruelty wreaked on A and B will deter the rest of the alphabet from similar indiscretions. History is against them. Unfortunately schoolmasters teach us to read history as though it was the story of a race that was entirely different from ourselves, whose social and political experiments have no bearing on our own lives. Whereas when you stumble on a book like Thomas Harman's *Caveat*, you meet a typical sensible county magistrate, whose ideas of sociology would be welcome in any first-class suburban railway carriage in Kent of to-day. The world moves very slowly and Harman only died quite recently, perhaps 350 years ago. Ideas do not alter much in these short periods of time.

The meaning of vagabond is well known, but rogue is a more elusive noun capable of many interpretations. It seems to have been a canting word of the sixteenth century not necessarily used with any evil meaning. With its inventors it probably connoted something endearing. A human rogue was youthful, pert, arch and saucy. You have the original sense of the word in Mrs. Mountstuart Jenkinson's description of Clara Middleton :

" A dainty rogue in porcelain."

" Why rogue ? " asks Sir Willoughby.

But as Mrs. Jenkinson, like the dictionary makers, knew nothing about the history and origin of the word she, woman-like, repeated it. Sir Willoughby Patterne shied at the sound of it. But he was a county magistrate, one of the statute-makers, and his tragedy was that he could not understand the psychology of statute-breakers.

Legislation, as far as I can make out, gave the word rogue its evil meaning, but we still use it pleasantly in the nursery. The etymology of roguery, however, is a simple affair compared with the psychology of the subject. Throughout the history of the world I find there have always been men doomed to wander the earth and others doomed to sit at home in the towns and villages of their birth. You may piously refer the phenomenon to the curse of Cain and leave it at that. Psychologists cannot explain why one man is a vagabond and another man is not, any more than mythologists can really satisfy you why " this little pig goes to market and this little pig stays at home." History records that these things happen, and perhaps the sanest course is to accept the truths we learn on our mothers' knees and not contend for further and better particulars.

For my part I think that the vagabond and the static are manifestations of youth and age. Gilbert's constable was, I suggest with submission, in error when he said that little boys and girls were born into the world either little Liberals or little Conservatives. History seems to show that they are born Liberal and grow Conservative, and probably they are born vagabond and become static, but a minority never grow up.

Vagabonds, youths, and Left Wing politicians are dominated by generous instincts for change and novelty. Statics, old men, and Right Wing politicians are obsessed with the value of the certainty of tradition. Both these aspects of life play their part in our evolution, and we must admit that if we are ever bereft of that instinct of adventure that leads weak men into vagrom ways it will be a poorer world than it is to-day. Dogberry possibly had some such reason as this at the back of his mind when he exercised his charity towards vagrom men.

The statics however are the men who frame our laws and from the earliest they have tried to make things as uncomfortable for the vagabonds as they could. The reason for this is not far to seek. The stay-at-homes, especially the employers of labour, objected to vagabonds because they diminished the amount of cheap and available labour. They included among rogues all men and women who amused and entertained the poor, because such entertainers gave an excuse to their labourers to knock off work and make holiday. All statutes against rogues and vagabonds were passed by a dominant class in the sacred cause of what industrialists call " production."

It is a curious fact that in our earliest code of law, The Ten Commandments, there is no actual commandment regulating labour, which is only incidentally mentioned in the clause which ordains a holiday. We cannot be too grateful to Moses for the careful drafting of the Fourth Commandment with its compulsory seventh day holiday. Nothing but a revolution would have wrung from any Government in modern historical times so great a blessing to mankind. Note too in the text that not only is the boss to take a holiday but a statutory right to an equal holiday is conferred upon servants and cattle. If it were decided to-day that cattle included motor-cars we could once more like Solomon say : " Come, my beloved, let us go forth into the field ; let us lodge in the villages," for there would then be Sabbath peace in the Weald of Kent.

Legislators, whether Radical or Conservative, have never shone in their dealings with holidays. Romme, the friend of the people, endeavoured with his New Calendar to repeal the commandment and cheat France and the world out of their seventh day holiday by substituting a tenth. Indignant humanity rejected this decimal fraud. Our own statutes have not done much to increase English holidays. James I it is true gave us a day off on November 5, Guy Fawkes Day, which was something of a holiday in my childhood, especially at Lewes where they had great bonfires, as I remember. Then there was May Day with Jack-in-the-Green, and May 29, when we wore oak leaves and went to church to rejoice over the restoration of the Stuarts. I think some dreary Government must have pinched these holidays for I no longer celebrate these anniversaries. But no modern politician ever gave the world a holiday except against his will, and we owe the Bank Holidays of 1871 to Lubbock and the Summer Time to Willett. Both these institutions are in the spirit of the Fourth Commandment.

Just as our rulers and masters thought we could get along without holidays so vagrom men have been under the delusion that a joyful life could be attained by perpetual holidays. The warfare between these two ideals has raged for many generations, as you may find by reading the history of vagrancy which has been treated of in many learned books.

If you study, for instance, Mr. Ribton-Turner's classic *History of Vagrants and Vagrancy* you will find that in this country there have been penal laws against vagrom men from the earliest days. Mr. Frank Aydelotte in his charming essay *Elizabethan Rogues and Vagabonds* sets out in great detail the law that Dogberry ought to have administered and the kind of people that he actually had to deal with. You cannot overrate the value of these books, but all historians appear to me to lose sight of the fact that the laws and regulations of the time merely represent the attitude of law-makers towards certain human habits and by no means accurately mirror the opinions and practice of the average citizen. Many laws of prohibition are not really desired by the majority of citizens, but are the outcome of the misplaced zeal of small-minded persons clothed in brief authority. Such laws never function smoothly. From the sixteenth to the eighteenth century what happened was, that though laws against vagrancy were passed they were often quietly ignored. For instance, until as late as 1824, actors were statutory rogues and vagabonds, but no sensible person thought any the worse of them and they were always welcomed by their countrymen from one end of the land to the other.

Another heresy, that must be guarded against, is that the rogue and vagabond was a human type that flourished in the Elizabethan age and has since died out. This is often expressed by writers on the subject, men of great learning who live in their studies and do not encounter the actual vagrom men of our own time. On the morning of the very day on which I am writing these words I have been engaged in trying a dispute relating to the estate of £1,000, left by a nomadic gentleman who lived in a caravan and hanged himself in a Sussex wood. Of six out of the seven witnesses, members of the family, all were nomadic and lived in caravans, only one could read and write, and though they were law-abiding and substantial citizens—the dispute related to a loan of £100—no member of the tribe had a bank account. There are still a large number of nomads among us, their manners and customs do not greatly differ from those of their ancestors, and many of them are worthy men and women.

Rogues and roguery are indeed for all time, and " coney-catching," as the Elizabethans called it, will continue as long as there are " conies " waiting at every corner for knaves to capture. The outward and visible methods of the vagrom man in outwitting his neighbour by tickling his vanity and self-conceit, may alter like the fashion of dress, but the human figure beneath is much the same to-day as it was in earlier historical periods. When the historian of Elizabethan rogues tells us that " in 1575 the poetry of their life began to decline and the literature of rogues and vagabonds to fall back upon tradition," he falls into the error that it is so difficult to avoid, when you spend your life in the literature of one period of time and have neither leisure nor opportunity to compare the facts you discover with what is going on in the world around you,

B

Take necromancy, for instance. Wise rulers and teachers have from the earliest times sought to put a stop to this neurotic and unhealthy pursuit. Moses at the end of his career was more outspoken about this " abomination " than any modern leader of thought in our own day. He forbade his people to be users of divination, observers of times, or enchanters or witches ; nor were they allowed to carry on the business of " a charmer, or a consulter with familiar spirits or a wizard or a necromancer."

The human " conies " of Moses's time were a ready prey to the coney-catchers of Israel who went about working on their fears and superstitions, and their love for their lost ones, just as is done to-day. Moses thought it was a bad, disreputable, swindling business and did his best to put it down. I understand that to-day Jews are more immune from these practices than Christians.

It is doubtless true that there is a human instinct which lures men, and especially women, to consult wizards and familiar spirits, and this instinct is perhaps as strong in our own day as it was in the time of Moses. The same old tricks still satisfy the same kind of people, and the idea that magic, witchcraft and necromancy were errors of our un-educated ancestors, which in our enlightened days have no hold on our minds, is quite untrue. Simon Forman or Cagliostro would have as many fashionable followers to-day as they had in their own time. Nor is there anything novel in the spectacle of men of learning and high social position patronizing these practices. King Saul himself passed some excellent legislation to " cut off those that have familiar spirits, and the wizards, out of the land," but he could not repress his own desire to visit the lady medium at Endor, with evil results to his health such as are known to modern neurologists whose foolish patients dabble in similar dissipa-tions to-day.

For it is one thing to make laws against a natural evil appetite of man and another to teach each new generation to eschew the evil they relate to. The appetite continues and, though the fashion of the manifestation alters to some extent, the basic idea of the superstition remains. This will no doubt continue with us from generation to generation until in a long course of evolution the evil appetite is acknowledged to be a futile superstition, and man will then be born without it as, generally speaking, he is now born without a tail.

And it is for this reason that vagrom men continue among us in spite of a long and vigorous warfare against them by Parliament and the Magistracy. The idea that vagrancy ceased in the sixteenth or seventeenth century is incorrect. Indeed in many ways its flagrancy was more remarkable in the eighteenth century than at any earlier time.

I have a quaint little volume, published in 1708 for Thomas Bever at the Hand and Star near Temple Bar, called *The Compleat Constable*. It contains directions to Constables, Head-Boroughs, Church Wardens and other Dogberries, how to deal with vagrom men. The statutes made for punishing rogues, vagabonds, night-walkers and such other idle persons are, says our anonymous legal author, " a large Branch of the Constable's office and herein two things are to be known :—

" 1. What a Rogue is and who is to be accounted a Vagabond ?

" 2. What is to be done with them ? "

The charming impersonal technical spirit of this little work is beyond all praise. Not a word is ever used to remind you that, after all, a rogue and a vagabond is a man and a brother. You are taught first to diagnose him, as Izaak Walton would teach the young angler how to discover the wise eel that did not usually stir in the daytime, and having captured your rogue and vagabond you are then enlightened as to the various methods of killing or curing him.

And first you are to note that all persons above the age of seven, man or woman, married or single, that wander abroad without a lawful passport and give no good account of their travel are accounted rogues. Then follows a very lengthy list of such as are " of a higher degree and are to be accounted as Rogues, Vagabonds and sturdy Beggars." Such are all Scholars and Sea-faring men that beg, wandering persons using unlawful games, subtle crafts, or plays, or pretending to have skill in telling fortunes by the marks or figures on the hands or face. All Jugglers or Slight-of-hand Artists pretending to do wonders by virtue of Hocus Pocus, the Powder of Pimper le Pimp, or the like ; all Tinkers, Pedlars, Chapmen, Glassmen, especially if they be not well known or have a sufficient testimonial. All collectors for Jails or Hospitals, Fencers, Bearwards, common players of interludes, and Fiddlers or Minstrels wandering abroad. Also Persons delivered out of Jails who beg their fees, such as go to and from the Baths and do not pursue their License, Soldiers and Mariners that beg and counterfeit certificates from their commanders. And, lastly : " All Labourers which wander abroad, out of their respective Parishes, and refuse to work for wages reasonably taxed, having no Livelyhood otherwise to maintain themselves, and such as go with general Passports not directed from Parish to Parish."

Having dealt in accurate detail with the classification and identification of rogues, we come next to the chapter on treatment, which is best given in the simple words of the original. " The Punishment is after this manner. The Constable, Headburrough or Tything-man assisted by the Minister and one other of the Parish, is to see (or do it himself), that such Rogues and Vagabonds, etc., be stript Naked from the middle upwards and openly Whipped till their Body be bloody and then forthwith to be sent away from Constable to Constable, the next straight way to the place of their Birth ; and if that cannot be known then to the place where they last Dwelt, by the space of one whole Year before the time of such their Punishment ; and if that cannot be known then to the Town through which they last passed unpunished." If, however, none of these habitats was discoverable, the vagrom man was sent to the House of Correction or common jail, where he was put to hard labour for twelve months.

It is only fair to remember, " that after such Vagabond is whipt as aforesaid he is to have a Testimonial "—is this the origin of people asking for testimonials ?—" under the hand and seal of the Constable or Tything-man and the Minister, testifying the day and place of his Punishment ; as also the place to which he is to be conveyed, and the time limited for his Passage thither :   And if by his own default he exceed that time then he is again to be whipt—and so from time to time till he arrive at the place limited."

One cannot shut one's eyes to the fact that this is pure class legislation actuated by a desire to uphold the social convenience of a large reserve of cheap labour which was not to be distracted from the duty of working for others by the insidious temptations to indolence introduced by travelling bands of entertainers.   It is all well meant but it naturally breeds discontent in its victims.

The vitality of vagrom men in the face of penalties such as these is indeed remarkable.   Men who are imbued with the desire to wander and seek adventure will, it seems, never be greatly hindered in their movements by statutes and rules and orders.   The overpowering longing for the open road, the call of " the long brown path before me leading wherever I choose ", is not to be stifled by fears of the stocks, the whipping-post or even the gallows.   Bampfylde-Moore Carew with his strange love of mendicancy, Jamie Allan fingering his beloved pipes, and Daniel Dunglass Home dreaming of strange visions and a new world of dupes, could not remain static like the home-keeping little pig, but all had to go out into the market of the world and sell their gifts and realize their fortunes. These are the kind of vagrom men that the statutes of the righteous sought to destroy. Luckily Dogberry has always been a man of strong common sense. He sees the futility of interfering with these favourites of the mob and wisely advises his watch " the less you meddle or make with them why the more for your honesty."

In selecting the lives of the various vagrom men and women in this volume I have endeavoured to choose types of the rogues and vagabonds described in the statutes. It is for this reason that a portrait of Samuel Foote figures in this gallery. He was an actor and dramatist and gentleman for whom I have a high regard, but not only was he technically a rogue and vagabond, as indeed all actors then were who were not His Majesty's servants, but as a " player of inter-ludes " the Shallows of Westminster actually interfered under their statutory powers with his performances, and the witty method by which he evaded their pedantic stupidity is worthy of remembrance. It is good to remember that the popular verdict overruled the decision of the Westminster Bench.

But because some of the men and women portrayed here are evil-doers it is not at all true that all vagrom men are worthy of the whipping-post. Many of them have excellent qualities, and even the worst of them are, as we shall see, followed and beloved by disciples whose self-deceit is the main factor in their hero's undoing.

Bampfylde-Moore Carew was a strange affectionate creature, and had troops of friends among the country gentlemen of Devonshire. Daniel Dunglass Home lived on his friends and followers, and in spite of his cupidity and deceit was nevertheless honoured by many of them to the last. Robin Hood, if he ever existed, was by all accounts a splendid fellow and a credit to the noble army of vagrom men. And it is curious to observe that, however obvious the ill-behaviour of vagrom men may be to magistrates and more serious citizens, they have all the divine gift that Falstaff—himself a delightful specimen of the race—possessed in a high degree, namely the power of inspiring love and faith and service in their followers.

Some day a psychologist will explain for us why we deceive ourselves about these vagrom brethren of ours. Why did we passionately believe in the claims of that absurdly vulgar impostor Arthur Orton ? Why did the county people of Cumberland entertain John Hatfield merely because he entered Keswick with fine horses and a travelling chariot ? Why should the sensitive Mrs. Browning tolerate a human sponge like Daniel Dunglass Home ? Why did the simple peasants of Kent follow the madman Tom to the grave or the gallows ? When you read of these things you are momentarily inclined to the belief that such beings must have given their supporters medicines to gain their love. In the cold grey light of a new generation these debauches of unreason read like fables and fairy tales.

In the future, scientists and physicians may be able to explain to us why Esau was a wanderer and a vagabond and Jacob stayed at home and was a knave. In spite of priestly explanations and apologies it seems to me that trickery and deceit did not at all periods of the world's history meet with divine disapproval, and it appears from Jacob's successful career that knavery is not necessarily a bar to worldly prosperity.

There is a very large literature both historical and scientific about the criminal and his why and wherefore. His

INTRODUCTION

younger cousin the rogue and vagabond has received far less attention, mainly, as I gather, because historians have concluded that when the phrase dropped out of the statutes the men and women who were so described ceased to function.

This I think is quite erroneous. A perusal of the daily newspapers, and especially the columns of *Truth*, would show us not only that vagrom men still fascinate and dupe mankind, in the same old agreeable way as of old, but that many of the ancient methods of coney-catching are still practised with much the same ritual as that used three hundred years ago. Moreover Providence still continues to supply a large reserve of simple, trusting conies as fodder for vagrom men.

VAGABONDS ALL

CHAPTER I

ARTHUR ORTON, THE CLAIMANT

ARTHUR ORTON, the Claimant to the Tichborne estates, was a vulgar rogue and vagabond. In Australia he lived the life of a roughrider, bushranger and cattleman, who might in middle age have settled down to a decent life, had not temptation and the greed and folly of others lured him into the limelight, and forced upon him the star part of a dangerous impostor, a reckless liar and, up to a point, an amazingly successful criminal.

The chief sinner against the wretched fool Orton was Henriette Félicité, Lady Tichborne, who, mourning for her lost son Roger long ago drowned at sea, was in a frame of mind ready, as one of the witnesses at the trial testified, to recognize an Egyptian mummy as her drowned son if they had brought one to her. Other dupes and knaves pushed or lured Arthur Orton along the path of destruction and the man himself was little more than a willing tool in their hands.

The imps of the Comic Spirit never before planned such an absurd tragic farce as this drama of the Claimant. Had they carried Caliban into the cradle of Sir Willoughby Patterne, the high priest of fiction must have failed in imposing the fraud on mankind. But men and women of all classes of society leapt to greet this coarse impostor and hailed the obviously " Bullocky " Orton as the new incarnation of the soldierly young baronet, Roger Tichborne.

Old Etheridge, the Alresford blacksmith, when Orton appeared to him and asked him, " Do you believe I am Roger Tichborne ? " looked at him and laughed.

" No, I'll be damned if you are," he replied ; " if you are you have turned from a race-horse to a cart-horse."

The smith knew all about the evolution of horses, and knowing that horses " don't do such things " argued that men and other animals followed a like rule.

But this obvious piece of reasoning was of no purpose to the fool multitude who scented a miracle. The mere fact that every word that fell from the rascal's lips bespoke his origin whetted their belief. The wish to believe is the broth on which the microbe of imposture feeds and multiplies. The man-monster was the hero of a fairy tale. Yes, here was a real fairy tale, and the mob loves fairy tales. *Quod homines volunt id facile credunt.* Men believe what they wish to believe to-day in London as they did in ancient Rome.

The real miracle is not the whale swallowing Jonah but the people swallowing the story. A study of legend, folk-lore and necromancy shows us that if the story had been that Jonah swallowed the whale it would have been received with equal simple, honest enthusiasm. Poor Orton, like many another weak-minded quack, medium or impostor, was carried to his doom on the shoulders of the imps of the Comic Spirit who dangle impostures before a gaping mob to enjoy the absurdity of their discomfiture. When you read the wretched man's story you will marvel how he ever got as far as he did on his career of fraud. That is accounted for by the folly of those who dragged him out of obscurity to act in their wicked comedy, and who in justice should have borne some of the punishment that fell so heavily on their star artist at the fall of the curtain.

ARTHUR ORTON

Arthur Orton was the son of old George Orton, a shipping butcher of High Street, Wapping, a respectable old man esteemed by his neighbours. He had twelve children, eight sons and four daughters. Arthur, the youngest, was born in March, 1834. Others we hear of later were Charles, Mary Ann (Mrs. Tredgett) and Margaret Ann (Mrs. Jury). Arthur went to local schools but was never much of a scholar, as from an early age he was afflicted with St. Vitus's dance. This was caused by fright due to a fire that broke out near his father's house, and the malady continued for some years and is said to have affected his intellect. He was early removed from school and taught the trade of a butcher in his father's shop.

His illness continuing, his father sent him to sea for his health, and he was apprenticed to Captain Brooks of the *Ocean* which sailed for Valparaiso. Here in June, 1849, Arthur Orton deserted his ship and started his vagabond career. Fearing to be arrested by the local police, he made his way inland forty miles to Melipilla. In this village he was befriended by a Dr. Hayley and lived with Don Thomas Castro, who kept a grocery store. Here he remained for two years and learned Spanish, and in June, 1851, he returned to Wapping and worked with his father. He stayed at home until November, 1852, during which time he became engaged to a young lady of the neighbourhood called Mary Anne Loder.

Wapping and Mary Anne Loder had not sufficient charms to overcome his vagabond instincts, and Mr. Chapman, a friend of his father, wanting a man to undertake the care of some Shetland ponies that he was exporting to Hobart Town, young Orton engaged to sail in the *Middleton* as butcher and take charge of the ponies. At that time he is described as weighing thirteen stone, standing 5 feet 9½ inches, and of fair complexion.

Arthur arrived at Hobart Town in April, 1853. He had a letter of introduction to Mrs. Mina Jury—the Jurys were a family connected by marriage with the Ortons. This lady knew him in Hobart Town for two years and was very kind to him. Before she came to England in June, 1855, she had lent him some money and gave him a five-pound note accidentally for a one-pound note, which he denied. Later on he wrote and acknowledged the theft and sent her a promissory note which I need hardly say the rascal did not honour.

He was in several employments as stock-keeper and cattleman, and Arthur Orton's career is easily followed until he determined to play the part of Roger Tichborne, when, of course, Orton had to disappear.

In 1855 he was employed by Mr. Johnstone at Mewburn Park. In 1856 he was with Mr. Foster at Boisdale, and afterwards at Dargo. On July 1, 1858, he rode up to Foster's house and told him Dargo was too lonely since the disappearance of his chum, " Ballarat Harry," who had been found murdered in the bush. Suspicion of the murder fell upon Orton, but there is no evidence of his guilt. He was then at Flodden Creek and at Sale. Then he went to Reedy Creek until the end of 1859, when there was a warrant out against him for stealing a horse, and he disappeared.

His own story of this episode, which is set down in his confession published after he came out of jail, is that when he was in the service of Mr. Mahon of Reedy Creek Diggings as a slaughterman he was without money and the wandering spirit seized him. He stole his employer's horse, rode fifty miles to Castlemaine, where, under the name of Johnny Paisley, a noted bushranger, he sold the horse. Thence he trained to Sandhurst, a hundred miles away, and came to Wagga Wagga, where he took the name of his old employer, Tom Castro. There is plenty of other evidence that Arthur

Orton and Tom Castro were the same person, but the above is his own account of the matter.

At Wagga Wagga he worked as a butcher and in January, 1865, married a servant girl named Mary Ann Bryant. He was married by a Wesleyan minister, giving the name of Castro and Orton's correct age, which was thirty.

Up to this date Arthur Orton had never conceived the idea of claiming the Tichborne estates and knew nothing whatever of Roger Tichborne or his family. The tragedy of his life was that they were ever introduced to his rascal greedy mind, and that after he had once allowed himself to pose as the lost Sir Roger every assistance of fools and knaves was thrust upon him, so that he could never escape from the chains of his own imposture. His life from this time onwards is an exhibit to the text :

> O, what a tangled web we weave,
> When first we practise to deceive!

Roger Charles Tichborne, a Catholic and the heir to a baronetcy and £20,000 a year, had been drowned at sea in 1854. The last letter he wrote home was on April 1 of that year. He went on board the *Bella* at Rio on the 20th and the ship foundered with all hands. There was no doubt of his death, which was duly presumed in the Courts, his will was proved and his brother succeeded to the estates, and when he died in 1866 this brother's infant child succeeded his father.

The trouble arose through the delusion of Lady Tichborne, Roger's mother, that her son was not dead and that some day he would return to her. Although in 1865 he had been dead for some eleven years she became every year more impressed with the belief that he would return, and spent considerable sums of money in issuing advertisements in foreign papers describing Roger's appearance and giving details of the properties and estates that he was heir to.

In 1865, when Arthur Orton married in the name of Tom Castro at the age of thirty, Roger Tichborne would have been thirty-six. Arthur Orton had been living a life of roguery, crime and penury, although, of course, if he had been Roger Tichborne he might have stepped back into wealth and comfort at any moment. But until 1865 Arthur Orton, or Tom Castro, had, as I have said, never heard of the Tichbornes, but on occasion being a liar and romancer he had told his pals that he had known better days, and so, in truth, he had in his father's house at Wapping.

His first introduction to the Tichborne affair was when his friend Dick Slade, or Slate, handed him a copy of the *Australian Times* and called his attention to a " funny advertisement." It was one of Lady Tichborne's appeals for her son to return. By way of a joke Tom Castro pretended to be very affected when he read it and Dick Slade, after the manner of his kind, was deeply impressed and asked Tom what he knew about it. Tom Castro only shook his head mysteriously and said nothing. This, of course, deepened the impression already formed in Dick's fertile imagination.

Now at this time Castro was in debt and Gibbes, a local attorney, was piloting him through the insolvency Court. He had boasted to Gibbes that he was coming into money, as bankrupts often do, and when Dick Slade told Gibbes what he had heard and seen, the attorney got very excited about it.

Meanwhile, " Bullocky " Orton pondered over the advertisement. The idea came into his dull mind that he might raise money by fraudulently personating Tichborne in Australia, sail for England by way of America, and disappear in the Far West. At this time Tom Castro was slaughterman to one Higgins of Wagga Wagga, and in a little pocket-book of his, which was afterwards discovered, you find some entries that show the trend of his mind.

He had been reading Miss Braddon's interesting novel, *Aurora Floyd*, and a passage in it had struck him as memorable and important. He sets it down as near as he can copy it in his illiterate way : " Some men has plenty of money and no brains, and some men has plenty of brains and no money. Surely men with plenty of money and no brains were made for men with plenty of brains and no money. R. C. Tichborne bart."

In the same book we find that he writes : " R. C. Tichborne, Tichborne Hall, Surrey," whereas Tichborne Park was in Hampshire. On another page is the name and address of Miss Mary Anne Loder, who, you remember, was Arthur Orton's sweetheart, the girl he had left behind him at Wapping.

Orton carves the initials " R. C. T. " on his pipe, and we find him practising an autograph signature in which he signs " Rodger " for Roger. As early as April 13, 1865, he writes to a Mr. Richardson at Wapping in the name of Castro asking for information about the Orton family. It is clear, therefore, that the idea of posing to the world as Roger Tichborne, who had been living under the disguise of Thomas Castro, began to ferment in his brain soon after he read the advertisement, but it was necessary to dispose of the Orton career. If his respectable old father, George, had been alive I do not think he would have dared to make his appearance in England.

There was a man named Cubitt who ran a missing friends' agency in Sydney at this time, who was in correspondence with Lady Tichborne and who got into touch with Gibbes, the attorney. It was Slade who excited Gibbes in the first instance and Orton kept the fires of his curiosity going by subtle hints of a strange past. He tells Gibbes that Castro is an assumed name ; that he is really heir to an English estate. He used to tell lies of this kind to the Castros when he was a boy. On another occasion he drops a hint that he has been shipwrecked and will never venture to sea again. He talks to his attorney of the climate of South America, and Gibbes hurries down to the local institution to read the advertisements again, having come to the absolute conclusion that his insolvent client is the missing heir.

The next day he visits Castro and finds him smoking a pipe on the veranda. He gazes at Tom in amazement, for his eyes are riveted on the pipe and the initials " R. C. T. " on the bowl of it.

" God bless my soul ! " he cries. " I have spotted you. You are Roger Tichborne ; they have been advertising for you. I see the initials on your pipe."

Tom Castro begs his friend to be quiet about it, but the attorney cannot contain himself.

" There you are ! You are the man ! " he cries gleefully. Tom pockets his pipe sulkily.

" I tell you what," said Gibbes sternly, " if you do not write to your mother in a month, I will."

From that moment Arthur Orton was launched on a career of crime that was to land him in jail for many years, ruin countless innocent enthusiasts, disturb the peace and happiness of an innocent family, and cast a heavy burden on the State in exposing and punishing the criminal. That Arthur Orton at the moment had any clear intention of following up the fraud by making an appearance in England, I think is quite unlikely. He himself in his after-confession declares that his original idea was to obtain money and clear away to America. But Fate was too strong for him. The lie once told he was forced by circumstances to live up to it, and in the end so popular was the delusion among his dupes that the man himself declared there were times when he almost believed himself that he was not Arthur Orton but Roger Tichborne.

The great art of successful imposture lies in permitting your dupes to cheat their willing selves. Gibbes, the attorney, was an enthusiast, and Cubitt, the agent in Sydney, was delighted to hear his good news. Both saw fees in the business no doubt, but there was money to be advanced before money could come in. Gibbes was not a very intelligent man and Orton found it easy to impose upon him. He knew little or nothing at that time about Roger Tichborne's career, but was careless enough to mention several things in his own career, such as the fact that his education was interfered with by St. Vitus's dance, a disease which Roger Tichborne had never suffered from.

He now wrote a very illiterate letter to his " dear Mama " and Cubitt and Gibbes wrote their accounts of him, which should, one thinks, have aroused her suspicions, but she was so eager to welcome a lost son that she sent money across to him, and herself advised that he should find and take into his service a negro named Bogle who was once a servant of Sir Edward Doughty, Roger's uncle, but who now resided at Sydney.

Here again is the hand of Fate pushing Arthur Orton vigorously along his road to jail. By June, 1866, he had been able to leave Wagga Wagga and go to Sydney with £50 borrowed from Gibbes and the bank. Before he does this he has had to make a ridiculous will as some sort of security, and sign bills for £500 in favour of Gibbes. Arthur Orton is already enjoying his new life. He lives at the Metropolitan Hotel, rides and drives about the place, and puts in a good deal of time in the billiard room. Bogle had read of his arrival and went down to the hotel to have a look at him.

Orton is coming out of the billiard room and sees the negro in the yard.

C

" Hello ! Bogle, is that you ? " he calls out.

" Yes, sir," says Bogle, much pleased.

" I shall see you shortly," says the other, and later on Bogle is taken up to Orton's room.

The conversation is a success. From the first Orton seems to have been extremely successful in doling out what information he possessed to simple people and satisfying their uncritical minds. Bogle is reminded of a few names and incidents that Orton had already collected and the old man recognizes Sir Roger without delay.

Orton took him into his service at once and borrowed his savings to the tune of £300. The recognition of Orton by Lady Tichborne was, of course, Orton's trump-card, but after that I think the touching devotion of the dear old white-polled negro, Bogle, went far with the common people to make them sure that the impostor was the real man. Lord Chief Justice Cockburn said that in his view old man Bogle was a good specimen of the negro race and an honest fellow at heart and that he believed in his new master. That Bogle was a godsend to Arthur Orton at the outset of his career as Tichborne is beyond doubt. He pumped him as to the names and habits of all the members of the Tichborne family and through his aid made a better show as Sir Roger on his arrival in England than anyone could have expected. In return for these services Orton ruined the old man and the small family pension that he had received from the Tichbornes was taken away from him.

It is an extraordinary thing in the history of finance that banks, and financiers, and even governments will readily give millions to fraudulent and wild-cat schemes, but to the poor and honest, who are ready to labour to repay, the purse is closed and the strings drawn tight. No one would have given Tom Castro, slaughterman of Wagga Wagga, in financial difficulties, £100 to open a new shop. But Tom

Castro swaggering around Sydney as Sir Roger Tichborne had as much money at his command as was necessary for his schemes. Greed and a gambling spirit seem at the bottom of the ease with which fools are fleeced.

Apart from Bogle's savings Orton got three separate sums of £600, £300 and £300 from three separate and credulous creditors, and having paid off Gibbes and enjoyed a good time at Sydney he sailed for Panama on September 2, 1866, on the *Rachaia* with £600 in gold. The party consisted of himself, his wife, child and a maid, old Bogle, and young Mr. Butts, the hotel-keeper's son at Sydney, who acted as the baronet's secretary and represented the financial interests of Australia in the recovery of the estates.

At Panama he was already hard up but had no difficulty in raising £300 on a bill, and found that the interest in him was so great that his idea of escaping to California and leaving Bogle and young Butts was quite out of the question, so he determined to face the music and come across to England, where he arrived on Christmas night, 1866.

When they reach the docks he asks Bogle what hotel he should go to and Bogle tells him the family always went to Ford's in Manchester Square, so he goes there and the party arrives about five or six in the afternoon. Now Arthur Orton was not only a rogue but a dull, stupid rogue at that. If he had had a glimmer of sense he must have recognized that openly to interest himself in his own family was courting destruction. Yet so greatly did he fear recognition by some of the Ortons, and so eager was he to learn what he could about the present members of the family, that the first act of the new-found baronet was to leave his comfortable hotel and putting himself into a four-wheeled cab drive down to Wapping.

About eight or nine o'clock he arrives at " The Globe " public-house muffled up in a pea-jacket with a big comforter round his throat and wearing a peaked cap. Mrs. Jackson, the landlady, gives him a cigar and a glass of sherry and he starts on his inquiries at once.

" What has become of the Ortons ? They used to live in High Street. I have been there knocking and I cannot get in."

Then the good lady tells him that old Orton and his wife are dead and the girls married and dispersed, but brother Charles is at the end of the street where he has a butcher's shop and shall they send for him ? But Arthur does not want to see any of them. Then Mrs. Fairhead, Mrs. Jackson's mother, comes in and Arthur has more cigars and sherry and surprises the old lady with his local knowledge of Wapping, so that at last she insists that he must be the Orton who went away twelve or fourteen years ago, because he is so like his father and mother, but this he stoutly denies and after an hour's chat passes out into the wintry night. But not out of the good ladies' memories, and in years to come they are called upon to relate the account of the mysterious stranger's visit to Wapping on Christmas night and to identify Arthur Orton as the prisoner at the bar.

That Orton was in considerable trepidation at the fraud he proposed to carry through was evident from his movements. He kept carefully out of the way of any members or agents of the Tichborne family. Leaving Bogle in London he and his family concealed themselves at Gravesend. One day, meeting with a brewer's traveller named Leete at Cannon Street Station, he scrapes acquaintance with him. That gentleman introduces him to Mr. Holmes, an attorney, and these two friends are in constant attendance upon him advising him how to proceed.

Before this, however, he makes a clandestine visit to Alresford on Saturday, December 30, and puts up at " The Swan," which was kept by Mr. Rous, a former clerk of the solicitors to the Tichborne family. He arrives as a Mr. Taylor, but on the 30th he announces to Mr. Rous that he is Roger Tichborne and Rous accepts him as the lost heir. Having made this valuable alliance he wires for Bogle, who comes down and is welcomed by four or five hundred inhabitants who remember the old negro and are ready to follow his lead in recognizing Sir Roger. On Sunday, January 1, Bogle goes to the Catholic Church at Tichborne and pays a visit to the house and looks at the old pictures. All this is done in order that when Arthur Orton does at last see Lady Tichborne he may have some knowledge of the home and county he is claiming as his own.

Mr. Holmes strongly advises him to go over to Paris to be identified by his mother and, taking his new friend, Mr. Leete, the three arrive in Paris on January 10. They put up at the Hôtel de Lille et d'Albion and Orton, who is undoubtedly in great dread of the interview, goes to bed and announces that he is ill. The next morning he dresses himself and lies on the bed. Holmes and Leete then go to the Place de la Madeleine to tell Lady Tichborne the news. She asks them whether they thought he would get the property and one of them replies : " As sure as you are sitting in that chair."

In the afternoon she visited the hotel to see him. Her servant, a man named Coyne, describes the eventful meeting. Orton himself could never give any connected account of the matter, and Holmes and Leete were never called as witnesses. Poor Lady Tichborne died, fortunately for her peace of mind, before the trials took place.

Coyne says : " I went with Lady Tichborne to the hotel, and showed her up to the room where the Claimant was. I went in myself and saw the Claimant. Lady Tichborne walked in first, and I and Mr. Holmes walked in afterwards. He was lying on the bed with the clothes on. He was lying with his face towards the wall. She stood over him and kissed him, and he stopped so with his face to the wall. She said : ' He looks like his father and his ears look like his uncle's.' As soon as she said that she turned round and told me to take the clothes off as he was nearly stifled. He told me to put some coals on the fire. Mr. Holmes said : ' You witness that ; you hear how she has identified him ? ' and I said : ' So do you.' Did he say anything ? No. Did he remain lying on the bed ? Yes."

In this strange fashion did Lady Tichborne identify and acknowledge Arthur Orton, the ex-slaughterman and horse thief of Wagga Wagga, as her dearly loved and long-sought-for son, Roger Charles Tichborne, baronet and heir to the Tichborne estates. It is clear that the poor lady had gone to the interview with the intention of identifying the man, and not even the repellent sight of him lying like a hog on the bed could alter her fixed determination, nor did she ever to the day of her death go back on her decision.

It was this act that created the great Tichborne myth. Up to now even Arthur Orton had gone about the fraud with strange hesitancy. His adherents were at present the faithful Bogle, the innkeeper Rous, his new-found friend, Leete, and Mr. Holmes, attorney, who was not, we may suppose, in the business for any sentimental reasons. A claimant recognized by his mother was from a legal, sporting and dramatic point of view a very different person from a man from the bush with a nigger retainer. Mr. Holmes was triumphant, Leete was jubilant and Arthur Orton himself rapidly got the better of his indisposition.

From this time forward there was no possibility of retreat except into the hands of the police. Nor did the rascal desire to go back on his fraud, as all that was required of him was to try and learn something of the past of the dead man in whose shoes he was standing and, for the rest, he could ride, play billiards, shoot pigeons and carouse with his low friends to his heart's content.

From this moment, though the Tichborne family refused to recognize him, Orton was a popular hero, the centre of a strange myth that he was kept out of his estates by a Jesuit conspiracy. Even the two long trials and the evidence collected from all parts of the world failed to convince everyone of the obvious history of Arthur Orton, so greatly does the mind of man prefer melodrama and mythology to the truth, the whole truth, and nothing but the truth.

It would be interesting to know what Mr. Holmes, attorney, thought of his strange client and how the matter was regarded by Mr. Leete, brewer's traveller, at this juncture. Had Lady Tichborne renounced Orton there would have been an end of the fraud, but who would dare to suggest that a mother could be mistaken as to her child? Lady Tichborne renewed her declaration of identity before Sir Joseph Olliffe, the physician to the Embassy, Arthur Orton got out of bed and dined and chatted with "dear Mama," and Mr. Attorney Holmes wrote a letter to *The Times* announcing these facts and stating that Sir Roger would come to England and take over his estates. The little grain of mustard seed that Gibbes and Cubitt had sowed in the greedy heart of Arthur Orton in far Australia had indeed burgeoned out into a mighty tree. Here was to be shelter for the obscene birds of the law and other scoundrels with their attendant flocks of greedy dupes, who, from this vantage-point, hoped to descend upon a wealthy estate and ruin the innocent in pursuit of riches for themselves. Never before had such a torrent of false witnessing flooded our courts, leaving behind it a wrack of mud and misery and destruction that was only cleaned up with the greatest difficulty by the devoted labour of the ministers of the law.

Lady Tichborne, as Orton said in his confession, " was

everything that was kind and good to me and if she had been an angel she could not possibly have done more for me than she did." A house was taken at Essex Lodge, Croydon, near to his solicitor, Holmes. Lady Tichborne allowed Orton £1,000 a year and lived with him and his family. Bogle was retained. Rous, the innkeeper of Alresford, was consulted. Old Mr. Hopkins, a former solicitor of the Tichborne family, joined the group, and a Mr. Baigent, an antiquary and genealogist of Hampshire, proved a most useful ally. Two old soldier servants of Sir Roger Tichborne were taken into service at Essex Lodge and Orton's memory began gradually to brighten up in an extraordinary way about the details of Sir Roger's early life. The friends and relations of the deceased declared the man an impostor, but many old acquaintances followed the example of Lady Tichborne. Meanwhile, the public, who only knew the bare fact that the Claimant was recognized by his mother, were at once convinced that he was the real Simon Pure.

No one at that time, either among his supporters or his opponents, had heard of Arthur Orton. He kept that part of his story locked in his own bosom. But it was necessary to watch the movements of his relations, and privately he posed to them as one who had met and known their brother in Australia and had so esteemed him that now he was coming into his own it was his pleasure to assist them.

You will remember his early visit to Wapping. After that he had corresponded with his family for a while under a false name and then, giving them an address at Liverpool, ceased connexion with them. But towards the end of 1867, when he began to take ejectment proceedings against the Tichbornes, the other side had found out something about Arthur Orton, so he reopened a correspondence with his brother Charles and his sisters, Mrs. Tredgett and Mrs. Jury, and sent them money. Charles had an allowance of £5 a month for several·months, and when it was necessary for Arthur to go to Chile, where a commission had been appointed to examine the Castro witnesses at Melipilla, he made no provision for brother Charles, who fraternally revenged himself by making an affidavit for the other side acknowledging that Sir Roger was brother Arthur.

When the Chile Commission was appointed the Claimant was to go to Chile to face the witnesses. We can imagine Arthur Orton's distaste for this task, for Sir Roger had never met them and they had known Orton well for nearly two years. However, he sails and returns, but he does not meet the witnesses and Mr. Holmes, his attorney, is so disgusted with him that he throws him over. Rous, the innkeeper, also deserts him, and to any ordinary impostor these defections would have been a serious check.

But by this time the Claimant was a public institution and a popular one at that. Arthur Orton, horse-slaughterer, was a myth and a cult, with high priests running the show and acolytes and disciples ready to lay down their fortunes at his feet. He could no more get away from the imposture he had set on foot than Canute could control the waves of the sea. There had been large subscriptions for him. Tichborne bonds had been the subject of investment of savings by enthusiastic dupes, and great men of business had lent him huge sums of money. It is alleged that Mr. Guildford Onslow lent him £80,000 and two ladies of his family £30,000 apiece, and Earl Rivers £163,000. But even if these amounts are exaggerated, immense sums of money were invested in Arthur Orton, the people were backing their favourite, and there was a public gamble on his winning the case.

On March 12, 1868, poor Lady Tichborne died suddenly of heart disease. Orton tried to get hold of her estate, but the law ruled that it must stay in the hands of a receiver until his case was decided. Later in the year Hopkins died.

Baigent was alarmed, but so much money was now at stake that Orton's backers, and the money-lenders to whom his suit was mortgaged, insisted on his going to the starting-post. More money was found, the new Tichborne bonds were well subscribed, fresh lawyers were retained and the litigation pursued its dignified course.

There was an Australian Commission to examine more witnesses, and it was not until January, 1871, that the case was opened. This is not the place to tell the story of the trial. Serjeant Ballantine led for the plaintiff and conducted the case with great tact and skill. Coleridge's cross-examination of our hero left little doubt in the minds of those who heard it that the man in the box was Arthur Orton. Hawkins demolished the crafty Baigent, but the public could not follow the complicated detail of the mass of evidence and a lot of respectable people who knew little about it honestly testified that he was Sir Roger Tichborne.

It was not until Coleridge opened the defendant's case that the world for the first time heard in a clear and consistent narrative the origin and growth of the myth that had been deceiving its dupes for so many years. It was certainly a marvellous piece of advocacy, pitiless and scathing, but well reasoned and restrained. He promised the jury in his opening words that he would prove to them that the plaintiff was Arthur Orton, the slaughterman of Wagga Wagga, " a conspirator, a perjurer, a forger, an impostor, and a villain," and from January 15 to February 21 he proceeded eloquently but methodically to keep his promise.

When Coleridge finished his speech it became known that Mr. Rose, afterwards Sir Philip Rose, a great friend of Lord Beaconsfield, of the firm of Baxter, Rose and Norton, the solicitors for the plaintiff, felt that he could no longer identify himself with the case and retired from the firm. But for some time longer witnesses were called until the jury stopped the case and the Lord Chief Justice ordered the plaintiff's arrest on the charge of perjury.

Even then there were some who still believed that Arthur Orton was not himself, and there was this excuse for them, that all the evidence had not been called. The public verdict at that date was summed up in a witty epigram :

> The firm of Baxter, Rose, and Norton,
> Deny the claimant's Arthur Orton ;
> But can't deny, what's more important,
> That Arthur did what Arthur oughtn't.

It was not until April 23, 1873, that Thomas Castro *alias* Arthur Orton was brought to the bar for the crimes he had committed. His friends, Lord Rivers, Mr. Onslow, M.P., Mr. Whalley, M.P., Mr. Skipworth and others with a charity and enthusiasm more honourable to their hearts than their heads, continued to give him financial support. The public still subscribed.

The time and cost of destroying the myth were enormous, but it was worth while, and in due course Arthur Orton was sentenced to fourteen years' penal servitude and disappeared and was forgotten. For a time, so difficult it is wholly to eradicate a lie that has been allowed to seed in the minds of men, there was some local excitement in the Potteries where his eccentric advocate, Dr. Kenealy, stood successfully for Parliament and petitions were signed and meetings held, but the bubble was really burst and those whose money and energy had blown it into its gross and unwholesome shape were not sorry when it vanished. After the rejection of Dr. Kenealy in 1880 by the electors of Stoke-on-Trent and his death soon afterwards, the believers in Arthur Orton ceased to be articulate, though like all strange sects, small congregations of them worshipped their idol in obscure places.

Arthur Orton was a well-behaved convict. On one

occasion at Dartmoor he was punished for ill-behaviour but
demanded a magisterial inquiry and his good conduct marks
were restored to him.   His confidence in judicial integrity
after his long experiences of our Courts is satisfactory and one
is glad to hear that his appeal was successful.   He was removed
to Portsmouth, where he was more content with his lot and
discharged from there on October 20, 1884, after serving
ten years, eight months and two days of his sentence, good
conduct having gained him this substantial remission.

He tried to address public meetings and went on as a
minor turn at the music-halls, but public interest could not
be aroused again.   He was employed in a public-house and
kept a tobacconist's shop, but had no success in business.

In 1898 he published a signed confession at great length
in the *People*.   Though no doubt he was assisted in this by
a trained journalist, for Orton himself was from first to last
illiterate, yet there are touches of the real Orton in it and the
basis of it is undoubtedly genuine.   It should be recorded
that one of the reasons he alleges for writing his confession
is a desire to make reparation to the Tichborne family for
the wrongs he had done them.   He maintains, what I believe
to be very true, that he was dragged into the business at
first almost against his will and without intent to prosecute
it seriously.   Also he says, what is not so easy to accept,
that towards the end of his mythical career he almost began
to believe that he was Sir Roger.

As to this a curious piece of evidence was given in Court
by a Captain Angel who identified him as Orton and said :
" He is Arthur Orton right enough, but I don't believe he
knows it.   I have conversed with him for many hours but I
cannot detect any instance when he really recognizes himself
as Orton."   How far the continued playing of a part can
destroy a man's belief in his own identity is a matter for
scientists.

Arthur Orton died in obscure lodgings at Marylebone in April, 1898, and his friends, true to the last, buried him as Sir Roger Tichborne. The impostor was a wicked rogue enough, but some of those who aided and abetted him had little excuse for their actions. It is always said in defence of easy dupes, when their pet rogue is unmasked, that they have been victimized, and the whole blame is laid upon the rascal they have flattered by their folly into dangerous criminal paths. Credulity and facile enthusiasm are the perilous and slippery approaches to the abyss of imposture. We are too easy-going with self-deceit and too ready to overlook the danger of letting our consciences slumber in a muddle-headed condition somewhere between self-delusion and voluntary fraud. Coleridge in his strictures on Baigent, who was certainly one of Orton's worst and wickedest advisers, quoted a great saying : " If people will be wicked they had far better be so from common vicious passions than from self-deceit, because it undermines the whole principle of good, darkens the light which guides our steps and corrupts the conscience which is the guide of life." Many a rogue and vagabond has been led to the gallows, the jail or the whipping-post by the self-deceit of his disciples. The life of Arthur Orton is a sermon against the sin of self-deceit in ourselves.

CHAPTER II

MARY ANNE CLARKE, THE COURTESAN

ROGUES and vagabonds are by no means always criminals, and their psychology requires separate scientific study. Some are guilty of crime whilst other typical rogues and vagabonds are very pleasant companions who win the love of the world by the charm of their errors. The true mark of vagrom men—do not forget that in law man embraces woman—is that they react to the call of the wild. Love of adventure leads them from the homes of their youth, they do not readily assimilate what are called by the elect " principles," and they have a happy instinct for erring and straying from the common highways of behaviour.

That Mary Anne Clarke was by way of being a rogue, and a moral vagabond to boot, cannot be gainsaid. Yet she was a dainty rogue. Not of the porcelain variety, it is true, but fashioned in common pottery, though if we picture her as a china figure her origin is Bow rather than Chelsea.

Mary Anne Clarke was born at Oxford about 1776. Her father was a respectable tradesman and gave her a fair education. Her handwriting is fluent, direct and of the approved feminine type. When she was about thirteen her father died and her mother married a journeyman printer named Farquhar. What her career might have been among impressionable undergraduates and unsympathetic proctors we may easily imagine, but fortunately her wanderings began with a move to London, where we find her in the narrow household of her stepfather in Black Raven Alley in Cursitor Street off Chancery Lane.

Here we may accept the testimony of one who knew her in early days that " her person and manners were infinitely above her condition." The gifts of the gods are the temptations that lure many vagrom men and women to lives of indiscretion. Mary Anne knew that she was beautiful. She was not content to be wooed by some young apprentice and after seven long years to settle down to life in our alley. Her native charm and ability attracted suitors from the outer world to the printer's lodgings in Black Raven Alley, and at the early age of eighteen—some say sixteen—she spread her wings and left her home, marrying young Mr. Clarke, the son of a respectable builder, in Angel Court, Snow Hill. The old gentleman at his death left his son an annuity of £50 and the business of a stonemason in Golden Lane.

For some three years the young man attended to his trade, but he and his brother were typical sons of the well-to-do eighteenth-century trader of the story-books. The elder brother, who inherited £7,000 from his father, ran through his money and shot himself in his chaise near Pentonville. Mary Anne's husband neglected his business and spent his days with dissolute and expensive company. Within three years of their marriage, to the delight, no doubt, of Mary Anne, they migrated West from Hoxton to Craven Place near Kensington Gravel Pits. The counting-house and the stoneyard were left to the supervision of servants. Mary Anne entertained her fashionable friends, and Mr. Clarke amused himself in the skittle-yard or the gambling-den.

The inevitable happened. With the aid of pawnbrokers and money-lenders the household was propped up for a few months, and then the crash came. Clarke seems to have gone his way leaving his wife to fend for herself and her children.

The story and its sequel are not dissimilar from Defoe's narrative of Roxana. The children were taken by friends or relations, the husband went out of her life and Mary Anne commenced rogue and vagabond. It is only fair to her character to note that she continued to support her children, and that her husband was content to draw an allowance of £5 a week from her in the days of her vanity.

She started on her career with all the enthusiasm and success of Defoe's heroine, but one cannot picture her framing her pouting lips to the moral phrases with which Roxana prefaced her various downward steps. Her portraits show her to have been an eminently prepossessing little woman, and all who met her fell under the spell of her easy manners and cheerful conversation. Her face was oval but not long. She had a small nose, broader than the poet's ideal but markedly " tip-tilted as the petal of a flower " which gave her an adorable pertness. Her eyes were dark, beaming with irresistible archness, and expressive of a captivating intelligence. Her mouth was small, her smiling rosy lips discovered dainty even teeth—a rare point in beauties of that date—her skin was delicately fair but wholesome, " not of a dead white " as an admirer notes. Her full cheeks were sufficiently adorned with the orthodox apple blossom, and her auburn hair carried across her brow and knotted into a fantastic bun, secured by a comb, set off her radiant face humorously. All agree that her whole air and deportment were absolutely untainted by affectation. " A happy creation," says one servant; " Nature in an undress," writes another enthusiast. Alas! Yes. Certainly a likely recruit to her new profession, being indeed as pretty a piece of Eve's flesh as any in Illyria. Sinner, if you please, but a merry sinner and a pretty one.

From the first she started on the career of rogue and vagabond with a business energy which if it had been devoted

MARY ANNE CLARKE

From an engraving by W. Hopwood.

to noble purposes would have been highly commendable. One utters this platitude too readily perhaps about many rogues and criminals, for it seems probable that these unhappy ones are only really capable of working in the medium suitable to their degree. They are like artists, poets and actors, who cannot use their gifts effectively in the dull honest trades and professions of the world.

That Mary Anne was greedy one cannot deny. A certain amount of greed is the basis of successful commerce, and Mary Anne had sound mercantile instincts and was out for profits. Do not forget that she had several children to provide for, a husband to pension, and that it was very necessary for her to acquire clothes and furniture suitable to success.

Her first protector was a baronet who met her at Willis's Rooms and, to the dismay of her world, carried her off to his country house in Wiltshire. Here she lived for six months, but finding her friend was deaf to her suggestions of a settlement she returned to town. There seem to have been several temporary alliances with men of fashion. We find her in elegantly furnished houses, and read of her from time to time in sumptuous lodgings at fashionable watering-places, surrounded by gay companions, to the grave discontent of Mrs. Homely and her friends, who would have very willingly seen her whipped at the cart's tail, a punishment to which she was then legally entitled under the statutes made and provided for rogues and vagabonds of her class.

But of course statutory penalties of this nature were only enforced against the poor and friendless. Pretty Mary Anne was never in danger of judgment, and after a few years' successful career in the fashionable world her name becomes connected with Frederick Augustus, Duke of York and Albany, the second son of His Majesty George III.

The Duke of York seems to have met Mary Anne either

D

in Weymouth or some other fashionable resort in the year 1803. He was forty years of age and she was about twenty-seven. The Duke was a popular figure in the English world, and though military critics of to-day might not agree with the verdict of his contemporaries, he was regarded as a very satisfactory Commander-in-Chief of the British Army. He was certainly credited with courage and energy and more doubtfully perhaps with soldierly skill, and a real desire for military reform. In an outburst of loyal enthusiasm on his decease Sir Walter Scott laments that " there has fallen this day in our Israel a Prince and a great man." And though we moderns may smile at this verdict let us be content to remember his good work at Chelsea Orphanage and Sandhurst, and acknowledge his courage and manliness even if we cannot accept him as a military genius.

Like the rest of his world, he fell an easy prey to Mary Anne. For Frederick was a burly, jolly, loud-voiced boon companion, with an income of £70,000 a year, with which he did not pay his debts, a wild passion for horse-racing, deep play and jovial company, holding a record of capacity for six bottles of claret after dinner without turning a hair.

Mrs. Clarke told the House of Commons that it was in 1803 that he first took her under his protection but that she had known him before. They lived in a furnished house in Park Lane. Gronow tells a romantic story of their meeting on Blackheath and of the lady going to the play with him and using his box without knowing his identity. This seems scarcely probable, but wherever the meeting took place no sooner did the Duke throw the handkerchief than pretty Mary Anne picked it up with a witching smile and, turning her back on her old admirers, became Frederick's grateful and obedient humble servant. Early in 1804 the world learned without surprise that Mrs. Clarke was installed in a great house at 18, Gloucester Place, where she began to entertain in a lavish and ostentatious manner, and the most honoured and constant guest at her revels and parties was Frederick, Duke of York.

The stories of her extravagance read like pages from *The Arabian Nights*. In the Gloucester Place household there were more than twenty servants, including two butlers and six footmen. Three or more chefs were often in attendance, at a guinea a day each, and the wages bill alone exceeded £1,000 a year. The furniture and appointments were the most splendid that money could buy. The pier-glasses cost £500, a dozen silver soup-plates cost 100 guineas and the wine-glasses two guineas apiece. Then there was the stable with the coaches and eight or ten horses, with lackeys in proportion. The Duke also provided her with a country house at Weybridge, near Oatlands, his own country seat. Here the Duchess spent the summer and the Duke went down and invited a number of guests from Saturday to Monday. The week-end habit is no new thing. The programme sounds modern enough. Dinner was from eight to eleven. Then whist. The Duke would sit up until all hours. His stakes were " fivers and ponies "—£5 points and £25 on the rubber. The Duchess had a half-crown table and retired early. At whatever hour the Duke went to bed, he was up early and went to church on Sunday, returning to a breakfast of cold meat and tea. He enjoyed riding or walking in the afternoons and evenings, and at nine on Monday morning was off to town again.

With Mary Anne near at hand at Weybridge the programme was doubtless altered and perhaps the Duke cut the evening whist short to visit his *chère amie*. For she, too, used to post down there from Saturday to Monday to be near the Duke. And the expense of this establishment, we are told by a wondering contemporary, " may be guessed from this single circumstance that the oilcloth, in the passage

only, cost fifty pounds." This oilcloth was not laid down
on the floor but was erected as a screen to hide the Duke on
his visits from the prying eyes of neighbours.

Of course all the world knew all about it and were not
particularly censorious. The Duke's marriage was not a
happy one. Lady Hester Stanhope in her outspoken way
pronounced society's verdict. " How should you," she asked
a bourgeois protester, " how should you like a painted wife,
with half a dozen gentlemen about her shaking the hair
powder in her face ? Or is it agreeable to have the window
opened at dinner-time on a cold November day to let out
the smells of a parcel of dogs ? I suppose if you had an
uncomfortable home, you would think yourself at liberty to
take a little pleasure elsewhere ? "

But the worst part of the Duke's conduct was perhaps
his failure to pay for his pleasures. Mrs. Clarke's account
of the finance of the establishments was given and cross-
examined to, in the House of Commons, and if there had
been any gross error in it, it would have been easy for the
Duke's agents to have corrected it. The Duke provided
£1,000 a year and the houses in Gloucester Place and Weybridge, and paid £1,300 on account to a silversmith and paid
a milliner's bill. He also purchased a landau. Mrs. Clarke,
who was responsible to the tradesmen for the upkeep of the
establishments and the food and drink consumed by servants
and guests, soon found that she was largely in debt and
began to be threatened by the tradesmen with processes
and executions. Of course they charged enormous prices, and
when one bill was paid they were only too ready to give
credit again. It was to keep the establishments going that
Mrs. Clarke started her trade in the sale of offices and pro-
motions that led to her appearance at the bar of the House
of Commons and the temporary retirement of the Commander-
in-Chief.

When the lady was asked what gave her the first idea of entering on this traffic she replied : " By persons applying to me ; and I found that His Royal Highness was very ready to oblige me when I asked him." Whatever may have been the degree of negligence or complicity in the Duke's conduct, no one can doubt that this extravagant household was financed by Mrs. Clarke in the way she described. When she went to Gloucester Place she had some property and money of her own, but when the Duke parted with her in 1806 she was over £2,000 in debt after the house and furniture had been sold. That Mrs. Clarke had lived in a glorious confusion of extravagance is clear, that the Duke of York had enjoyed the hospitality of the house is also beyond doubt.

The outer world, who knew nothing of the Duke's affairs, supposed that he was paying for this magnificence out of his income of £70,000 a year, but the inner circle of the Court, knowing something of his financial affairs, were puzzled over the problem.

In 1806 the Duke's more sensible friends endeavoured to detach him from his mistress, but he was by no means eager to give her up. At length his agent, Mr. William Adam, M.P., was successful and the parting took place. Now if, when Mrs. Clarke retired from Gloucester Place, the Duke had agreed to settle £400 a year on the lady and pay her debts of £2,000, incurred to keep up his establishments, all had been well. Unfortunately, this reasonable proposition was turned down by the Duke's agent.

Mr. William Adam, Member for Kincardineshire, was a Scots barrister and also Attorney-General to the Prince of Wales. He had undertaken some kind of management of the Duke of York's affairs and it seems probable that he was, in fact, a trustee for the benefit of creditors. Naturally and rightly, he desired to get rid of the liability of Mary Anne at the cheapest, and though he had persuaded the Duke to break away from her, His Grace still seems to have desired that she should be reasonably treated.

Adam, when describing his negotiations with Mary Anne made a great point in the House of Commons that he was acting gratuitously, but it appeared that he had had the good fortune to obtain for a son of fourteen a commission in the Army, and this young fellow, who afterwards saw some service and was no doubt brave and capable, had through the Duke's influence become a Lieutenant-Colonel of a regiment at the early age of one-and-twenty.

This was the man who came to Mary Anne to arrange the terms of her separation from the Duke. His sole offer was £400 a year to be paid quarterly " as long as her conduct was correct," but there was to be nothing in writing and no bond, and it must rest entirely on the Duke's word. Mary Anne was indignant. She wanted security for the annuity and payment of her debts and showed Mr. Adam the door.

The annuity was paid for a time. There were further futile negotiations which came to nothing, and after a while the annuity was stopped. One cannot deny that Mrs. Clarke was shabbily treated. She had her children to maintain, she was threatened with a debtors' prison and was in poverty and distress. She had already been approached by the political opponents of the Duke to publish her reminiscences, but before she would agree to do so she made a last offer to Mr. Adam. She also appealed to the Duke and in June, 1808, she wrote two last letters to Mr. Adam. Her annuity was over a year in arrear and neither the Duke nor Mr. Adam would answer her letters. There were, however, customers for her reminiscences and the letters that the Duke had written to her from time to time, and she explained quite openly to Mr. Adam what she proposed to do with them. " It is to gentlemen and not to my publisher they will be committed ; and those gentlemen are just as obstinate as His

Royal Highness and more independent : they are acquaintances of yours ; and to relieve my wants in pique to others
will do what the Duke will not." If Adam understood the
allusion it seems a pity for his client that he did not re-open
negotiations with Mrs. Clarke, but he held silence and the
matter proceeded on its unseemly course.

The " gentlemen " referred to in Mrs. Clarke's letters
were a Colonel Gwyllym Lloyd Wardle, M.P. for Oke-
hampton, and other Parliamentarians who were interested in
Army reform. The purchase system in the Army at that
date was a part of our Constitution and, as Sir Walter Scott
asserted, " indispensable to the freedom of the country."
It was no uncommon thing for a commission to be obtained
for a child in a cradle and when he came from college he
was already a lieutenant of some standing by dint of due
promotion. Even young ladies received commissions when
pensions could not be arranged. These things were gravely
disliked by Sir Francis Burdett and the party of reformers
who followed his leadership. Wardle seems to have discovered that Mrs. Clarke had, during the period that she
lived with the Duke of York, made large sums by receiving
money from officers, who had been promoted or received
commissions, and hearing she had been deserted by the Duke
he approached her to see if he could obtain her evidence.

The details of these negotiations are obscure and contra-
dictory. Mrs. Clarke's story is that Wardle assured her
that he was authorized by the Duke of Kent to promise her
more than the annuity of £400 promised by his brother, and
that she should be placed in a well-furnished house and freed
from debts if she would give up her papers and letters and
give evidence of the way in which she had trafficked in places
and offices. To assure her of the good faith of his offer he
handed the lady a letter of Major Dodd, the Duke of Kent's
confidential secretary. How far anyone of authority in these

promises was acting with Colonel Wardle it is difficult to
say. In the end they were repudiated and poor Mrs. Clarke
was as grievously treated by Wardle as she had been by the
Duke of York. But for the moment she was satisfied, handing
all her papers to the Colonel and promising to appear and
give evidence of the facts in the House of Commons. The
Reformers were jubilant. Colonel Wardle was entrusted
with the attack and looked forward to a great parliamentary
triumph. On January 27, 1809, he moved for an inquiry
into the conduct of the Commander-in-Chief in relation to
promotion in the Army, which was seconded by Sir Francis
Burdett. The House agreed to an inquiry, and for nearly
two months amidst great public excitement the world listened
to the strange stories of Mary Anne Clarke.

On Wednesday, February 1, the House went into Committee on the charges against the Duke of York and examined
witnesses until two in the morning. Lord Byron on his
arrival in town writes to a friend : " London is full of the
Duke's business," and for a couple of months among high
and low it was the only town talk.

The man in the street, who has a natural affection for
the rogue and vagabond, made pretty Mary Anne his pet
heroine. Even in the House of Commons her frank, saucy
manner, and witty, sensible replies to her examiners, gained
her a great deal of sympathy as she stood at the bar of the
House and detailed the methods by which money was raised
for the upkeep of the Gloucester Place establishment. It
was beyond doubt that in the main her story was true.
Gloucester Place had certainly been financed by the sales of
commissions in the Army, but how far the Duke was a party
to this was of course another question.

A certain Mr. Dowler, from whom she had received
£1,000, the price of an appointment in the Commis-
sariat, used to act as a sort of " runner " for the lady and

was a constant visitor at Gloucester Place. But even with the business introduced by Dowler and others the establishment was difficult to run. In answer to Lord Folkestone, Mrs. Clarke said she had suits and executions against her, and when she asked the Duke for more money all he said was " that if I was clever I should never ask for money." There is no doubt that she was clever, that she did obtain large sums of money and that she spent them on her household.

Mr. Sheridan, who clearly had some inner knowledge of the facts of the case, inquired of the witness whether she did any business in ecclesiastical patronage ? She remembered that a Dr. O'Meara approached her as to a bishopric, and she persuaded the Duke to use his influence to allow him to preach before the King. This he was allowed to do on one Sunday at Weymouth, but the Duke reported that there was no chance for O'Meara " as the King did not like the great O in his name." Another of Mrs. Clarke's friends, a Lieutenant Donovan, obtained an offer from two pious old ladies of 3,000 guineas for a deanery in the West of England for their favourite parson, the Rev. Bazeley. But Mrs. Clarke had to admit that she was not successful in ecclesiastical patronage, and accounted for it by saying " the person who takes all the patronage of the Church into her hands is the first female personage in England."

But in Army and Customs Office affairs a brisk trade was done. An Inspector of Customs went for £1,000 and a Paymaster to a battalion for £500. Her influence was paramount. We find that her own footman, Samuel Carter, a likely young fellow, was made colonel of a regiment in the West Indies. He writes a piteous letter to the lady from the transport at Spithead asking for money to pay for the necessaries of life on the journey, which no doubt she sent to him if she could. This promotion certainly cannot be put down to bribery and may have been a pure act of kindness on the part of the Duke. Colonel Carter was as likely to turn out a good soldier as any of the others who purchased commissions.

That a very widespread system of corruption existed is clearly proved. That Mrs. Clarke obtained large sums of money and influenced her lover to obtain appointments seems certain, but how far the Duke was himself an actual party to the system is by no means so clear. If we are to believe Mary Anne Clarke, the business was openly discussed between them. She had a list of candidates' names pinned on her bed-curtains and discussed their affairs with her lover before he went down to the War Office in the morning.

Mrs. Clarke gave much detailed evidence of her requests to the Duke, but in the nature of things there could be no corroboration of her statements, except in so far as the fact that money was paid and promotion followed. On one occasion, however, Miss Taylor, an intimate friend of Mrs. Clarke, swore that she was present when the question of Colonel French and his levy was mentioned and gave evidence of a very incriminating conversation. The Duke said : " I am continually worried by Colonel French—he worries me continually about the levy business and is always wanting something more in his favour," and turning to Mrs. Clarke he asked : " How does French behave to darling ? "

Mrs. Clarke replied : " Only middling, not very well."

On which the Duke replied : " Master French must mind what he is about or I shall cut up him and his levy too."

Whether this evidence was truth or fiction it caught the fancy of the town, which made merry over it, and Speaker Abbot records that, " the joke in the streets among the people is not to cry ' Heads and Tails ' when they toss up half-pence but ' Duke and Darling.' "

And though the Duke was never called as a witness to deny these things it must be remembered that he wrote a letter to the House of Commons in which " in the most solemn manner upon my honour as a Prince " he denied all knowledge of any corrupt participation in the infamous transactions which appeared in the evidence at the bar of the House.

No one would convict the meanest citizen on the un- supported evidence of Mary Anne Clarke. That the Duke discussed military matters with her is certain, and that she was an influence with him in the matter of appointments is clear. It is a mistake to mix up love and business. It has been the ruin of many a great man. Of this error of judgment the Duke was obviously guilty. Here is an extract from a letter that greatly delighted the House of Commons.

SANDGATE, *August* 24, 1804.

How can I sufficiently express to my darling love my thanks for her dear dear letter, or the delight which the assurances of her love have given me ? Oh, my angel ! do me justice and be convinced, that there never was a woman adored as you are. Every day, every hour, convinces me more and more that my whole happiness depends upon you alone. What a time it appears to be since we parted and with what impatience do I look forward to the day after to-morrow ; here are still however two whole nights before I shall clasp my darling in my arms !

How happy am I to learn that you are better ; I still however will not give up hopes of the cause of you feeling uncomfortable. Clavering is mistaken, my angel, in thinking that any new regiments are to be raised ; it is not intended ; only second battalion to the existing corps ; you had better therefore tell him so and that you were sure there would be no use in applying for him.

Mrs. Clarke did not produce this letter until General Clavering had denied that she had used her influence for him, and later on, in course of the inquiry, she produced several letters from General Clavering showing that he wrote to her asking for information about new military projects, and he was clearly one of her customers.

But the case of Captain Tonyn, which was the first charge put forward by Mr. Wardle and was strenuously fought by the Duke's friends, was perhaps the most remarkable story investigated by the House. Tonyn was introduced to Mrs. Clarke by Captain Sandon and Lieutenant Donovan, who bargained that he should obtain his majority for a payment of £500 to Mrs. Clarke. This was done, and the £500 went in part payment of a service of plate for use at Gloucester Place. The transaction was spoken to by Donovan and Mrs. Clarke and admitted by Sandon, who paid her the £500. Sandon, however, omitted to state that he had been given by Mrs. Clarke a note purporting to be written to her by the Duke about Tonyn's business, and this coming to the ears of the Chancellor of the Exchequer, Mr. Perceval, who had put forward Sandon as a witness of truth, he at once very honourably ordered him back to the bar of the House.

Sandon at first denied any recollection of any such letters, then he " remembered there was something of a note," then he thought he had destroyed it or it was mislaid, then he admitted it was in his bureau and he saw it five or six days ago and had looked for it two days ago and could not find it, and at last he expressed the hope that he could find it.

The House heard this prevarication with natural indignation, and at the request of Speaker Abbot the Chairman ordered the witness to withdraw. The Speaker then moved amid general cheering that Captain Sandon had been guilty of gross prevarication. The question was put and amidst continued cries of " Aye, aye," carried *nemine contradicente*. Mr. Perceval then moved that he should be taken into custody by the Serjeant-at-Arms.

Returning in custody, Sandon offered a humble apology and set off with the Serjeant-at-Arms to produce the note alleged to have been written by the Duke, and, the House waiting for him for a considerable time, he returned with the note which he said he had received from Mrs. Clarke.

It was addressed " George Farquhar, Esq.," an address often used by Mrs. Clarke in her correspondence with the Duke. It read : " I have just received Your Note and Tonyn's business shall remain as it is—God bless you."

Mrs. Clarke was now recalled and stated that the note was in the Duke's writing and that she had given it to Sandon to show him that Tonyn's business was progressing. There was some cross-examination of the lady to suggest she had imitated the Duke's handwriting, and the sitting closed with a unanimous resolution to commit Captain Sandon to Newgate.

Some evidence was afterwards called to substantiate the suggestion of forgery, but all Colonel Gordon, who knew the Duke's writing, could say was that " it bore a strong resemblance to his handwriting, but whether it was or not he could not say," and that was the view of other witnesses. If, indeed, Sandon or anyone who knew of it thought it was a forgery one would have expected that it would not have been kept back by Sandon but produced as a forgery in the first instance. The suggestion of forgery was an after-thought.

One cannot help thinking that the advisers of the Duke acted unwisely in putting forward the military witnesses, who had approached and been served by Mrs. Clarke, as opponents to her stories. Their evidence broke down badly and was contradicted by written documents. There is no doubt that she carried on her nefarious traffic and that it was done by means of her influence with the Duke ; but it seems probable that he was so infatuated with the woman that his motive in obliging her was to please her rather than to obtain money for her establishment, though incidentally supplies were raised of which he enjoyed his share.

But when the House came to deliver judgment on their

inquiry you could not expect any dispassionate verdict. The Government were out to whitewash the Duke and his doings and uphold the system under which the Army was managed. The Whigs were out to show the rottenness of the system and the managers of it, and to prove that they alone could work reforms. The debate is as modern in its party bias as if it had taken place yesterday. The voting on a Parliamentary inquiry can always be accurately forecast and has seldom any genuine relation to evidence or facts proved. The figures of the divisions would have been much the same before Mrs. Clarke and the witnesses were heard as they were afterwards.

The debate lasted several days. Spencer Perceval, the Chancellor of the Exchequer, was a typical Crown prosecutor, whose motto might have been " My brief right or wrong, but always my brief." He led for the defence of the Duke of York and made a most telling speech. To say that it might have been made by Sir Edward Clarke at the Old Bailey is to give expression to the excellence of its advocacy. Although he had engaged the time of the House by calling witnesses to prove that corruption did not exist, he threw that point over, and admitting the evil practices to be proved, boldly took the line that if Mrs. Clarke was a witness of truth His Royal Highness had allowed her to use her influence with him corruptly. He did not deny that her influence might have been used corruptly, but was the Duke actor, act and part in the conspiracy?

He pointed out the contemptible sums of bribes that had been proved—£3,000 at the most. He chaffed the Opposition on their simple faith in Mary Anne and their eager reaction to her " engaging manners and fascinating deportment," and pointed out that by payment of a paltry £400 a year the Duke could have stopped the inquiry. Then he told the House that he proposed to move resolutions not only stating that no personal corruption had been proved against the Duke, but that there was no one in the country who could fill his place as Commander-in-Chief.

At half-past three in the morning, so interested was the House in his argument, that the members would not let him stop, but insisted on adjourning to hear him further. When he finished the next day, his party, for the first time, seemed to feel that they could vote as they were directed without conscientious inconvenience.

Perceval was followed by Samuel Whitbread, the Non-conformist brewer, a typical Radical, whose vehemence against the corruption and oppression of the times caused the younger aristocrats much offence. That a brewer should pretend to statesmanship vexed their spirit, and when he rose to flights of eloquence they pretended amusement at the fellow's efforts " to teach his dray horse to caper."

But when they listened to his direct indictment of the Duke of York, though his arguments did not dissolve the pleasant atmosphere with which silver-tongued Perceval had surrounded the business, yet many must have felt uneasy. For the gist of his contention was eminently businesslike and for a moment the House cheered the common sense of it when he asked the Chancellor and his colleagues " Would it be said, that if such a mass of evidence had come, out respecting the conduct of any private individual in that situation, that he could be permitted any longer to retain the command of the Army ? "

The good Mr. Wilberforce, the abolitionist, displeased both parties by the dispassionate survey of the evidence that had been called. He pointed out how the defence had first suggested that Dr. O'Meara and General Clavering and others had never approached Mrs. Clarke, and that when they were called and cross-examined her evidence was confirmed and they were found to be the deceivers. and he rallied the Duke's friends on their sagacity in calling no further evidence and at long last admitting that Mrs. Clarke's facts were correct. His conclusion was to my thinking a sensible one and probably was the ultimate verdict of the people when party passions had died away. It sounds vague and inconclusive, but it is perhaps as near the truth of the matter as can be reached. " Many suspicions," he says, " must have rested on the Duke's mind, as to these corrupt practices, and I cannot go the length of acquitting him of all connivance, but undoubtedly I do free him from any real knowledge amounting to participation in that corruption." He concluded by expressing the opinion that the Duke could no longer be Commander-in-Chief.

After a four days' debate the House on Monday, March 15, 1809, accepted Mr. Perceval's resolution negativing Mr. Wardle's resolution by a majority of 241. There was still further debate over Mr. Perceval's second resolution declaring the Duke's innocence. This was ultimately carried on March 17 by 82.

The Duke of York now, of his own motion, tendered his resignation, which His Majesty was graciously pleased to accept. After an absence of two years, a reasonable statutory limitation for any public scandal, he returned to his high office, to the content of his friends and companions.

But Mary Anne Clarke had many troubles to encounter before she reached a safe haven, and poor Wardle found that the rewards of patriotism were very Dead Sea fruit. At first it was " roses, roses all the way." He was voted the freedom of the City of London. Medals were struck, portraits were painted and illuminated addresses poured into his house from all parts of the kingdom. But with the summer his popularity was gone, and he found to his dismay that one cannot live and pay one's way on the dying echo of popular applause.

When Mary Anne claimed the reward of her good work Wardle found that his backers, true to type, were of one accord and did their backing by backing out of their promises. The upholsterer who had furnished Mary Anne a new and fitting house sued poor Wardle, who was cast in damages. Then Wardle indicted Mrs. Clarke and her upholsterer for conspiracy, but Mary Anne's star was still in the ascendant and she was acquitted.

At the dissolution of 1812 Wardle was not re-elected. Friends among the patriots subscribed a few thousand pounds for him and he started a milk business at Tonbridge, but this failed and he retired from a world of sheriffs and bailiffs to Florence, where he lived to a ripe old age.

Mrs. Clarke, having defeated Wardle, now produced in two volumes an attack on his conduct, called *The Rival Princes*, in which she threw the blame of bringing the charges against the Duke of York upon his brother of Kent, and vilified Wardle and his friends. The book is a worthless pamphlet and was certainly not written by the lady without assistance.

She was now without money, but she still possessed many letters of the Duke's which had not found their way into the reports of the inquiry or the several histories of Mrs. Clarke which were prepared in Grub Street. Her own reminiscences would no doubt have kept the wolf from the door for a time, but she had the wit to appreciate that the threat of them was worth more than their publication. Like the books of the Sibyl Amalthea, these volumes of Mary Anne might have been bought by Mr. Adam for a very reasonable sum before the inquiry, and the Duke might have remained in office, the State saved large sums of money and all scandal have been averted. Now we find Mary Anne in her hour of need and victory offering them to the publisher for a high sum, but to the Duke's friends, to whom they have

E

a real money value, at a higher price than mere literature is worth.

The masterful Adam was set aside and the negotiations left to the Duke's private secretary, Sir Herbert Taylor, a soldier of distinction untouched by the past scandals. Mary Anne's volumes were already printed and Sir Herbert arranged that the printed edition should be destroyed, Mrs. Clarke accepting compensation in £7,000 down and a pension of £400 a year.

With that the story of Mrs. Clarke may be said to end happily. She removed to Paris with her daughters, whom she brought up virtuously and she had the satisfaction of seeing them happily married.

Then she retired to Boulogne, " that refuge of much exiled innocence," where you may picture her, like Mrs. Rawdon Crawley, living in a genteel widowed manner in a couple of rooms with her *femme de chambre*. But still she was not lonely. Her salon in the 'forties was visited by many of the great ones of the world who rested at Boulogne on their way to Paris. The livelier of the English contingent living there greatly appreciated her presence among them and sought her society. For to the last she had a ready wit, merry memories of the great ones of the past, and was, within her means, a gracious hostess. She died on the 21st of June, 1852, at the age of seventy-six, respected by all who knew her.

CHAPTER III

DANIEL DUNGLASS HOME, THE MEDIUM

THERE may still be devout believers who credit Daniel Dunglass Home with supernatural gifts, but, whatever his physical abnormalities, if any, may have been, the man himself must be classified as a " vagrom man " of the type of Cagliostro and the astrologers and other high priests of the shrine of Hocus Pocus. And though he was a rogue and vagabond in the true Elizabethan sense of the word, yet one must allow that he had his temptations. The idle rich of his day were all agog for table-turning and spirit-rapping, and he had all the necessary gifts to minister to their entertainment.

Home left two volumes of *Incidents of My Life* and his widow wrote his life, but these authorities cannot be accepted without criticism, any more than it would be fair to Home to receive every word of Robert Browning's *Mr. Sludge the Medium* as evidence against him. To get at the true facts of his career can only be attempted by searching contemporary reminiscences.

Home claimed to be the grandson of Alexander, tenth Earl of Home and Baron of Dunglass. It is said that his father was one William Home, a natural son of the earl, and his mother's name was McNeill. He was born near Edinburgh on March 20, 1833. His aunt adopted him in infancy and he went with her and her husband to America when he was nine years old. His mother also went to America, but did not live with the others. What became of his father or what his status was, we know not. His mother died in 1850 at the age of forty-two. She was a seer and gifted with what is called second sight, which she claimed was hereditary, and she had an uncanny habit of foreseeing the passing away of her relatives and foretold her own death.

Young Home was now about seventeen and, to his aunt's annoyance, had joined the Wesleyan body. Soon after his mother's death Home became the medium of rappings and noises in the house and caused movements of furniture similar to the celebrated noises that disturbed Samuel Wesley in the parsonage at Epworth.

In 1850 spiritualism was very popular in America. A Baptist minister named Scott, and a preacher named Harris, were working successful miracles with a medium called Mrs. Benedict in Auburn, New York. Mrs. Benedict and the ministers put their dupes in touch with the Prophet Daniel and St. John and St. Paul. Scott and Harris were " chosen vessels," and a small mob of deluded men and women followed them to Mountain Cove in Virginia, the people of Auburn being disgusted with their blasphemies. Home went to one of their meetings and in after life expressed his disapprobation of their methods. They were probably quacks and humbugs, or at best religious maniacs, but they did all the medium business and table-tilting or turning that was popular in their day, and Harris had considerable success both in England and America.

Table-tilting in 1853 was a well recognized method of obtaining spiritual advice from mediums and had hundreds of followers and believers. Faraday investigated it and showed conclusively that it was the work of the medium assisted by his willing patients.

Faraday was a little ashamed of having condescended to trouble about the imposture of table-tilting, but in the weak, credulous age in which he lived he considered it a duty to do so. His verdict on the average minds of the spiritualists he came in contact with was that rather than be endowed with their understandings he would prefer to be limited to " the obedience, affections and instincts of a dog."

Of table-tilting and similar tricks even Home himself—in a book called *Lights and Shadows of Spiritualism*, which was largely written by Howitt—wisely says that though he would not say they were " deliberate imposture," yet he is " perfectly satisfied that they constituted a monstrous delusion in which disembodied spirits had not the slightest share." Home in after life was very impatient of the lesser pretenders. He writes of his rivals as quacks and humbugs, and went so far on one occasion as to visit the séance of a boy who was doing a thriving trade with the " cabinet trick." As Home apparently was fully versed in the way the lad was working it, the manifestations ceased and Home himself was voted an " adverse influence." In early life he also records that he visited a Mr. Gordon, an established medium at Springfield, Massachusetts. He was invited to a séance, but he notes " the contending influences prevented the occurrence of manifestations." One medium cannot easily deceive another.

Home, as a lad in his aunt's house, was afflicted with visions, telepathic warnings and mysterious " raps " followed him about. His aunt found him a domestic nuisance, and after calling in the local clergy to exorcise the evil spirits by which she supposed he was haunted, and finding their efforts were useless, she turned him out of the house.

But the fame of the young man had gone forth to the world and, in a community where mediums were welcome, he found many good people ready to offer him a home. It would have been instructive if Home's widow and disciples had given us more details of his financial history, but they are nearly silent about it. We know that he was turned out of his aunt's house in 1853 a penniless youth, but we shall find that he fared luxuriously all the days of his life, travelled in Europe and America, lived expensively in the capitals and pleasure cities of the world, and associated on terms of intimacy with royalty and the aristocrats.

All this was done on the fame of his manifestations. And if indeed he was, as he alleged, afflicted by spirits whose movements he could not control, the misfortune had its worldly compensations, and probably there is no recorded instance of a medium who was financed by his disciples so substantially or for such a length of time.

It is notable that from the first Home laid down two principles of action to which he strictly adhered during his long and successful career. In the first place, he never held himself out directly as a man who could call spirits to his aid. He announced his " passivity " in the business and kept to it. Of course, his spirits were less passive and more active among believers, and he was careful in choosing his sitters. But " passivity " enabled him to decline any séances he did not wish to attend on the plea that his powers were for the moment absent. In the second place, he never held séances in a public hall for money, or tickets bought by the public, and was only to be found at the houses of faithful friends. His powers rarely worked except in the evenings and generally in darkened rooms. He refused fees for séances, but the gifts that he accepted and received must have been enormous, judging from his expenditure and the one case that found its way into the Law Courts.

For four years after his departure from his aunt's house he lived comfortably enough at friends' houses, where his " rapping " business was very popular. The vogue then was for a few initiates to sit round with the medium until raps began, when the alphabet was spelt out and, a rap being given at the right letter, the spirit in attendance gave his message from the dead. This method was so obviously open to fraudulent use that it fell into disgrace, but at that date it was highly popular and remained so during the greater part of Home's career. Home also did table-turning or tilting, the medium and the circle placing their hands upon the table. This, of course, is to-day wholly discredited as a display of supernatural agency. It is interesting to note that at the age of eighteen, rapping, and furniture moving, and visions, were all the manifestations with which he was troubled.

In March, 1851, a table-turning exploit got into the papers and, to use his own phrase, " I found myself finally embarked without any volition of my own and indeed greatly against my will upon the tempestuous sea of a public life." It must have been very pleasant for an indolent lad of eighteen—there is no evidence that he ever did a day's work in his life—to wander about among well-to-do friends in America, and to be received into the society of educated and interesting men and women at the price of manifestations in which, according to his own account, he was a mere conduit-pipe. He lived on and among these people for about four or five years.

At this period he used to go into a trance. As a disciple describes it, " he was thrown into a spiritually magnetic state, discovering great rigidity of muscle and the ordinary pheno-mena of the psycho-magnetic condition including a magnetic locking of the jaws." His eyes were then bound, and by rapidly pointing out letters on a card before him he spelt messages which were taken down. If they were obscure one of the company suggested a meaning and if the spirits approved they rapped vigorously.

He must have had a great fascination for simple folk. A Mr. and Mrs. Elmer, who were amongst his most devoted adherents, offered to adopt him when he was about nineteen, but he had the vagrant nature in him, and he declined the proposal, though he lived with them for some considerable time.

It was suggested to Home that he should enter the medical profession, and he played with the study of it a while, but work had no attractions for him. He made, however, one or two attempts at study and learned some German and French, but the manifestations became daily more interesting both to himself and his friends. Spirit-hands were now commonly felt by the sitters and they continued to increase their familiarities among certain circles who longed for the touch of a vanished hand, but adverse influences or even mere indifference easily affected their movements.

These spirit-hands, which were much admired, are often described. Thomas Adolphus Trollope thought they looked like "long kid gloves stuffed with some substance," but he was somewhat of an adverse influence. The Emperor Napoleon and the Empress Eugénie were allowed to kiss a spirit-hand.

On one occasion, in America, Home declares he himself was levitated, as the tables had been, and in his later career this immunity from the law of gravitation is said to have affected him, and there were some who believed they had witnessed this levitation. These witnesses are certainly worthy of the same credit that is readily given to people who have seen a common miracle done by Indian conjurers who throw a rope into the air and climb up it and disappear into the skies.

The spirits at this time were very lively. Home thought nothing of six séances a week and seldom drew blank. Friendly doctors who diagnosed lung trouble suggested that he should go slower and cut down the weekly séances to two. But his popularity made this very difficult and his "passivity" did not enable him to keep the spirits away even for one night a week.

Home now began to think of a wider career than that open to him in the States. He had made influential friends, he had overtopped the exploits of all contemporary mediums, and at the age of twenty-two he determined to set forth into the wide world in search of fame and fortune. He achieved both.

In April, 1855, he arrived in London, where he soon found the leisured classes as eager for séances as his American friends. He was taken up at the onset by an ardent spiritualist, Mr. Cox, an hotel-keeper in Jermyn Street. His house "was a home for mediums arriving from every country" and his spiritualistic hobbies made his hotel famous.

Cox invited Lord Brougham and Sir David Brewster to a private view of Home, out of which arose a great controversy which was a splendid advertisement for Home. Brougham was seventy-eight and Sir David seventy-four, and the two old gentlemen, with Cox and Home, sat round a table. Nothing very sensational occurred. Brewster agreed that tables moved, rappings were heard, an accordion in Lord Brougham's hands gave out a single note but would not play a tune. A bell, he says, rang without being touched " and came over to me and placed itself in my hand. It did the same to Lord Brougham." Hands were sometimes seen and felt. Although Brewster truly records what he thought he saw, he is convinced that whatever did occur was not the work of spirits and he so asserted. Lord Brougham never gave any account of the business, though it would have been important to know how far he corroborated Brewster. In the public controversy that ensued, Brewster pointed out that during the séance Home left the room and returned, and though Sir David frankly admitted that the effects produced puzzled him, yet he could see no reason why they could not have been produced by Home by mechanical contrivance.

Nothing was shown on this occasion by Home that was

not in the programme of any ordinary medium, and whatever the manifestations were they did not convert either Lord Brougham or Professor Brewster into a belief in spiritualism.

Home himself, in later years, agreed that spirit-writing, in which at one time he indulged, was probably not of spirit origin and freely charged his fellow-mediums with jugglery and trickery in producing spirit-rapping. Mr. Faulkner, the instrument-maker of Endell Street, had for many years a large demand for spirit-rapping magnets and batteries especially made for concealment under the floor and in cupboards. One cannot imagine a spiritualist of to-day innocent enough to accept the spirit-rapping produced by Home as anything but a mechanical device controlled by the medium. But in those days people who had the wish to believe were readily impressed by it.

A family named Rymer at Ealing, who were enthusiastic spiritualists, held many séances for Home, and he was soon the centre of a crowd of admirers. Mr. Rymer was a wealthy Australian and it seems probable he financed Home at this time. Someone must have provided ways and means, for he lived in good style and frequented the best society.

Thomas Adolphus Trollope met him here and describes him as flirting with one of the Rymer girls in a way which showed he was a petted member of the household. He would talk of the phenomena of his existence, but was unable or unwilling to formulate any theory of their origin. He was a loosely built youth of twenty with red hair, blue eyes, a sensual mouth and a phthisical complexion. It was in a trance at Rymer's that a spirit spoke through him saying : " When Daniel recovers give him some bottled porter." This most sensible message did not please the faithful, and was not, so far as we can learn, ever repeated.

It was at Rymer's house that Browning attended a séance. Mrs. Browning was a believer and her husband was not.

In preparation for the séance Home and Miss Rymer made a clematis wreath, which was laid on the table in the room where the manifestations occurred. At the sitting this wreath was raised by spirit-hands and placed on the head of Mrs. Browning, who was much touched and delighted. Browning always maintained that the whole thing was a trick, and stated to Hawthorne that he believed the spirit-hands were worked by Home's feet, and he said afterwards that he caught hold of Home's foot when it was moving about under the table. No exposé was made at the time. Browning suggested a second séance, but Home refused. Later on, Home called on the Brownings with Mrs. Rymer, and Browning told him to his face he believed he was guilty of fraud. In later years he made him the hero of *Mr. Sludge the Medium*, which contains perhaps the most sensible apology for the medium that can be put forward. The rogue is blamed for his imposture, but those who encourage him are equally blamed for leading him into temptation.

And the temptation offered by wealthy idle men and women to a penniless youth like Home must be recognized. The man had never done a day's work in his life, he had no means, and had learned no trade or profession by which he could earn his living. If he could impose himself upon the world as a medium he could live a life of idleness and ease :

> Sweet and clean, dining daintily, dizened smart ;
> Set on a stool buttressed by ladies' knees,
> Every soft smiler calling me her pet.

Home was in Victorian phrase a lady-killer, and his attractions for feminine and dependent natures of either sex cannot be doubted. A lady present at one of his readings when he was about thirty describes him for the benefit of her friends as, " the most *distingué* man you have seen for years and then you will not have reached the plane on which

Home stands." Her adoration for his beauty cannot find adequate words : " His figure is singularly fine and graceful, his hands and feet beautiful, the former being the embodiment of artistic genius," whatever that may mean. " He is of the blonde type with beautiful hair, fine teeth, a good mouth and eyes that really look as though they saw things in heaven and earth not dreamed of in our philosophy."

About the same date a male writer in *Echoes from the Clubs* sees nothing in the fellow but " a dark-complexioned person with quick-shifting eyes, curly black hair, and a nose which seemed to vouch for a purely Caucasian descent."

Of such is the nature of evidence. For my part I gather from these two statements that the woman is more nearly correct than the man, who, disgusted at the rogue's pretensions and behaviour, unfairly denied him that outward male daintiness which since the days of Helen and Paris has always been an unwholesome lure for women.

Mrs. Browning was too sensible a woman to be foolishly interested in the personality of Home. She notes that he was " weak and vain," and excuses certain moral shortcomings that have reached her ears on the ground that he was " exposed to gross flatteries " from the foolish coteries that took him up. She, like many other convinced spiritualists, believed that he was a medium and considered the fact that he was also a rogue irrelevant.

In the early autumn of 1855 Home went to Florence to stay with Mrs. Trollope, the mother of the novelist, and Thomas Adolphus. Here he was in great vogue and was taken up by the fashionable world, though Mrs. Trollope threw him over later on, owing to some discontent with his moral character. The more sensible of his followers recognized that as a citizen and a human being he was a worthless person, but nevertheless, being eager for the manifestations he could produce, they accepted him as a physical curiosity.

Nathaniel Hawthorne, who was in Italy a few years later, heard a good deal about Home when he was in Florence. He met Mr. and Mrs. Browning over " tea and strawberries," and the talk turned on what Hawthorne called the " disagreeable and now wearisome topic of spiritual communications." Browning expressed his belief that the spirit-hands that he had witnessed were worked by Home with his feet. Hawthorne also met in Florence Mr. Hiram Powers, the American sculptor, a Swedenborgian and a believer in spiritualism. Powers, who described a séance, " gave a decided opinion that Home is a knave, but thinks him so organized nevertheless as to be a particularly good medium." There is a shrewd simplicity in this verdict that makes it a sound foundation on which to enter judgment.

Hawthorne found, as everyone must who reads the dreary accounts of séances, that the stories they contain are " idle and empty." His own womenkind dabbled in the business with a female medium, and Hawthorne notes that there was " a lack of substance in her talk, a want of grip, a delusive show, a sentimental surface with no bottom beneath it. The same sort of thing has struck me in all the poetry and prose that I have read from spiritual sources. I should judge that these effusions emanated from earthly minds, but had undergone some process that had deprived them of solidity and warmth."

Hawthorne tried the lady medium with test questions which failed egregiously, and these failures were set down to an evil spirit, but this excuse did not appeal to his common sense. Hawthorne also records that another friend of his, a quasi believer, was much affrighted and puzzled by Home's manifestations, and declared that Home is " unquestionably a knave " and that " when his spiritual powers fall short he does his best to eke them out with imposture." Hawthorne himself did not desire to meet Home, having a natural dislike

" to receive a message from a dead friend through the organism of a rogue."

From this time onward Home's career was a splendid romantic success. Like all other vagabonds he did not overstay his welcome in any one city. Florence becoming lukewarm about him, he accepts the invitation of Count Branicka, a Polish nobleman with whom he lives in Naples. He tests his friendship very high, for he writes and tells him that his power has left him since February 10, 1856, but that the spirits inform him that it would return in twelve months. The Branicka family are so fond of him that this makes no difference, and he becomes their guest and they take him to Rome. Here he seemed inclined to give up the medium business and enter a monastery. At Rome he joined the Catholic Church and was received by the Pope, but the idea of a monastic cell did not continue to satisfy him and the Branicka family carried him off to the more congenial atmosphere of Paris. Here Père de Ravignan, his confessor, assured him that as he was now a good Catholic the spirits would not worry him any more, and perhaps if he had entered a monastery discipline might have hindered further manifestations.

The 10th of February, 1857, arrived and Home's spiritual friends were all agog. Punctual to the moment, if we may believe Home, " as the clock struck twelve I was in bed, to which I had been confined, when there came loud rappings in my room, a hand was placed gently upon my brow and a voice said, ' Be of good cheer, Daniel, you will soon be well.' "

Père de Ravignan was sent for and expressed considerable annoyance at the news, and Home notes that " as he was about to give me his benediction before leaving, loud raps came on the bedstead. He left me without expressing any opinion whatever on the subject of the phenomena."

It is stated in Father Ponlevoy's life of Ravignan that

on Home being received into the Church and abjuring Protestantism he also repudiated magic, and that all his old practices " of invoking the dead to amuse the living were absolutely forbidden. The unhappy medium," says Ponlevoy, "violated his promise and was once forgiven, but there came another backsliding which made such a noise (*rechute éclatante*) " that Ravignan told him " never again to appear in his presence."

Now if this is the true story it would appear that Home was at one time really desirous, from religious motives, of dropping the medium business and more or less kept out of it for twelve months, but finding that his wealthy friends tired of him decided to take it on again. As a good Catholic there was nothing before him but the workhouse or the monastery; as a medium all the Courts of Europe were open to him, and the faithful who delighted in his manifestations were ready to endow him with riches and jewels and to quarrel for the honour of receiving him as a guest.

The return of Home's power was known at the French Court at once. The Marquis de Belmont, Chamberlain of the Emperor, came with kind inquiries about his miraculous powers and, learning the welcome truth, fixed up a séance for the evening of February 13 at the Tuileries. On that night Home was at his best. He dictated to the Emperor how many should be present—and the manifestations took place as usual. Rappings were heard, the Empress felt her robe pulled, which frightened her, and Home asked her to put her hand under the table when a spirit-hand should touch hers. This she did and informed the audience with tears in her eyes that she felt the hand of her father in hers. The Emperor afterwards was allowed to feel the hand. It was recognized by a defective finger.

A second séance with table-turning effects was given, and

at a third, where the writing business was done, a hand lifted
a pencil and wrote " Napoleon " in the autograph of the
great Emperor. It is to be noted that the same persons were
constantly present and the marvels increased each time.
When the spirits returned after their year's vacation they
were in good form, and the Emperor and Empress were
delighted with all they saw.

Home now left Paris for America. The newspapers were
full of his doings and many scandalous reasons were given
for his departure. But he had certainly secured the interest
of the Court, and he returned to Paris in a few months with
his sister, who was adopted and educated by the Empress.
It is said that Home refused large sums of money for proposed séances, and this may be true, but the gifts that he did
receive must have been considerable, and he was constantly
billeting himself on wealthy families, who at all events for
a time were eager to receive him. Mrs. Browning was
delighted to hear that " the Empress Eugénie protects his
little sister," and even more pleased that " Home, my protégé
prophet," has got an annuity of £240 English " left to him
by an English woman." She also refers to the gifts he has
received and records that she hears " his manners as well
as his morals are wonderfully improved."

Whether Home's continued changes of scene and address
were part of a careful plan of campaign or merely due to
" passivity " impelled by the spirit of vagabondage it is hard
to say. At Paris he became acquainted with Lord Howden,
who had been British Minister at Madrid. From him he
obtained introductions to the Embassies at Vienna and
Constantinople, and we find him flitting from city to city
and Court to Court holding his séances and amazing drawing-
room audiences at the palaces of those counts, barons, dukes
and even kings, who tolerated their wives' appetites for
necromancy, or were entertained by it themselves. Home's

D. D. HOME

*From the painting in the possession of the London
Spiritualist Alliance.*

spirits were nothing if not aristocratic and their best miracles were reserved for the best people.

In March, 1858, he happened to be in Rome and was introduced to a very rich Russian nobleman, Count Koucheleff-Besborodka. Home relates that he and a friend were walking " to the Pynchon," as he spells it, when a carriage passed them and stopped. He was introduced to the Countess and accepted an invitation to supper. " I went about ten," he writes, " and found a large party assembled. At twelve as we entered the supper room the Countess introduced me to a young lady, whom I then observed for the first time as her sister. A strange impression came over me at once and I knew that she was to be my wife." It was quick work. In twelve days they were engaged, and Home accompanied the family to Naples for a few weeks.

In June, Home was in St. Petersburg. There were difficulties with his papers and it seemed as if the marriage was to be postponed. A week spent at the Peterhof Palace entertaining the Emperor with manifestations, " and all the obstacles in the way of my marriage were removed by his most gracious Majesty."

His bride, Mademoiselle Alexandrina de Kroll, was the daughter of a Russian general, and as soon as the Emperor's approval was notified the wedding took place on August 1, 1858. The lady brought him a fortune which involved him in a Russian lawsuit at her death some four years later. The Emperor's wedding gift to Home was a wonderful diamond ring, and on the christening of his child, a year after, His Majesty gave him another valuable ring. These imperial jewels were much in evidence in later years and greatly impressed the groundlings at lectures and séances.

Home made no settled establishment for his wife and child. He continued his vagrant life, and he and his family were guests at country houses in England and châteaux and palaces abroad.

F

The consideration for his entertainment was the counter-entertainment of manifestations which he provided for his hosts.

In spite of his so-called " passivity " the spirits were generally available several evenings a week. The manifestations were of the same character, rapping, furniture-moving, accordion-playing, etc., but occasionally among favoured sitters Home would appear to levitate and float about the room as figures do in dreams.

The best authenticated levitation story is that told by three witnesses, Lord Lindsay, Lord Adare, and a cousin, Captain Wynne. They all testified that they were sitting in an upper room in Ashley House and saw Home float into the room through the window from an adjoining room, where they had left him in a trance. It was a dark séance with moonlight outside and, as Lord Adare says, " so dark that I could not clearly see how he was supported outside." It begins, as do so many of the strange stories told about Home, with a suggestion to the frightened sitters in the dark as to what was going to happen. Lord Adare tells the story thus :

Home went into a trance.
Lindsay suddenly said : " Oh, good heavens ! I know what he is going to do ; it is too fearful."
Adare : " What is it ? "
Lindsay : " I cannot tell you, it is too horrible. A spirit says that I must tell you. He is going out of the window in the other room and coming in at this window."
We heard Home go into the next room, heard the window thrown up and presently Home appeared standing upright outside our window. He opened the window and walked in quite coolly.

Lord Lindsay, in his account, said, " he raised the window and glided into the room feet foremost." Nobody seemed in the least interested as to how a man floating in the air managed to open a sash-window from the outside.

In another account, which Lord Adare wrote for Sir Francis Burnand, with a plan of the rooms, he states that

" a tapping was heard at the window and they perceived Home erect on the ledge. Lord Adare opened the window." The various accounts are entirely unsatisfactory, but Lord Adare left behind and published a large number of strange stories about Home, with whom at one time he was on terms of great intimacy, and he was allowed to see more wonders than any other sitter.

Whatever the witnesses did see, or thought they saw, all this occurred in a dark room with the moonshine outside. In later years, when Home wrote his book *Lights and Shadows*, to prove that he was the only Simon Pure and that all his competitors were quacks and impostors, he derides all manifestations in the dark. " I implore you," he writes to Dr. Sexton, " to advocate the suppression of dark séances. Every form of phenomena ever occurring through me at the few dark séances has been repeated over and over again in the light, and I now regret ever having had other than light séances." This is incorrect. He never floated out of the window in the daylight, though many thought they saw him raised from the ground, and not only did he use dark or dim séances continually, but at times his familiars rapped out a command to put out all lights as a condition precedent to fuller and better manifestations.

His more foolish disciples thought nothing of allowing him to mesmerize them during a séance, and were rewarded by seeing great wonders. A Mr. Jencken, who describes many séances, says : " Home walked round our circle mesmerizing each in turn." They then thought they saw that " an extraordinary manifestation of elongation and shortening occurred. The height he attained must have been quite six feet nine inches ; and again as he became shorter and shorter the waistcoat descended down to his hips, Mrs. —— holding the end of his waistcoat to make certain of the elongation."

On another occasion he mesmerized the same circle, and
they saw him grow up to six feet nine inches and then down
to five feet like Alice in Wonderland. These valuable
spiritual experiences were the privilege of the mesmerized.

Professor Crookes, who was a believer in Home and an
eager searcher after spirits, made some experiments of doubtful value to prove Home's abnormality. But even he noted
at the séances that some sitters saw some things and others
saw others. The apparitions " were seldom visible to all
persons present at a séance." When a hand appeared and
took hold of some grass " only two persons saw the hand,
but all in the room saw the grass moving." Lord Adare
repeatedly records this phenomenon and so do others.

This seems to show that the " manifestations " were not
akin to earthly facts or were entirely subjective. If a crowd
is sitting round watching a cricket match and a ball is hit to
the boundary everyone in the crowd sees the same thing if
he is on the look-out. In a " manifestation " where five or
six people are looking for spirits, one sees a hand, one sees a
luminous appearance and another sees nothing.

It was suggested by Professor Balfour Stewart that
mesmerism was at the bottom of much that people imagined
they saw. Probably he is right. Trollope tells us he could
not be mesmerized ; neither could he see Home's best
miracles or receive his spirits' messages. Jencken was in fact
mesmerized, and Lord Adare and Lord Lindsay were obviously
more susceptible than observant. Home insisted on a small
number of sitters, and the accounts show that the more often
a sitter attended the greater the miracles he saw. Nothing
important came off where " adverse influences " were present,
and Home would not attempt a séance at all with some
people. Whatever the solution may have been, it is difficult
to read the accounts of these séances with any respect for
the persons who took part in them. Home in his attack on

his rivals speaks of their trickiness with a very proper contempt. But that he himself was an adept at all the tricks
of the trade is beyond doubt, though he may have had
abilities not possessed by the meaner professors of mediumship. Home, too, writes very wisely about the sitters at the
feet of mediums who accept every miracle offered to them
and " seem to experience an insane pleasure in being duped,"
and he is certainly right in blaming the sitters, as Robert
Browning did, for the frauds of his fellow-mediums.

He was very jealous of a popular necromancer named.
Allan Kardec, and writing of him in the chapter on " Delusions " says :

His intensity of conviction mastered not only himself but others
His earnestness was projected on the minds of the sensitive magnetic
subjects whom he termed his mediums. The thoughts thus forced into
their brains their hands committed to paper, and Kardec received
his own doctrines as messages of the spirit-world.

When you read the absurd accounts recorded by Home's
sitters of the foolish and useless things they thought they
saw and heard, they certainly read more like the inventions
of a trickster inspiring the minds of his dupes than the
actions and sayings of any sane or sensible being.

That Home had his dupes and fooled them to the top
of their bent to his own profit cannot be gainsaid. The most
notorious case that was made public was that of Mrs. Lyon.
In 1866 Home was down on his luck. He was now thirty-
three, and for over ten years had lived in affluence, sponging
on his friends and supported by the gifts of his dupes and
his late wife's money. But a Russian brother-in-law had
stopped supplies and he had started an action against him.
He had also been expelled from Rome as an undesirable,
having incurred the displeasure of the Catholic Church, and
had returned to England in want of funds.

Dickens, in a letter to Trollope written before the Lyon

case, says that Home was trying to come out as an actor at
Fechter's, " where I had the honour of stopping him short."
Dickens relates some other theatrical efforts he made which
were not successful, and concludes, " I believe the public
to have found out the scoundrel, in which lively and sustaining hope this leaves me at present." Browning's poem,
Mr. Sludge the Medium, had further injured his position
among the more thoughtful. Neither Dickens nor Browning
had any doubt that the man was a rogue, and mankind
generally were beginning to find his manifestations rather
futile and boring. They were tired of his pinchbeck
miracles.

Spiritualism, like other necromancies, has always been
a hobby of the idle well-to-do, and for the moment it was
becoming unfashionable. Some of Home's friends in England, however, tried to assist him by starting a Spiritual
Athenæum in Sloane Street, with a hundred five-guinea
subscribers and Home as resident secretary.

The Spiritual Athenæum did not catch on, but it did
attract a foolish, vulgar, wealthy and lonely old woman named
Mrs. Lyon. Home gave her private séances, when the spirit
of her deceased husband told her that he was the father of
Dan and " therefore Dan is your son." Home has the
promise of a £10 subscription to the Athenæum out of this
old lady the first time he meets her. The next day she gives
him £30 instead of the £10, and two days afterwards another
present of £50 under the direction of the spirit of her deceased
husband, " so that our son may not be without the means
of living."

Within three months the rascal has deeds of gift to the
amount of £60,000 out of the old lady and has been adopted
by her and taken her name. But he was a restless vagabond
and found his adopted mother a tedious bore. " I have sold
my liberty," he sighed. Instead of introducing his new

mamma to his aristocratic friends he gads round to watering-places and enjoys himself with her money. At length she hears he is off to Germany and, fearing her son is going to desert her, she consults a solicitor, Home is arrested and liberated on depositing in Court the deeds of gift.

The case in the Chancery Court created a stir in the fashionable world. Many believed that there would be a demonstration of spiritual forces in Court and the alphabet would be spelled out before the Vice-Chancellor. It is hard to understand why any decent disembodied spirit should desert Home in his hour of need. Mrs. Lyon's counsel, in cross-examining the defendant, took the bold course of asking Home if a rap would be forthcoming? This I think would have made the raps evidence. But the familiars that played accordions and tilted tables in the darkened drawing-rooms of the well-to-do refused the more practical service of giving evidence in a Court of Justice to sustain the character of their chosen medium. The Vice-Chancellor very properly declared the gifts fraudulent and void, and Home was ordered to return the plunder. Home's circle of friends made light of the result of the trial and their hero resumed his wanderings. He gave some readings at this period of his career and also lectured on spiritualism with some success, people flocking to see him and the imperial jewels with which he was always adorned.

His good luck did not desert him, and in 1871 he married another Russian lady of good family, a Madame Aksakoff. About the same time he was successful in his Russian law-suit and once more he was a rich man ; we find him living in Paris and Italy and touring in Russia, where he is received again by the Emperor.

His séances were now fewer and even more select. He and his friend Howitt published *Lights and Shadows of Spiritualism*, in which, as we have seen, dark séances are sensibly condemned and the trickery and delusion of all mediumship, except his own, amply acknowledged. This and a second instalment of *Incidents in My Life* were doubtless written to reinstate him in the eyes of the world after the disclosures in the Lyon case. He now posed as the Master-medium more or less retired from active business.

Towards the end of the 'seventies the spirits seem to have given him a rest and he travelled for health and amusement, but his fame still brought him a considerable correspondence with spiritualists all over the world. He had always had a tendency to consumption, and for some years before his death, which occurred at Auteuil on June 21, 1886, he was in bad health.

Whatever may have been Home's physical abnormalities, if any, there can be no doubt that the bulk of his manifestations were the same tricks and delusions that he exposes and condemns in his own book. For the rest, as Home was never under any real scientific observation when his more startling manifestations came off, it is impossible to dogmatize about how they were produced. His more sensible patrons, men like Thomas Adolphus Trollope, for instance, never saw any very stupendous miracles and came to the conclusion that such phenomena as they saw were " natural or in accordance with some law in nature."

Whilst no doubt the man fascinated many people, especially women, he repelled others. Whatever gifts he had he used them to selfish ends. By means of his manifestations and his methods of exploiting them he lived in wealth and comfort and complete idleness at other people's expense for over thirty years, wandering about the earth in search of pleasure. A charming and undoubtedly a beloved vagabond, both in many ways and to many people, it is to be regretted that he could not resist the temptation of despoiling poor helpless Mrs. Lyon, as but for that discreditable incident it would have been unnecessary to write him down a rogue.

CHAPTER IV

JOHN HATFIELD, THE IMPOSTOR

ON Tuesday, August 16, 1803, Wordsworth and his sister Dorothy accompanied by Coleridge set out on their tour to Scotland and dined at Carlisle. They found the town in a bustle with the Assizes. It was the day John Hatfield was sentenced to death for forgery. At eight o'clock in the morning Hatfield, who had been found guilty overnight, had been taken across the street in a post-chaise to the Town Hall for sentence and he was now in custody at the jailer's house, which became a centre of attraction to the mob. It is interesting to note that Wordsworth and Coleridge shared with the common herd the somewhat morbid desire to interview a man about to be hanged.

Miss Wordsworth, who was rather shy of the crowd of fine ladies and county people who mobbed the streets of the old city on this interesting occasion, accompanied her brother and his friend to the jailer's house but did not go in to see Hatfield. " I stood at the door of the jailer's house where he was ; William entered the house and Coleridge saw him." Miss Wordsworth may be wrong about this because others say that Hatfield refused to see Coleridge, whose letters to the *Morning Post* had been instrumental in bringing about his downfall, though he granted Wordsworth an interview.

However, whilst they were within, Dorothy talked to the folk at the door. One of the debtor prisoners came up to her and claimed to have been a fellow-sailor on brother John's ship, on the strength of which tale the old sailor drew a shilling and confided to his benefactress that in his view Hatfield was " far overlearned." Another prisoner observed to William that " we might learn from Hatfield's fate not to meddle with pens and ink." Afterwards at the " Graham Arms " at Longtown, Dorothy finds that, " here, as everywhere else, the people seem utterly insensible of the enormity of Hatfield's offences, the ostler told William that he was quite a gentleman and paid everyone genteelly." Always remembering that what the ostler told William is not evidence, Miss Wordsworth's account of what she heard and saw goes to show that a hundred years ago society, both high and low, was as curious and sympathetic about a criminal under sentence of death as it is to-day.

Now Hatfield was a rogue and criminal of a low type, but he had the true instinct of the vagabond in squandering freely among those who ministered to his pleasures the money he obtained from others. Moreover, like all claimants and pretenders, he found some who believed in his pretensions to the last, or at least regarded him as a victim of the law. People exist to-day who fancy that Arthur Orton was Roger Tichborne. And we must remember that Hatfield was not executed for marrying women and deserting his wives and children, but for forgery, and this, as Wordsworth's friend had said, was clearly the result of his ill-fortune in being educated " to meddle with pens and ink."

Reading the history of this unpleasing rogue and vagabond, it is difficult to understand how anyone could regret his fate. But every execution not unnaturally turns the pity of the people from the victim to the criminal ; and in this case the illogical public managed to bewail the fate of both Hatfield and the woman he wronged with one flood of tears.

John Hatfield was born early in the seventeen-fifties, of poor but honest parents, at Mottram-in-Longden-Dale, Cheshire. He was unfortunate in many ways. He had natural abilities and received a poor education ; he was good-looking, " his face was handsome, the shape of which in his youth was oval, his person genteel, his eyes blue, and his complexion fair ; " furthermore he had the instinct of the vagabond and the selfish desires of the rogue. It seems typical of the rogue and vagabond that he or she should possess strong attraction for the opposite sex. Perhaps this was an added misfortune for Hatfield, but be that as it may, he had a fatal fascination for women.

His native village had no use for him, and as a young man he left his home and found congenial employment as " a rider " or traveller for a linen-draper in the North of England. A neighbour of his master, a farmer, had a pretty daughter, who became acquainted with Hatfield and fell in love with him. The farmer now told the girl that he was in fact only her poor guardian, and that she was the natural daughter of Lord Robert Manners, who proposed to give her £1,000 when she married. Hatfield, as soon as he learned this, made formal proposal for her hand. The farmer acquainted his lordship with the young linen-draper's honourable and prudent intentions, and Hatfield was interviewed by the " noble and unsuspecting parent," who was so pleased with his demeanour that he presented him with a banker's draft for £1,500 and the young people were married to everyone's content in or about 1772. At least so the chronicles say, but I am very doubtful about this date and think it must have been much later.

This last stroke of luck or ill-fortune, whichever you will, started him merrily on the gay road to the gallows. The rogue and his pretty bride set off for London. There he bought a phaeton—it would have been a motor-car to-day —and swaggered about the town as a man of wealth. He haunted the coffee-houses of Covent Garden where he posed as a near relation of the Rutland family, his talk was of his horses, parks and hounds, but the men of the world scented the linen-draper in him and he was known to the habitués as " Lying Hatfield."

Even £1,500 cannot last for ever, and after a few years Hatfield disappeared and there is a gap in his history until we find him in 1782 in the King's Bench prison. He had deserted his wife and three children, and she, poor thing, had returned to the farm to die. Perhaps the good farmer took care of the orphans, or the beadle carried them off and the parish apprenticed them. John Hatfield cared nothing whatever about it.

For the fellow was in congenial surroundings in the prison, where he met many of his former acquaintances whom he had feasted in the days of his vanity. He had cast his bread—or rather his wife's and children's bread— upon the waters of waste, and here in jail, true to the text, it was returned to him. His old friends invited him to dinner, listened in these squalid surroundings to his fairy tales of the Rutlandshire estate settled on his wife, and his annoyance at being lagged for £160, when he was cutting a new lake in the Yorkshire family park and ought to be super-vising his thirty workmen.

Pleasant as this life was compared with any form of honest toil, Hatfield yearned for liberty. It appears that a venerable clergyman of the simplicity of Dr. Primrose was in the habit of visiting Valentine Morris, an unfortunate Colonial Governor who had retired to a debtors' prison. To him Hatfield posed as a minor star of nobility under a cloud of despair. In strictest confidence he told him he was nearly allied to the house of Rutland, and was here in jail for £160. " But," he added most impressively, " the truth is, sir, I would not have my situation known to any man in the world but my worthy relative, His Grace of Rutland. Indeed, I would rather remain a captive for ever. But, sir, if you would

have the goodness to pay your respects to this worthy nobleman, and frankly describe how matters are, he will send me
the money by you, and this mighty business will not only
be instantly settled, but I shall have the satisfaction of introducing you to a connexion which may be attended with
happy consequences."

The honest clergyman could not refuse a mission to a
duke, and the hint of " happy consequences " worked as was
intended. He paid his respects to His Grace of Rutland,
who flatly told him that the whole thing was the idle tale of
some impostor. The good man faltered out his apologies,
which were graciously received, for the Duke now remembered that his kinsman, Lord Robert Manners, had a natural
daughter married to a draper of the name of Hatfield. There
were no " happy consequences " for the kindly mediator ;
these were reserved, as the way of the world is, for the rogue.
Herein we must commend the insight of the linen-draper.
He foresaw that His Grace would not approve of the husband
of a relation's daughter lying poverty-stricken in jail. It
would offend his notion of what was due to the princely
standing of the House of Manners. He was right. The
Duke's agent was set to work. Inquiries were made. A
messenger arrived at the prison with £200, and Hatfield
started off once again with a light heart on his road to the
gallows.

Now Charles Manners, Duke of Rutland, himself a young
man of thirty, was in 1784 persuaded by his friend Pitt to
become Lord-Lieutenant of Ireland. Shortly after his
arrival in Dublin the rascal Hatfield makes another appearance above the horizon. We find him landing at Kings-
town, posting to Dublin and engaging a suite of rooms at
the best hotel in College Green, telling the landlord of his
relationship to the Viceroy and impatiently awaiting the
arrival of his horses and carriages. These, he says, he has

shipped from Liverpool so that he can pay his devoirs at the Castle in proper state.

He was a regular attendant at Lucas's Coffee-house, where the rank and fashion of Dublin were to be found. Here his fairy tales of the Yorkshire park and the Rutland-shire estates were amiably received. But after a month, the landlord of the hotel, finding no servants or horses arriving from England, desired that his bill of £60 should be met. Hatfield was equal to the emergency. He gave him the name of his agent, who was a man holding high appoint-ment in the county, but at the moment not in Dublin, and told him to present the bill to him. By this means he got three days' respite.

Whether he meant to return to England or what his in-tentions were, who can say ? The landlord presented the bill and was informed by the supposed agent that his customer was well known in London as " a romantic simpleton whose plausibilities had imposed on several people and plunged himself into repeated difficulties." The indignant landlord posted off to his lawyer and before nightfall Hatfield was lodged in the prison of the Marshalsea.

But the man is never to be daunted, and if there is a woman to appeal to, you may be certain you will not find him lonely and forlorn. The jailer's wife is allowed to dis-cover that she is entertaining one of the nobility. In strict confidence he whispers to her that he is a near relation of the Viceroy, and she, good woman, moves him into her best parlour where a good table is provided, and she and her fond husband and the delightful prisoner enjoy each other's society with the utmost harmony and good humour for a space of three weeks.

During this time he has petitioned His Grace for further supplies, and to get rid of the ignominy of such a pretender, the Viceroy orders his release on condition of his quitting

Ireland at once, and sends one of his servants to see him on to the packet and wait until it sails for Holyhead. Whether his bills were settled by the Castle authorities is not recorded, but very probably they were, as it was important for the Viceroy to be popular among his new subjects.

Again Hatfield disappears from public view for several years and when next heard of we find him at Scarborough, visiting the landed gentry of the neighbourhood and insinuating that His Grace the Duke of Rutland intended him to be the new parliamentary representative of the borough. His old patron, Charles Manners, was dead and the present Duke, John Henry Manners, was a youth of fourteen. Hatfield's career of imposture at Scarborough was cut short by the landlord of the hotel where he was staying presenting his bill. As he was again without money he was arrested, and thrown into Scarborough jail, where he languished for some seven years.

One would have thought that experiences such as these would have satisfied his appetite for roguery and vagabondage, and that if another chance were given to him he might have turned away from the fatal road upon which he had travelled for so long and with such evil results. But this was not to be, and doubtless his vanity and insane belief in his own abilities were flattered and confirmed by the incidents of his release.

In a house opposite the jail at Scarborough lived a Mrs. Nation and her daughter. How the young lady and Hatfield became acquainted, how the courtship was conducted, what Mamma was doing, and how her daughter outwitted her vigilance remains a mystery. That Miss Nation paid Hatfield's debts and obtained his release is clear, and the legend goes that she never even spoke to him until he quitted the jail and then she married him on the morning afterwards, which was September 14, 1800.

Here was a chance to begin a new century with a better life. But that was not Hatfield's way. His bride was a Devonshire woman and they first settled in Dulverton. Here she introduced him to useful friends, and some highly respectable merchants took him into partnership and an unfortunate clergyman accepted his drafts.

Again we find him in London living in splendid style and once more pretending to parliamentary honours, for we hear of him canvassing the rotten borough of Queensborough A general election was in view and the immunity from arrest which was a privilege of Parliament, would have been very useful to him. But all his wild-cat schemes came to nothing His creditors discovered the man they were dealing with The inevitable crash came. He was declared a bankrupt and took to flight, deserting his unhappy and penniless wife, who, with her child, retired to some charitable relations at Tiverton.

By your true rogue and vagabond these little set-backs in the luxury of vain imagination are not to be treated too seriously. To a rogue of resource there are always more worlds to conquer, more dupes to swindle, more women to seduce. John Hatfield was not going to turn back, he was nearing the end of his journey, the gallows was over the edge of the hill, but the road still seemed to him to lead to a land of promise. This last adventure was to be his masterpiece, the great drama of his life, with entirely new effects and a part to play worthy of his heroic vanity.

On a summer morning in July of 1802, a handsome and well-appointed travelling carriage mounted Dunmail Raise and, passing Thirlspot, crossed the Greta and leaving Causeway Foot rattled over the cobble-stones into the little town of Keswick, where it drew up at the " Queen's Head." From it alighted Colonel The Hon. Alexander Augustus Hope, M.P. for Linlithgow and brother of the Earl of Hope-

JOHN HATFIELD.

The Famous Seducer &c &c

(Aged 46)

From a contemporary engraving in Kirby's
"The Wonderful and Scientific Museum."

toun. He came without servant, which seemed strange to the citizens of Keswick at first, but he was such a pleasant affable fellow that he soon won the hearts of the inhabitants ; and as he was always ready to frank their letters—which was then the privilege of a Member of Parliament—it was not wonderful that no one had the least suspicion of his identity. Perhaps John Hatfield had not at that time duly considered that forging a frank on a letter was not only a forgery but a forgery on the Post Office, and a capital offence not likely to be condoned.

However, for the time all went well. The neighbouring landed gentry called and invited him to their houses. He returned their calls, leaving much-envied pasteboards on those he honoured, with the magic title " The Honourable Alexander Augustus Hope " engraved upon them in a flowing Italian hand. He was for the last time, to the delight of his vanity, a splendid success. " All doors," says his chronicler, " flew open at his approach ; boats, boatmen, nets, and the most unlimited sporting privileges were placed at the disposal of the ' Honourable ' gentleman ; and the hospitality of the whole county taxed itself to offer a suitable reception to the patrician Scotsman."

No one at that time came to Keswick without going to Buttermere, not only to visit Scale Force but to see Mary Robinson, the beauty of the village. Joseph Budworth, antiquary and poet, had visited the little village in 1795 and had so described the rustic beauty of Sally of Buttermere—her real name was Mary—that no tourist omitted a visit to the little ale-house, " The Char," at the bottom end of the lake.

Mr. Robinson was a " Statesman " and looked after the char fishing. What with his land, his sheep and his inn, he had saved a little money. Budworth, in his *Fortnight's Ramble in the Lake District*, had portrayed the Beauty of

G

Buttermere in alluring phrases. At his first approach the
girl left her spinning-wheel and " flew away as fast as a
mountain sheep," but when the party came back from the
waterfall to dinner she waited on them, and Budworth
extolled her fine oval face and full eyes, her lips as red as
vermilion and the lily hue of her cheeks. Her charm of
manner was even more angel-like than her face. She " was
a very Lavinia," wrote the enraptured Budworth quoting
his favourite Thomson :

> for loveliness
> Needs not the foreign aid of ornament,
> But is when unadorned adorned the most.

Two years afterwards Budworth revisited the little ale-
house, and had a pleasant meal off " a cold sirloin of most
excellent marbled beef." But he found the parlour whitewash scribbled with Greek, Latin, French and English
compliments to the beauty of the parlour-maid. He regretted
that he had written up Mary in his guide book, and thought
it right as he was leaving, to suggest to Mary that she should
be very careful of encouraging strangers, who were not all
Josephs and might have evil intentions. He added that it
was only just to tell her plainly that : " You really are not so
handsome as you promised to be, and I have long intended
by conversation like this to do away what mischief the flattering character I gave you may expose you to." Mary sincerely
thanked Mr. Budworth and said she was very well able to
take care of herself, and Joseph kissed her heartily and said
farewell.

It is not to be wondered at that John Hatfield, in the
guise of Colonel Hope, drove over to " The Char " in his
splendid coach and put up there to spend his time in fishing
and making love to Mary. Not that she was by any means
his only love. There was a fisherman's daughter at Keswick,
and another girl of the same class, and a young and beautiful

heiress staying with an Irish colonel and Member of Parliament, to all of whom in these summer months did Colonel Hope become engaged to be married.

The young heiress was so infatuated that the trousseau was ordered, and the wedding-day would have been fixed, but that for some reason or other Colonel Hope delayed to approach formally her family and ask for her hand.

Finding his schemes against this young lady were likely to come to naught Hatfield determined to carry off the Beauty of Buttermere, who is described by his biographer as a " fine young woman of eighteen." She was probably much older, but neither she nor her simple parents were proof against the temptation of so grand a marriage as that proposed by Colonel Hope.

Unfortunately for poor Mary, the one man in the valley who might have given her good advice and saved her from this scoundrel was the Reverend John Nicholson, chaplain of Loweswater. He was, however, a firm friend and believer in the Hon. Colonel Hope, up to the last, Hatfield having won his heart by attending his church, praising his sermons, and driving him over to Keswick in his splendid chariot to dine with him at the " Queen's Head."

About a week before October 2 the Rev. Mr. Nicholson drove with Colonel Hope to Whitehaven, where they got a marriage licence that the Colonel might marry Mary Robinson of Buttermere. The clergyman had heard his friend speak of Mary as " a lovely girl," but he " had not seen any signs of intimacy previous to marriage." Colonel Hope suggested to old Robinson that he should sell up his holding in the valley and come and live near them in Scotland, but nothing came of that and Hatfield does not seem to have got any money out of him.

The excess of charity in the clergy, and their habit of thinking no evil of mankind, make them very easy prey to the rogue and vagabond, who, without a respectable colleague, would often find it difficult to accomplish his aims. Had Nicholson asked for some proofs of Hope's identity, which was already suspect among some of the more cautious gentry in the neighbourhood, he might have saved the flower of his parish from undeserved misery. As it was he was the instrument of her undoing.

On Saturday, October 2, 1802, at Lorton Church, on the road between Keswick and Cockermouth, the Rev. John Nicholson married " Alexander Augustus Hope of Scotland and Mary Robinson of the parish of Lorton," and the happy pair drove away in the handsome carriage to Scotland to spend the honeymoon. The week-end was spent at Longtown, a little town eight miles north of Carlisle, from which on Monday Hatfield wrote a characteristic letter to his friend Nicholson. It is indeed hard to understand the psychology of the writer of such a letter, but it helps to explain the success of his deceits.

LONGTOWN, *Monday Evening*, *4th October*.
MY DEAR AND REV. SIR,
We arrived here on Saturday evening about eight, went to the Church on Sunday and Mr. Graham, the brother of Sir James, gave one of the finest lectures I ever heard. We attended his evening discourse, at the end of which he addressed me, begging I would not return to my quarters without a light, and his footman stood ready with one. All this flurried my dear Mary a little, but nothing can be more pleasing than the manner she at all times possesses. To-morrow evening we may perhaps proceed further ; but Mrs. Hope likes the quietude of this place much, and her wishes are my laws.

In the churchyard we found the following inscription which I copied on purpose to send you, thinking it may amuse some of our friends ; pray read it to Dr. Head and present him my best respects :

Our life is but a winter day
Some only breakfast and away ;
Others, to dinner stay, and are full fed ;
The oldest man but sups, and goes to bed.
Large is his debt, who lingers out the day ;
Who goes the soonest, has the least to pay.

Be pleased to say for us both, whatever you think will be acceptable to those, who from kind motives, may inquire after us ; and at Buttermere, Mary desires you will tender to father and mother the most affectionate duty and the most lively assurances of our mutual happiness. I find happiness is not very loquacious so this will be a short letter ; let us have a long one as soon as possible addressed for Col. Hope, M.P., Post Office, Longtown, Cumberland, and you will greatly oblige.

Very dear and Rev. Sir,

Yours most truly,

A. HOPE.

At this time Coleridge was living at Greta Hall, Keswick, and was contributing to the *Morning Post*. With true journalistic instinct he saw that the story of poor Mary's marriage would make good copy and that the publicity given to the activities of Colonel Hope would lead to his family either acknowledging the relationship or denying it. Coleridge himself did not share the local enthusiasm about the Colonel and obviously mistrusted him. The article appeared in the paper of Monday, October 11, and began as follows :

On the 2nd instant, a gentleman calling himself Alexander Augustus Hope, member for Linlithgowshire and brother to the Earl of Hopetoun, was married at the church of Lorton, near Keswick, to a young woman celebrated by the tourists, under the name of the Beauty of Buttermere. To beauty, however, in the strict sense of the word, she has small pretensions, for she is rather sap-toothed and somewhat pock-fretten. But her face is very expressive and the expression extremely interesting, and her figure and movements are graceful to a miracle. She ought, indeed to have been called the Grace of Buttermere rather than the Beauty. She is the daughter of an old couple, named Robinson, who keep a little pot-house at the foot of the small lake of Buttermere with the sign of the Char, and has been all her life the attendant and waiter, for they have no servant. She is now about thirty and has long attracted the notice of every visitor by her exquisite elegance and the becoming manner in which she is used to fillet her beautiful long hair ; likewise by the uncommonly fine Italian handwriting in which the little bill is made out. Added to this she has ever maintained an irreproachable character, is a good daughter, and is a modest, sensible and observant woman.

Coleridge then details Colonel Hope's descent upon Keswick and his courtship of the Irish gentleman's lady guest, and concludes by alluding to the anxiety caused to the friends and neighbours of Mary and their desire to have " decisive proofs that the bridegroom is the real person whom he describes himself to be."

On October 14 the *Morning Post* prints a letter from Charles Hope saying that the Hon. Col. Alexander Hope has been abroad the whole summer and is now at Vienna.

Before these papers reach Keswick rumours have grown stronger about the doings of Colonel Hope. Even friend Nicholson thinks they cannot be treated with contempt and writes to his patron that he had better come home and face the music. The chief complaint against him seems to be his desertion of the young heiress. Colonel Hope writes bravely to his friend denying that he proposed to the lady and says he will return at once to Buttermere " that I may properly answer all such persons as assume the privilege of censuring my conduct and are mean enough to disturb the peace of our parents." The honeymoon is abandoned. Colonel and Mrs. Hope come south in the beautiful carriage and within ten or eleven days of her marriage Mary is at home again.

Now it happened that about this time George Hardinge, the Welsh judge and an author well known to society, was touring in the Lakes. Hearing at the " Queen's Head," where he stayed, that Colonel Hope had been residing there, and had married the Beauty of Buttermere, he expressed his surprise and his desire to meet him as he knew the colonel very well. He therefore wrote to Buttermere asking Colonel Hope to dinner. This invitation the Colonel did not accept, but he arrived later bringing the Reverend Mr. Nicholson with him in his carriage. This was on October 18.

He explained at once to Mr. Hardinge that he was not his

friend Colonel Hope and had never assumed that name. He had said his name was Hope but not that he was member for Linlithgow. This did not accord with the information Hardinge had received and he dismissed him very coolly. He then wrote to Sir Frederick Vane, a county magistrate, advising the man's arrest and suggested to Mr. Wood, the landlord, that he should detain the horses so that he could not escape.

Hatfield complained of Hardinge's conduct and Wood sympathized with him but said he must obey the judge's commands. So Hatfield ordered dinner and persuaded Wood to cash him a bill for £20 on the security of his carriage, which for the want of horses must perforce remain at the " Queen's Head," and he and Nicholson sauntered down to the lake.

Here he told his friend that he would cross the lake and go over the mountains to Buttermere and suggested to Nicholson that he should go back to the " Queen's Head " and eat the ordered dinner and pay for it. This his good friend agreed to do and saw him into his boat at the lakeside and walked back to the town. But when he had gone, the boatman was ordered not to cross the lake but to land at Lodore, at the head of Derwentwater, where Hatfield stepped ashore and was last seen walking up the gorge of Borrowdale.

This was the end of Colonel Hope, and his poor wife saw him no more. Her parents, his friend Nicholson, Mr. Wood, landlord of the " Queen's Head," and the gentry of Keswick who had entertained him so royally never saw their splendid guest again until he stood in the dock at Carlisle.

Coleridge thinks that Hatfield made his way over " the Stake, a fearful Alpine Pass, over Glaramara into Langdale." But I think it far more likely he was piloted across Sty Head down to Wastdale, for he was seen on October 25 at Ravenglass on board a sloop wrapped in a sailor's great-coat and disguised. His profusion in ordering good things from the inn aroused the curiosity of the sailors, and he did not sail with them but took coach to Ulverston and thence made his way into Chester. Here he had a good supper and a bottle of Madeira, took a chaise to Northwich and could be traced no farther.

By now there was a hue and cry raised and his description was in all the papers. Coleridge continued his articles about poor Mary in the *Morning Post* and the people throughout the country were all on the look-out for the scoundrel who had betrayed her. Coleridge is not even content with the romance of the story as it stands, and the pitiful description of the poor girl's misery in her desertion, but in best journalistic style tries to heighten popular interest by hinting " that there are some circumstances attending her birth and true parentage which would account for her striking personality in mind and manners in a way extremely flattering to the prejudices of rank and birth." Indeed, he goes so far as to write of poor Mr. Robinson as " her nominal father." This libel on the Robinsons seems to have escaped the blue pencil of the editor and fortunately never caught the eye of any speculative Cumberland attorney—or maybe no forbears of Dodson & Fogg had then penetrated that Arcadian county. It is right, perhaps, to add that there seems no basis of truth in Coleridge's unnecessary excursion into scandal.

The hunted man was at last run to earth near Swansea. When he was arrested his vain imagination did not desert him. On being brought before the Welsh magistrates he told them that he was Henry Tudor, and boasted that he was descended from an old Welsh family, and had always entertained great love and respect for the Welsh people. He was, however, satisfactorily identified as John Hatfield and carried to London. In due course he was taken on to Cumberland and committed for trial by the county magistrates for forgery and bigamy.

His trial took place on Monday, August 15, 1803. James Scarlett, afterwards Lord Abinger, who was then a junior in large practice, conducted the prosecution. The charge was forgery of franks, which was a serious offence in those days against the Post Office and the State. Scarlett, however, in opening the case took care to remind the jury of the general character of the prisoner and his conduct to Mary Robinson, as juries in those days often hesitated to send a man to the gallows for the offence of forgery. Had he been indicted for bigamy he would have been transported but could not have been sentenced to death.

The evidence against him was conclusive, and the jury, who desired he should be punished for his conduct to Mary, only consulted for ten minutes before finding him guilty. It was thought that he might possibly be reprieved, but, no pardon arriving, Saturday, September 8, was fixed for his execution and a gallows was erected on an island in the River Eden on the north side of the town between two bridges.

No friends visited him in jail, but his father sent him some money at the last, and he at once assumed his former airs of grandeur, making presents to his brother felons and patronizing his jailers who were proud of their show prisoner and treated him " as a kind of emperor." He was driven to the place of execution in a chaise escorted by a troop of yeomanry, and was exceedingly annoyed that the jailers would not draw up the window blinds so that the prodigious crowd that had collected for the execution could see the hero of the day. He behaved with dignity and fortitude at the gallows and, having handed the hangman his last half-crown, which he had saved for the occasion, he gave his blessing to the assembled people as a signal that the cart should be drawn from under his feet.

Mary of Buttermere became the heroine of ballads, broadsides and melodramas, and a subscription was started for her which unfortunately did not bring in very much money. Mary Lamb writes to Dorothy Wordsworth an amusing account of a Sadler's Wells drama in which Mary of Buttermere was happily married to a sailor sweetheart. A prodigious new view of Buttermere with " mountains like haycocks and a lake like nothing at all " was the best part of the play. Charles and Miss Rickman laughed merrily through all the tragic scenes and Southey went to sleep over it.

In due course Mary of Buttermere was forgotten and those who saw her in later life could not understand why so much pother had been made of her beauty. She became fat and well-looking, married a neighbouring farmer and was seen no more at the sign of " The Char."

Among Hatfield's papers were found many verses, including at least two epitaphs written apparently during one of his many imprisonments. The one below is worth recording as it shows how lightly his villainies weighed upon his soul and how real his vain imaginings were in his own eyes.

To where the ancient marbles weep,
And all the worthy Hatfields sleep,
Amongst them soon may I recline.
Oh ! pray their hallow'd tombs be mine.
When in that sacred vault I'm laid,
Heaven grant it may with truth be said,
His heart was warm'd with faith sincere
And soft humanity dwelt there.
My children oft will mourn their father's love,
Heart-easing tears from their sweet eyes will flow ;
My . . . too, relenting, when I'm dead,
O'er past unkindness, tender tears will shed.

Which of his deserted wives was to shed tears for the rogue he does not say, but to my mind these and other verses, coupled with the extravagant nature of his crimes, suggest that the wretched man was not wholly responsible for his wickedness.

CHAPTER V

ROBIN HOOD, THE BRIGAND

I CONFESS that it was with real dismay that on opening the volume of my beloved *Dictionary of National Biography*, which treats of all famous Englishmen from Harris to Hovenden, I found that so gracious and learned a scholar as Sir Sidney Lee had succumbed to the modern heresy of deeming Robin Hood a " legendary hero," and only faintly murmured his disapproval of those who announced him to be a sun-myth. These sayings are a stumbling-block to faith. I found myself rehearsing the hymn of Truthful James with a cold feeling that he too might be only a sun-myth.

> Do I sleep ? do I dream ?
> Do I wonder and doubt ?
> Are things what they seem ?
> Or is visions about ?
> Is our civilization a failure ?
> Or is the Caucasian played out ?

I remembered that had it not been for the splendid stand made by Sir Sidney Lee, our great national hero William Shakespeare might by this time have become a Yankee sun-myth and his works mere Chicago Bacon. That an English writer who could accept not only William himself but his little poaching adventure in Charlecote Great Park as " a credible tradition," should turn down that other great English hero, Robin Hood, was a shock to my young mind, for though I am stricken in years my mind remains young enough, I am glad to say, to believe in the great truths that I learned in the nursery.

Merely because a man lived a long time ago in an age when there were no journalists to interview him, and stories have grown up around his name that sound like fairy tales, there is no reason in rejecting his physical existence altogether, especially when you can find sufficient evidence of the real body of a man, doing great actions, in the background of his story. I had always pictured Robin Hood as a typical English hero. He was a rogue and vagabond perhaps, but one that gave both great and poor medicines to make them love him, and I must plead guilty to having drunk his medicines in ballad form. He was a vagabond that lived a strenuous and active life. He was an outdoor man who had no use for the effeminacy of cities. He was the greatest English bowman of his own or, indeed, any other time. He was a strong anti-prohibitionist, and in an age when there was a perpetual closing time in the forest, and the killing and eating of deer were absolutely forbidden and punished by horrible and cruel penalties, Robin Hood and his merry men defied the sheriffs and shot and ate venison at any time of the day that pleased them.

Politically he seems to have been the only effective Opposition to the Government of the day, and though towards the end of his career he accepted a royal invitation to London, his innate Radicalism saved him from the fate of dying in a palace and he escaped to end his days in his beloved greenwood.

Moreover, he was a simple Christian ; and yet he was in constant warfare with the monks and abbots, who, as the bureaucrats and tax-gatherers of the age, were always honestly hated by the normal Englishman. In so far as the fathers forgot their task of selling all their goods and giving to the poor, Robin Hood became their almoner ; and many a good story is told of how he lightened their " portmantles " of gold and used the proceeds for merry charities.

These were my memories of the good Robin Hood, and it was a mournful day when, for the first time in my life, I drew blank in the covers of the *Dictionary of National Biography*, and on seeking for further and better particulars of Robin Hood's career was answered by a learned paraphrase of those memorable and tremendous words, " I don't believe there's no sich a person."

And though I felt at the moment that my faith in Robin Hood had received a blow, yet it was not wholly shattered. Faith has always been a strong point of mine. What I believe I believe. In spite of the modernists and the theory of relativity, I continue to hold that two and two are approximately four, even on the golf links where simple addition is often a complex affair. My faith is of the quality defined by the schoolboy who said that " true faith consists in believing what you *know* to be untrue." No sooner had I learned from the Dictionary that Robin Hood had never existed than I believed in the details of his career more passionately than ever. I re-read the *Lyttel Geste*, and all the old ballads of his story, and they seemed to me more obviously true than ever they had been before. I had enjoyed them as a child and I got a greater enjoyment of them to-day. I mentioned all this to a friendly psychologist, who was also an authority on folk-lore, and he thoughtfully reminded me that there was such a human condition as second childhood.

The academic verdict was evidently against me, and I should have given up the notion of writing a biographical essay about my English hero had I not by accident come across a passage in that glorious work, the *Institutes* of Lord Chief Justice Sir Edward Coke. On the hundred and ninety-seventh page of the third *Institute*, where I was looking for legal light and guidance on the Elizabethan rule of the road in relation to collisions on land in cases where the speed limit is exceeded by both vehicles, I found the following statement : " Robin Hood lived in the reign of King Richard I " !

Never before had I realized what a true prophet old Fuller was when he wrote of Coke's *Institutes* : " His learned and laborious works will be admired by judicious posterity, while fame has a trumpet left her and any breath to blow therein." Had the rules of the library allowed of it and an intrument been at hand I could have blown his praises on a saxophone. For not only as a citizen who claims to be classed among the " judicious posterity " was I entitled to accept the Lord Chief Justice's dictum, but as judicial posterity I was bound to follow his judgment. If, for instance, Robin Hood cropped up at Bromley County Court, I should be bound to follow Coke and to take judicial notice, not only of his existence, but of the fact that he lived in the time of Richard I. Scholars may take what line they please, but to a judge of an inferior Court the existence of Robin Hood is *res judicata*, *chose jugée*, and finally decided by a competent authority, and must remain binding on my judicial conscience until his entity is overruled by the Court of Appeal. Even then I fancy he will be restored and resurrected by the House of Lords, a phenomenon which occurs more often than the layman would suppose. Gaily I renewed my researches into the history of my beloved vagabond who was now lawfully living—though not living lawfully—as we shall see —in the reign of Richard I.

And when Coke settled once for all that Robin Hood lived in that reign he was well within the common law of England, which, to hinder futile suits about what happened earlier, has wisely decreed that the memory of legal man has been ascertained by the law to commence from the reign of Richard I. And Coke goes on to insist that " unless it be known what this Robin Hood was " it would not be possible to understand such statutes as 13 Edward I and 5 Edward III. For these statues deal with " Roberdsmen," who were imitators of the great Robin Hood, as well as draw-latches, night-walkers and other vagabonds. Herein the philologist may see the strange romance of the word "Robert," which in one age provides a statutory term for a misdemeanant and in another a familiar name for a policeman. And the fact that there are statutes against Robin Hood is conclusive of his existence, since, as Chief Justice Hale pointed out in a later age, there must be such things as witches, because there were laws made against witches, and it is not conceivable that laws should be made against that which did not exist. Blackstone concurs in all this and, to my mind, it is at least as sensible as much that is reported in the Law Reports of to-day.

I do not propose, for I am no antiquary, and my purpose is but descriptive biography, to burden my readers with arguments for or against legend and history. But there is one other fact that seems worth setting down, for though it has not legal sanction, yet it is spoken to by a Dean of the Church of England and therefore should command that respect due to ecclesiastical authority. Robin Hood died on December 24, 1247.

This we know from his epitaph, which the learned antiquary, Ralph Thoresby of Leeds, printed in his *Ducatus Leodiensis*. This he found among the papers of his predecessor, Thomas Gale, Dean of York, who some time in the seventeenth century must have copied it from Robin Hood's tomb at Kirkleys Nunnery. It runs in this way :

> Here, underneath this little stone,
> Lies Robin Earl of Huntingdon,
> Ne'er archer was as he so good,
> And people called him Robin Hood.
> Such outlaws as he and his men
> Will England never see again.
>   Died 24 December, 1247.

The original is in black letter but the above seems a fair translation, and for aught I know the original may still be among the dean's papers which were ultimately given to Trinity College, Cambridge. Thoresby, when he went to see Robin Hood's grave in later years, found the stone with the inscription on it, but says that the latter was " scarce legible." But what would you have ? The dean could not have dreamt the inscription, and that he forged it is unthinkable to any right-minded person. Anyhow, it was good enough for Thoresby and it is good enough for me.

Once you are satisfied that Robin Hood lived in the reign of Richard I and died and was buried at Kirkleys Nunnery in 1247, there is plenty of biographical material for a life of him in the ballads that rehearse his splendid exploits. And that ballads are a reasonable source of history is laid down by Andrew Fletcher of Saltoun, who notes with approval that he " knew a very wise man that believed that, if a man were permitted to make all the ballads, he need not care who should make the laws of a nation," which, looking at the comparative popularity and good sense of the *Bab Ballads* and the " Rent Restriction Acts," seems wisdom in our own day.

Reading these ballads again, with more than half a century of experience of human life since I first enjoyed their great adventures, I am impressed by the reality of them. They seem to me like pages from a daily newspaper of the time. The things that happen might happen to-day. The horrors and crimes are similar to those we read of as occurring in ill-governed countries in recent historical times. The rulers behave in the same ineffective bat-like way that modern rulers behave, the rebels behave in the bad bold adventurous way that rebels always behave, the high sheriffs, tax-gatherers and other bureaucrats follow their duties with loyal narrow pertinacity, get heavily let down by the mandarins above them, and in the end the higher powers and the rebels make it up at the expense of the tax-payers and peace falls on the land until next time. Well may we moderns raise our glasses to our hero and sing the old refrain :

> For though bold Robin's gone
> Still his soul lives on,
> And we drink to him with three times three.

But to biography. Robin Hood was born at Locksley in the County of Nottingham. Whether he was a Fitzooth or an Earl of Huntingdon is no matter. He was an aristocrat and a ruler of men. That, like William Shakespeare in later years, he was of a wild and extravagant disposition and fond of hunting the deer goes without saying. But in Robin's day to kill a deer meant loss of both eyes and mutilation, whilst in Shakespeare's more merciful age the penalty had been reduced to three months without the option.

Whether it was debt or deer that brought about Robin's downfall is a disputed point, but he was pronounced an outlaw, such of his inheritance as he had not wasted was forfeit, and he sought an asylum in the woods. At that time there were immense tracts of forest in the North of England, and Robin Hood and his followers—for he soon surrounded himself with a worthy band of brothers-in-arms—chose as their head-quarters Sherwood Forest in Nottinghamshire. Thence when necessity arose they roamed across to Barnsdale in Yorkshire, and on more than one occasion were found at Plompton Park in Cumberland, which was a preserved deer forest as late as the reign of Henry VIII. One of his visits to the latter place was, according to the ballad, to engage in a professional county match with those celebrated Cumberland archers, Adam Bell, Clym of the Clough and William of Cloudesly. Robin Hood returned to Notts three up on his opponents, to the delight of his native county.

A forest in those days was a waste reserved for royal

H

hunting. The lord of the manor might hunt " hare, fox, cat and squirrel with dogs and hounds," but could only kill deer in these forests by royal permission. There were at least 100,000 acres of Sherwood Forest in Robin Hood's day, and it was about twenty miles long and eight broad. There are many surveys of the forest boundaries, the earliest in date being made in the reign of Henry III. For practical purposes we may say that in Robin Hood's time it stretched south and north from Nottingham to Doncaster and east and west from the Trent to the south Derbyshire hills.

Within these limits was Robin Hood's kingdom. You may picture it to yourself as well-wooded forest-land, with a few clearings of farmers and swineherds, a tract of land at least twice the size of Jersey with rich towns on its borders. In this domain Robin Hood and his *meyne*, as his band of yeomen were called, held sway by force of arms. If he were seriously invaded he could slip away north to the Yorkshire forest of Barnsdale, for he ruled " from Barnsdale's shrogs to Nottingham's red cliffs," or he could hide himself in the caves of the Derbyshire hills. We read of his adventures in all these places, but Sherwood Forest was the real home and territory of Robin Hood and his merry men, and here he ruled, defying the jurisdiction of the unfortunate sheriffs of Nottingham.

He seems to have picked his men carefully. Like himself they were outlaws and expert bowmen, and the names of his lieutenants were well known throughout the north. There was the famous giant and archer, Little John, who lies in Hathersage churchyard near Castleton. There was that astute dwarf, Much, the miller's son, nicknamed Much on the same principle that John was called Little. After Little and Much there was George-a-Green, the former pound-keeper of Wakefield, who after some breach of trust seems to have retired to the forest, and the sweet minstrel with the tuneful name of Allen-a-Dale, and that delightful rogue, Will Scarlet, who owed his bride to Robin Hood's masterful intervention. Last, but not least, there was his domestic chaplain, Friar Tuck, a personality as dear to the English heart as Falstaff himself. As to Maid Marian, the daughter of Lord Fitzwalter, who lies buried in Little Dunmow in Essex, she must have belonged to the early period of his outlawry, if there is any truth in the story of his second marriage to the black-eyed Clorinda of Gamwell Hall.

The *meyne* he had gathered round him were not only a splendid set of yeoman soldiers but well clothed in uniforms of Lincoln green, well armed and well fed. By picking his men carefully, treating them well and commanding them with skill and success, Robin Hood was enabled to hold his kingdom to the end. He himself is always pictured as clad in coat and hood of green, carrying a mighty bow and a sheaf of peacock arrows. On one side he wore a sword and buckler and on the other a gay dagger bravely harnessed and sharp as point of spear.

Nor need we suppose that the neighbouring townsmen were afraid of him or sought to do him injury, any more than the Sussex farmers and Rye and Seaford shopkeepers were at enmity with the Free Traders in the smuggling days. Robin Hood could not have equipped his army without commerce with the townsfolk, who doubtless were glad of an occasional haunch of venison and not averse to some of their tithe gold back again when Robin had taken it from the monks. The Merry Men had many friends at Bradford, Wakefield and Barnsley. The nuns of Farnsfield gave the courteous yeomen napkins, shirts and bands. Bateman of Kendal provided Kendal green, Sharpe of Leeds was their fletcher and Jackson of Rotherham made their bows. Of course if they were all sun-myths, they would not want these things, but if their adventures were real adventures and they shot real deer with real bows and arrows this is how they were equipped.

It is difficult to a modern to understand the apathy among respectable citizens over law and order. Yet such a phenomenon is not unknown in our own civilization. It is generally a complement of unwise prohibition and unsympathetic alien rule. In this way your Garibaldi, or Michael Collins, or the local rogue who runs a forbidden cargo past the sheriff's officer, is always a popular hero, and his exploits are repeated with advantages by eager lips to eager ears.

Now all the ballads agree in certain characteristics of their hero that are by no means typical of the average rogue and vagabond. Something started those stories. If it was a sun-myth it managed to create a very human solar-plexus. If there was a Robin Hood he was certainly a man of religion and would boldly enter a parish church to hear a Mass. It was said that it was his habit to hear three Masses daily.

> The one to worship the Father,
>   And one the Holy Ghost,
> The third was of our dear Ladye,
>   For he loved her of all the most.

> Robin, he loved our dear Ladye,
>   In dread of deadly sin ;
> For her sake would he no company harm
>   That any woman was in.

If women joined the Merry Men they went voluntarily, and there is no record of any force being used toward them by the chief or any of his followers.

Another rule that he laid down and enforced was that no harm was to be done to any husbandmen or farmers that tilled the land. With regard to knights and their squires they were not to be attacked if they were " good fellows " and acted courteously :

> But proud archbishops and bishops,
>   Them shall ye beat and bind ;
> And for the high sheriff of Nottingham
>   Ye shall ever hold him in mind.

That was the spirit and letter of the law that Robin Hood laid down, and one can see what valuable allies it brought him in his fierce struggle with the authority of the Crown.

There was a poor but gentle knight, Sir Richard of the Lee, whose castle of Uterysdale was on the edge of the forest. Robin Hood, hearing that he was riding north through his demesne towards Doncaster, sent Little John to bring him to dinner, and he, having heard many good things of the yeoman king, accepted the invitation. A splendid repast of pheasant, swan, and river-fowl was spread for him beneath the greenwood tree, such a feast as the poor knight had not seen for many weary weeks. At the end of it Robin Hood, to try him, asked him to pay for his repast, when the knight confessed with blushes that he had but ten shillings in the world. Little John was sent to inspect his portmantle and it was found that the good fellow was speaking the truth and had only half a pound in his coffer.

Thereupon Robin called for more wine to toast his honest guest and asked for the story of his poverty. It appeared that the knight's son had slain a knight of Lancashire, and the rich abbot of St. Mary's at York had, in punishment of the manslaughter, taken his land in pledge of a fine of £400, which, if not paid within a few days, would render him landless, and there would then be nothing left for him but to sail across the salt sea for Palestine.

Robin Hood, courteous robber that he was, sent Little John to his treasury for the money which he lent Sir Richard on the surety " of our Ladye dear " as the poor knight's worldly friends had all deserted him. Sir Richard promised to return on a certain day to the forest bringing back the loan, for if he could get his lands out of the abbot's clutches he could easily raise the money. This being settled the generous yeomen lapped his body in good Lincoln cloth, scarlet and green, they found him a grey courser, and a new saddle, boots and spurs, and started him off on his journey with Little John as his squire to guide him through the forest.

The proud and greedy abbot had not expected that Sir Richard could raise the money, and his chagrin may be imagined when the gentle knight, whose poverty was well known, returned to the day and, after much parleying and requests for time and mercy which were brutally refused, strode to a round table and " shook out of a bag even four hundred pound." In vain did Sir Abbot ask the knight to take back his money, and when this was refused begged the justice, whom he had summoned to deliver judgment, at least to return him the hearing fee. But the law never returns hearing fees and the abbot had to be content with his £400, whilst the knight rode back to his castle singing merrily once more, now that he was out of the abbot's debt.

Robin Hood was never in doubt that Sir Richard would return to pay his debt, or at least to report progress of the business on the appointed day, and ordered a feast to be prepared, but no one came. So he sent Much and Little John and Will Scarlet up to Watling Street to see if there were any strange guests on the road, with orders to compel them to the feast. For a time they looked east and west and saw no man, but at last they espied two black monks each astride a good palfrey with a retinue of fifty and seven sumpter horses besides.

" Look to your bows," said Little John. " I'll wager these monks have brought our pay."

Little John explained to the monks that their master, Robin Hood, had ordered them to bring any travellers they met to dine with him. Instead of accepting the invitation in good part the elder monk began abusing their master as a stout strong thief and a waster, which so enraged Much that he let fly a bolt at him and he went to ground. The whole posse now fled in terror except a little page and a groom who led one of the sumpter horses carrying the monks' coffers, and these with the other monk were escorted to Robin Hood's bower.

The captured monk turned out to be the High Cellarer of St. Mary's Abbey, and Robin Hood served him the feast he had prepared for Sir Richard with much reverence and ceremony. He made a point when he learned his official status to fill him up with the very best wine in his own cellar, of which the monk highly approved. He then explained to the fellow that Our Ladye had been appointed surety between him and a poor knight for a little money he had lent to him, and opined in his devout, simple way that the Cellarer had been sent as Her servant to repay the debt.

The Cellarer absolutely denied that there had been any such divine intention and swore an oath that he had but twenty marks with him.

" If that be all," said Robin with unfailing generosity, " I will not touch a penny, but if thou art in such need I will lend thee twice as much."

Little John, according to the ritual, was sent to examine the monk's coffer, and spreading his mantle on the ground counted out over £800.

Robin Hood, when he heard this, gave pious thanks to Our Ladye, who had thus paid the knight's debt two-fold, and having filled the cellarer with more wine, tied him on his palfrey back to front and sent him on his journey, bidding him greet his abbot and his prior and tell them that they might send such another monk to dine with him every day of the year.

Before sunset, Sir Richard, who had been delayed in doing good services to a poor yeoman, arrived with the £400 which he owed to Robin and 20 marks to boot. When he heard that Our Ladye had not only paid the debt but had left another £400 which Robin Hood insisted was intended for the knight, he greatly marvelled. But he was at length persuaded to accept the money and rode home again through the green-wood singing more merrily than ever.

All this may be mere legend, but to my ears it rings true. The way it appeals to me is that here was an outlaw whose only chance of living and holding his kingdom was to rule over a contented people. The monks and abbots and the sheriff, as representing the King, were bound to be his enemies, and try to destroy him, but by generosity on a lavish scale to other citizens he could at least hope that those who had been ill-treated by his enemies and well treated by himself would remain neutral in his struggle with authority. His policy was in effect the modern economic policy of all rulers. He robbed the coffers of the rich who were few in number and, keeping sufficient for himself and his immediate hench-men, made himself popular and beloved by scattering the taxes among those who wanted them most. In this conduct he seems to me to act more like an enlightened Chancellor of the Exchequer than a sun-myth.

Thomas Fuller and other moralists have boggled at the legality of Robin Hood's action. Quaint old Tom in his precise way asks, not without reason, " Who made Robin Hood a judge or gave him a commission to take where it might be spared and give where it was most wanted ? " Here I think the seraphic doctor has a lot to say for himself. Legally his position is sound. Certainly Robin Hood had no statutory posture from which he could fling forth Schedules D commanding the monks to assess themselves for super-tax. He could only assess it and recover it in his own wild woodland way. But then let us remember that even Henry VIII, who was nothing if not a constitutional monarch, has been blamed by many for his even more drastic treatment of the monks' successors in title. Nor can I as a lawyer follow the example of Ritson, my hero's gravest biographer, and stoop to excuse Robin Hood by citing as a precedent the pirate's case. Ritson was a bit of a Jacobin and defends our hero by reminding us what the pirate said to Alexander the Great ; of which I cannot approve, knowing that what the pirate said is not evidence. What the pirate did say when Alexander called on him for his defence was : " Because I do that with a single ship, which thou dost with a great fleet, I am called a thief and thou art called a King."

I think it is far more honest to admit that in law Robin Hood was a thief. But then it must be remembered that Robin Hood was not *in* law but *out*law. As an outlaw it did not matter whether he thieved or starved, lived a wicked or a virtuous life ; he was equally certain of being hanged if he was caught loafing about within the curtilage of a sheriff. It would have been moral suicide for him to have given himself up or allowed himself to be captured. What he did, seeing the age he lived in, and the way it had treated him, was to my mind actuated by sound common sense, if you grant to a human being the elementary right to preserve his life from destruction. He annexed Sherwood Forest and ran it as a hostel for himself and others similarly circumstanced, with unique courtesy and efficiency. True, Richard I was its owner *de jure*, but Robin Hood was proprietor *de facto*, and when the two met the former wisely recognized how excellently his *locum tenens* had acted in his absence. I have no doubt Richard was inwardly tickled at the way the monks had been treated ; and as for the sheriffs, no ruling authority has much compassion for the ill-fate of an unsuccessful bureaucracy.

I confess that my heart often goes out to the Sheriff of Nottingham of that day. His job was something far different from the pageantry of to-day, with prancing steeds, gorgeous uniforms, and trumpeters dear to modern sheriffdom. He was, too, a worthy enemy of Robin Hood, and Robin must have been a big man—if he was not a sun-myth—to have got the better of him. Unless, of course, a sheriff could also be a sun-myth, but that, as Euclid would say, is absurd.

Soon after the events already related the sheriff proclaimed in Nottingham an open national archery competition, the prize for which was to be the title of Champion of England symbolized by " an arrow with a shaft of silver white, with head and feathers of rich red gold." The shrewd sheriff knew well that Robin Hood must enter for the competition or lose status in the archery world. He was not wrong. Robin Hood immediately ordered seven score of strong bowmen to attend him. Six were to shoot with him and the remainder were to stand by and see that he was not treacherously attacked. The team were Robin Hood, Gilbert, Little John, Will Scarlet, Much and Reynold, who seem to have won the " six-somes," if so they were called, but Robin Hood splitting the wand on every occasion took the championship for the singles and carried off the silver arrow.

After the prize had been presented by the sheriff's lady and Robin Hood and his Merry Men were returning to the forest, a very regrettable incident occurred. Nottingham City had been badly beaten by Nottingham Forest, and the archers of that day were not so chivalrous and polite as the football crowds of to-day. Several horns were blown as the foresters went for the city gate and they were suddenly attacked by a superior force. It was soon seen that the sheriff and his men were leading the attack. Little John was shot in the knee and disabled, but was carried off the field of battle by his plucky little companion, Much. They were hard-pressed, and from time to time Much had to set his burden down and shoot at the enemy. Robin Hood conducted a masterly retreat and they ultimately reached the castle of Sir Richard of the Lee, who, in spite of the fact that they were being pursued by the sheriff and his friends, welcomed them all within the castle and offered them sanctuary for twelve days. Once the troop were within the castle the gates were closed, the bridge drawn and the walls manned within. But the sheriff and his posse withdrew, and Sir Richard ordering boards to be set and cloths to be laid, the triumph of Robin Hood was celebrated in right English style.

Next morning the sheriff returned with a trumpeter and summoned the knight to deliver up his guests on peril of being denounced to the King as a traitor. Here, I think, the sheriff had the thick end of the law. Sir Richard, although he had no attorney to advise him, refused to parley with the sheriff until he could produce to him the royal mandate, which he humbly and courteously proffered to obey. This was a shrewd rebutter, for the sheriff remembered that a Judge of Assize had once laid down as good law that " every man's house is his castle," and cast his predecessor in damages for " forcible entry," and he doubted how far it would be legal to assault Sir Richard's stronghold.

His next move was entirely in accordance with modern practice. Like any other provincial official, finding himself in difficulties, he knew that the right course was to pay a visit to London at the expense of the ratepayers to ask the authorities at Whitehall what he ought to do. The sheriff therefore rode up to town.

One cannot suppose that he would sully the ears of Richard I, who was a sportsman and a gentleman, with the story of his own treachery. But he could easily keep within the truth about Robin Hood and yet pile up a very sufficient indictment against him. He seems to have reported to the King that the outlaw " set him at naught and ruled the North," which is exactly what was happening, and the King sent him back to Nottingham with the promise that he would be there in a fortnight to put an end to the reign of Robin Hood and to punish Sir Richard of the Lee.

By now Little John was on his way to recovery, and Robin Hood and his men had returned to the greenwood. A week or two afterwards the sheriff's men sent a strong armed band into the forest, who found nothing of the foresters, but happening upon Sir Richard who was out at the river-side trying a hawk, took him and bound him hand and foot and carried him into Nottingham.

Sir Richard's terror-stricken wife, hearing this shocking news, saddled her palfrey and rode out into the forest in search of Robin Hood and told him her tale of woe.

The chronicles say that Robin behaved " as one who was mad and raved." This was very excusable. He knew the sheriff had referred the matter to the King, and the King was on his way north. The matter could then be thrashed out between the two monarchs *de jure* and *de facto* either by force of arms or at a diplomatic conference. For an underling like the sheriff to butt in at this moment and capture, and probably execute his friend Sir Richard, was an exasperating impertinence. Even a sun-myth might have expressed himself with some heat at such a juncture.

Robin Hood was as prompt in his movements as Richard. He blew his horn and assembled seven score men and marched on Nottingham. There was a pitched battle in the streets of the city in which the treacherous sheriff was slain and Sir Richard was set at liberty. But Robin Hood urged him not to return to the castle and carried him through mire, moss and fen to a fastness in the forest to which my lady had already withdrawn under the sturdy escort of Friar Tuck.

The King was now riding north and it became necessary for Robin Hood to find out how things were going forward in Nottingham. To this end he captured a potter who was carrying his ware through the forest, and disguising himself in his clothes he drove off in his cart with a cargo of pots to Nottingham market. Here he put up his horse and, standing on his cart in the midst of the throng right opposite the new sheriff's gate—for sheriffs, like kings, never die—he proceeded to sell his wares, shouting, " What d'ye lack ? " like any common chapman.

He had no difficulty in getting rid of his stock, for he gave for threepence what was worth fivepence. Here, again, we see his sound political instinct in selling what was not his own under cost price. The modern Chancellor of the Exchequer who invented the cry of " ninepence for fourpence " was a plagiarist on Robin Hood whose " fivepence for threepence " seems to have been the original precedent for gaining popular favour by such means.

When his stock was nearly cleared and he had but five pots left, he walked to the door of the sheriff's house and courteously presented the sheriff's lady with the remainder of his stock. This so pleased the good dame that she invited the pleasant potter to dine with them, and the new sheriff, hearing he had come across the forest, began to make inquiry if he knew anything of the whereabouts of Robin Hood. He told the potter that the King could not arrive for a week or two, the ways being bad, and that he intended before the King came to put up a big archery prize of no less than forty shillings, and he hoped that Robin Hood would let bygones be bygones and come to the contest. For in those parts an archery contest without any of Robin Hood's men drew no gate money.

The pretended potter said he knew Robin Hood, who had given him a bow, which was in his cart. Upon hearing this the sheriff and his guest went out to the butts and had a friendly match for a crown, which Robin Hood won skilfully by only a small margin. They spent a jovial and convivial evening, and it was arranged that the potter should lead the sheriff into the woods on the morrow to see if he could bring him into touch with Robin Hood.

Mounted on his best steed and attended by the potter and his cart, the sheriff started for the forest early in the morning. They had not travelled many miles when in the midst of a dense glade the potter sounded a horn and the two were immediately surrounded by a body of foresters headed by Little John.

The unhappy sheriff found himself tied and bound by the men in green, and the potter, throwing off his disguise, was welcomed by his faithful *meyne* with shouts and acclamations. Inasmuch as the sheriff had treated him hospitably, Robin Hood forbade his men to ill-treat their captive. His horse and gear were taken from him, it is true, for that form of capital levy was a custom of the forest whilst it was under Robin Hood's rule, but the chief told his men to loose the sheriff and let him go, saying, " Hither you come on horse, and home you shall go on foot, Mr. Sheriff. Greet well the good woman, your wife : I send her as a present a white palfrey, which ambles as the wind. For her sake you shall receive no further harm."

The disconsolate sheriff ambled home as best he might, and told his wife his woes. But she, being a woman of wit, burst into loud laughter at his recital and swore a merry oath that all were quits, since her good man had now handsomely paid for all the pots that Robin had given her so courteously.

At length the King and a small army of knights arrived at Nottingham. Attended by the sheriff's posse, the forest was scoured from end to end, but there was no sign of Robin

Hood and his Merry Men. Doubtless they had slipped away into Derbyshire or Yorkshire. The King, having enjoyed a month's hunting, began to think he would never see his famous subject, Robin Hood, and being a brave man he determined to disguise himself as an abbot and ride into the forest with a small retinue of five knights to see if he could come upon him. Thanks to a friendly forester Robin Hood was, it appears, easily to be met with.

The abbot showed him the King's seal and gave him a royal invitation to come to Nottingham. Robin Hood explained to the abbot that he loved no man in all the world as he did the King, and for his sake and the tidings he brought him from his beloved monarch, he insisted upon his dining with him under his trysting-tree.

Although the chronicles and ballads are silent upon the point, one cannot but surmise that Robin Hood knew well who he was entertaining, and the King must have been well pleased to meet as an equal a man of such sterling common sense, gentle courtesy and noble hospitality. However, the horn was sounded. The whole *meyne* of seven score men appeared in their splendid equipment and habiliments and bent the knee to Robin Hood and his guest, the King remarking to himself the discipline and loyalty of the troop, which rivalled anything in his own experience. The banquet was of the best and after dinner there was shooting.

The terms were that anyone who missed the mark should lose an arrow and receive a buffet on the head. Robin had been raking in arrows and handing out buffets right merrily until it came to his own turn, when he failed at the garland, at which there was much secret satisfaction.

Robin, however, was ready to play the game, and kneeling to Sir Abbot, he gave him his arrow and awaited the buffet. The Abbot demurred to smiting so good a yeoman for fear of doing him hurt, but Robin insisted upon the penalty. Whereupon the King rolled up his sleeve and dealt Robin Hood such a hefty blow that it full nigh knocked him out. Any doubts that Robin and his men may have had as to the identity of the stalwart friar were set at rest. No one but a right-down regular royal king could have knocked out Robin Hood in one. The outlaws fell on their knees before their beloved monarch. They all received pardon for their trespasses, Sir Richard of the Lee was restored to his estates, and Robin Hood was invited to ride to London with the King. This royal invitation was a command that could not be disobeyed and, leaving Little John in charge of his men and his dominions, Robin Hood rode at the right hand of his sovereign in friendly state to London.

No one who has lived in the hospitable north can exist for long with any sense of freedom in the artificial society of London and the Home Counties. Robin Hood was not the man to hang about a Court, and though he was hospitable and lavish of his money he was too good a shot to be a welcome guest at south-country pot hunts. For the archers of the south were a poor crowd compared with the bowmen of Nottingham and Yorkshire. At last, having spent his gold and silver, he sickened and pined for the good greenwood, and the King, who loved and honoured the man to the last, gave him leave to return to Sherwood Forest.

His life there continued in the old way. The outlaws gathered round him and he was once again monarch of the good greenwood. But old age at length overcame him and he found that he could no longer get his shots away and hole out his arrows in the flying deer. Like many simple men to-day, he seemed to think that the ravages of age could be repaired by the magic of medicine. It appears that the prioress of Kirkleys Nunnery was a cousin of Robin Hood, and, moreover, this lady was said to have had a secret affection for Sir Roger of Doncaster, a worthy knight, who had had some differences with the *meyne* and their chief over the taking of Yorkshire venison in the knight's demesne. The prioress was a noted wise woman and skilled in leechcraft. To this unregistered practitioner Robin Hood, assisted by Little John, went for treatment.

It is only fair to the lady's memory to mention that on Robin's arrival she invited him to sit down and drink beer with her ; but Robin, who had made up his mind in his rude, strong way as to what he had come for, replied : " I will neither eat nor drink till I am blooded by thee." The lady smiled and accepted the task with alacrity, offering him her lily-white hand to lead him to a private room.

Here, if the chronicles are correct, she blooded him in the vein of the arm and then locked him up in the room, where, it is said, he continued to bleed all the livelong day until noon on the morrow. This looks black against the prioress, and gave rise to the strong suspicion that Robin Hood was murdered by his cousin at Sir Roger of Doncaster's instigation. It is quite as probable that the operation of bleeding was unskilfully done, and when the lady found she could not stop the hæmorrhage she lost her head and ran away and left him to die. In which case the charge must be reduced to manslaughter. However that may be, Little John seems to have sat in the buttery drinking ale all night whilst his master bled to death upstairs.

When Robin Hood found that things were wrong with him he bethought him to leap out of the casement, but he was too weak. He managed, however, to put his horn to his lips and blow three weak blasts, the sound of which reached the ears of the faithful Little John. He at once scented danger from the weary notes of the horn, and rushing up the priory stairs broke open several doors until at last he came to his dying master. Instead of sending for a respectable barber-surgeon to see if he could remedy the patient's con-

I

dition, Little John began worrying his master to allow him
to burn down the nunnery. Robin Hood, who was fast
sinking, reminded him that he had never hurt a woman nor
man in woman's company during his long career as an outlaw,
and that Little John's suggestion, though well meant, was
distasteful to him. He then asked his friend to bend his
bow for him for the last time and put it in his hand. With
that he shot a feeble arrow through the open casement into
the nunnery garden. Falling back into his friend's arms he
whispered to him that there where the arrow should fall
was the spot he had chosen for his grave in which they were
to place his body and his bow. The grave was to be fitly
made of " gravel and green " and his head was to be pillowed
on a green sod. All this was done as Robin Hood commanded, and the funeral at Kirkleys was attended by the
sorrowing *meyne* and all the peasants and farmers for miles
round.

The human affection which he inspired in life remains
with him to this day among those of us who are simple
enough to accept the truth of the well-known facts of his
life which I have here set down. As I read them they are
statements of real adventures, exaggerated perhaps and
coloured by the enthusiasm of the narrators, but having at
the base of them a typical Englishman of all time. I do
not propose to argue in favour of his existence any more
than Mistress Gamp condescended to argue with her sister
nurse about the existence of Mrs. Harris. Indeed, I think
the cases are parallel. Deeply as I respect Mistress Betsey
Prig, I take the side of Mistress Gamp in the dispute. That
Mrs. Harris was a sun-myth I can never allow. But I have
met many of Mistress Prig's great-nephews and nieces. They
are no longer in the nursing profession, the Prigs being now
mostly to be found in academic circles. But they have
the family failing. They lack faith. And, speaking as a

lawyer, they seem to me to take up a wrong attitude in their quarrel with the man in the street. The Prigs who tell you that Mrs. Harris or Robin Hood or even more sacred characters are sun-myths or what not, forget that the onus of proof is upon them. Robin Hood is in possession, as it were. In Mrs. Harris's case we have a large number of intimate biographical details told at first hand by a narrator of unimpeachable honesty. In Robin Hood's case we have exactly similar details handed down to us, as all the best stories in the world are, by oral tradition. That these traditions should be flouted and despised is deplorable, but do not let us take it too seriously to heart, for such a course, as Mistress Gamp observed, only leads to anger, broken friendship, and despair of humanity.

It would be sad to end the story of Robin Hood on a note of discord. Faith, after all, is a better gift than reason, and we should pity rather than abuse those who in the vain pursuit of academic shadows lose the glorious companionship of living men of action. It is good to remember that there was such a man as Robin Hood and that there was such a place as Merry England. There is comfort in the thought that history repeats itself. There is piety in the prayer of the ballad-monger :

> May God that sitteth in heaven high,
> Grant us as well to fare.

CHAPTER VII

MADAME RACHEL, THE GO-BETWEEN

SARAH RACHEL LEVERSON was a rogue and vaga-
bond, and her trade was as ancient as it was disreputable.
The type is unfortunately eternal. Rachel was "your
herb woman; she that sets seeds and roots of shame and
iniquity." Samuel Richardson portrays her to the life in
Clarissa Harlowe as Mrs. Sinclair, who in the pay of Love-
lace conspires with him against the peace and honour of
the heroine of the story. And you may see the picture
of Madame Rachel or Mrs. Sinclair in Hogarth's first plate
of the *Harlot's Progress*. The pleasant-looking lady there
portrayed was Mother Needham, an infamous woman of the
day who, poor wretch, ended her career in the pillory on a
May morning in 1734, when the virtuous mob pelted her so
roughly that she died a few days afterwards. Fortunately
for Mrs. Leverson, she lived in a softer age. For had she
carried on her devil's trade in an earlier century she would
doubtless have been whipped at the cart's tail, and her aristocratic patrons would not have raised a hand to save her.

Madame Rachel was born about 1806; her father, a man
named Russell, was said to have been a professional humorist,
and maybe there was some sense of hereditary humour in
Madame's methods of trade. She first married Mr. Jacob
Moses, who was lost in the wreck of the *Royal Charter*,
leaving her with a young family to provide for. Later she
married Mr. Phillip Leverson, or Levison, but there is no

evidence that he played any part in the crimes and swindles for which she was prosecuted.

In her early days Madame was a clothes-dealer and carried on her trade of hawking finery among the small-part girls in the theatre. Serjeant Ballantine, who successfully prosecuted the woman and put an end to her foul activities, remembers seeing her on one occasion behind the scenes at Drury Lane Theatre. She was chaffering with a girl about the price of a dress and made an insulting proposal to her customer, who replied by throwing the contents of a pot of porter into her face. This Hogarthian episode led to Madame being warned off the premises, and Drury Lane Theatre was cleansed of her presence.

The police and the magistrates of Middlesex Sessions had Mrs. Leverson's dossier and knew all about her infamous trade. That she was an industrious and saving woman seems beyond doubt, and some time in the 'sixties she gave up her old business and opened a beauty shop in New Bond Street under the name of Madame Rachel. There was a shop and a small back room and she was assisted in the business by her two daughters, Rachel aged twenty-seven and Leonti aged twenty. Later on she took a house in Maddox Street as well, where her patrons visited her for treatment. Her younger children lived out at Blackheath. All these establishments were paid for by Madame's industry.

There is a curious true story attached to her entrance into the world of cosmetics. The poor woman had been stricken down with a fever and had been a patient at King's College Hospital in Lincoln's Inn Fields. Here she lost her beautiful hair, of which she was very proud. The doctor at the hospital gave her a lotion by which she recovered her hair in all its former beauty. She begged from the doctor the recipe for this wonder-working lotion, and this recipe was probably the whole scientific basis of her marvellous lotions and essences which in her notorious pamphlet, *Beautiful for Ever*, she described as " the purest and most fragrant productions of the East."

Who composed her flowery and audacious advertisements I cannot tell. There is no evidence that her husband assisted in her business, but there was a solicitor in St. James's Street named Haynes who, it is clear, was often consulted by her in the finance of her trade. He was the mortgagee of the house in New Bond Street, and his interest in the matter was to get £250 a year in rent from Madame Rachel, a task to which he scrupulously and successfully devoted his energies.

Whether he was the master-spirit in the advertisement department one cannot say, but the methods of attracting fools into her clutches were so impudently clever that one can scarcely credit their authorship to the illiterate Mrs. Leverson.

Antiquaries tell us that there is no ancient civilization which has yet disclosed itself to modern investigation in which evidences are not discovered of some wise woman carrying on the beauty business. The folk-lore and fairy tales of the magic water that rejuvenates the elderly are to be found in every language of the world, and in these matters the women of to-day seem true to the type of their maternal ancestors of prehistoric times.

I suppose it would be possible for a beauty specialist to carry on an honest trade and earn a rent of £250 a year in a Bond Street shop, and a handsome income to boot. But, for certain, Mrs. Leverson never made any attempt to do so. She was a quack and a blackmailer and worse, and the wild absurdity of her advertisements suggests to my mind that she was aided by some cynical literary misogynist, whose contempt for feminine intellect was boundless, and whose success at least goes to show that the limits of human folly have not yet been fully explored.

The Bond Street shop was an immediate success. The things you could buy there, if you had money to fling away, were certainly remarkable, and many a middle-aged woman must have gloated longingly over Madame Rachel's promises.

Beautiful Women !—The Peach Blossom Cream and Alabaster Powder, the Magnetic Rock Dew Water from Sahara, Circassian Bloom, Arabian Soaps and Alabaster Liquid. These costly and inimitable toilet preparations render the hair, teeth and complexion beautiful beyond comparison. Can be had only at Madame Rachel's, 47A New Bond Street, where she can be consulted daily. All communications are strictly confidential. Madame Rachel's Royal Arabian perfume baths are open daily. *Beautiful for Ever*, Book of Beauty just published by Madame Rachel.

Madame claimed to be the sole possessor of delicate and costly arts whereby the appearance of youth could be reproduced in the face and figure of women " however advanced in years," and when the glad tidings flashed upon Mayfair you may be sure that they were responded to by a cheerful rattle of many elderly bones. That her wares were expensive was according to all precedent. Who would grudge two guineas for " Magnetic Rock Dew Water of Sahara for removing wrinkles "—if it did the trick ? Remember, too, that this wonderful remedy, which " gives the appearance of youth to persons of considerable antiquity," was carried from Sahara to Morocco, " on swift dromedaries for the use of the Court, and its virtues are much extolled by the Court physicians. It might be called the antipodes of the Lethean Styx of ancient times." Obviously, dromedaries cost money and you cannot expect to get an elixir of that type for nothing.

Madame's business flourished, as no doubt it would to-day. But you must not suppose that so many Victorian women were victims of the cosmetic habit as there are in our own day. The market was more limited ; the customers

fewer and more select. Nowadays, when every girl carries
a bag of outfit and implements and does the running repairs
to her complexion in the tram or the train, when desert
transport is worked by Ford cars instead of dromedaries, a
trade in Sahara Rock Water must be worked on cheaper and
more popular lines. But the real truth is that Madame's
marvels were only intended to lure wealthy clients to her
shop and the privacy of her little back parlour. Women of
fashion and position visited her, but they did not talk of
their adventures. Men about town dropped into the shop
for a chat with the girls and bought scent and pomade, but
whether they had any business with Madame, who can say ?
Whether the ladies ever met the gentlemen, or whether
Madame became cognizant of strange secrets, there is hardly
evidence that amounts to proof, but that the scents and
lotions were in every sense mere eyewash, and that the money-
making part of her trade was fraud and blackmail, cannot be
doubted, and though the police could not move against her
without proof they kept a watch on the beauty shop and
bided their time.

Rogues of this type often flourish for a long period because
their victims can only expose their wickedness at the cost
of exposing their own folly, or even their own profligacy.
Several cases were heard of in solicitors' offices and advised
upon in the Temple, before Madame found herself in the
dock.

There was the matter of the admiral's wife, in which the
poor lady had merely entered the shop to buy ordinary per-
fumes but was induced to buy some of the more expensive
cosmetics. After a while the admiral got a bill for £1,000
for curing his wife of an unpleasant skin affection, and scandals
were hinted at in the letters of request for payment. These
could not have been written by the illiterate woman herself,
and she must have had a partner in such villainies. The

admiral went to his lawyers and rightly refused to pay a penny, and Madame dropped the claim.

But others were not so successful in escaping from her clutches. A lady of fashion, a respectable and indeed a very attractive woman, was foolish enough to be wheedled by the old lady into taking a course of wonder-working baths under her supervision at the Maddox Street establishment. The heavy fees for cosmetics and treatment were paid in advance. One day when the lady was taking a bath she took off some valuable jewels she was wearing and placed them in a drawer in the dressing-room. On her return she found to her horror they had disappeared. She rang the bell and summoned Madame and told her of her loss. The rogue fell into a towering passion and declared that she did not believe she had any jewellery with her.

Upon this the lady was indignant and insisted upon the return of her property. Madame's reply was crushing. " It's no good you giving yourself airs here. I know who you are. I have had you watched. I know where you live. How would you like your husband to know the real reason for your coming here, and about the gentleman who has visited you here ? "

The poor woman slunk home in despair ; and though there was not a word of truth in the woman's wicked suggestions, she did not dare to tell her husband her story until after the conviction of Madame Rachel. Mr. Montagu Williams, who tells the story in his excellent reminiscences, wisely advised the husband that it was better to leave the business where it stood rather than expose his foolish wife to the ridicule and censure of the world.

The victim who turned on Madame Rachel and slew her was indeed a veritable human worm. Rarely has a Court of Justice been called upon to champion the cause of so despicable and contemptible a citizen. So absurd was her behaviour, so inconsistent and ludicrous was her conduct, that the editor of *The Times*, though he was satisfied with Rachel Leverson's downfall, was by no means satisfied that Mary Tucker Borradaile, the prosecutrix, was telling the truth, the whole truth and nothing but the truth, or that the charge against the prisoner was legally proven.

Madame was tried twice, the first jury disagreeing. She was on both occasions defended by Mr. Digby Seymour, Q.C., my father, Serjeant Parry, and other eminent counsel. Serjeant Ballantine and Mr. Montagu Williams prosecuted. On the first trial the Recorder of London, the Rt. Hon. Russell Gurney, Q.C., who did not believe Mrs. Borradaile's story, summed up for an acquittal. On the second occasion she was tried before Mr. Commissioner Kerr, who gave her no loophole of escape and accepted all Mrs. Borradaile's story without serious criticism. *The Times* considered that the result of the trial struck a serious blow at our system of not allowing a prisoner to give evidence. But looking at the fact that Madame would have had to face the cross-examination of Serjeant Ballantine, one cannot but believe she was at least as safe in the dock as she would have been in the witness-box.

Ballantine had a wholesome contempt for Mrs. Borradaile, the chief witness for the prosecution. He describes her as a " quondam beauty—a skeleton encased apparently in plaster of Paris, painted pink and white, and surmounted with a juvenile wig," who tottered in to the witness-box and gave the evidence of her incredible folly in a childish and affected manner. Reading her story one can imagine no useful purpose such a woman could serve, except as fodder for scoundrels of the Rachel type.

She was the widow of an Indian colonel, and at the time of the trial in August, 1868, her husband had been dead for seven years. She indignantly refused to give her age, but was married in 1846, so that we shall not be doing her an injustice if we set her down as between forty and fifty. She had a married sister in Wales, but she lived by herself in different lodgings in London, apparently on her pension and the interest of her fortune of a few thousand pounds. It is difficult to understand how she spent her time and among what class of society she moved, but that she was vain and shallow-witted and irresponsible is beyond doubt. Her charge against Madame Rachel was that she had obtained her money by false pretences and practically ruined her, the false pretences being that she had told her that Lord Ranelagh desired to marry her and that the money she advanced to Madame would be expended to that desirable end. The defence was that there was no truth whatever in the marriage story and that the money had been expended upon a mysterious paramour of Mrs. Borradaile named " William," whose actual existence remains not proven to this day. This was the legal and immoral problem with which the jury were invited to puzzle their brains.

Mrs. Borradaile's story is worth reading as a classic example of human credulity, always assuming, as the second jury found by their verdict, that she was speaking the truth. She fluttered into Madame's web some time in 1864, having read in some advertisement that the proprietor of the web was " purveyor to the Queen." On her first visit she spent £10 and during the next year further sums amounting to £170. In 1866, Madame Rachel informed her that there was a gentleman who was very much in love with her, who had seen her both before and after her marriage, and was a very good man and a rich man. The lady was surprised and excited. A few days after this extraordinary announcement, when she was sitting in Madame's parlour, the door was opened and Madame called to a gentleman in the shop, whom she addressed as " Lord Ranelagh."

Mrs. Borradaile said : " Are you Lord Ranelagh ? "

He replied, " Yes, and here is my card."

Madame closed the door and the interview ended.

On several occasions Mrs. Borradaile saw his lordship in the shop, and once he bowed to her, and on another occasion said a few words to her that she could not remember.

Upon that slender basis Madame proceeded with her plot. In May, 1866, she told Mrs. Borradaile that before she could marry Lord Ranelagh she must be made " beautiful for ever " and this operation would cost £1,000. She was now taken, with Mr. Haynes, the solicitor, to the City, and stock amounting to £1,300 was sold out for £963, she signing a paper directing Haynes to pay Madame £800. Madame now began to bring her letters, which she said came from Lord Ranelagh. She told her victim that she was to be " married by proxy." She said it was to be done by letter-writing ; that she had married two parties before by proxy, and that Mrs. Borradaile should be the third. Madame also explained that his lordship's letters should be signed " William " for fear they should be seen by others.

One of the first letters she received, which was written on paper decorated with Lord Ranelagh's crest and mono-gram, was handed to her by Madame together with a vinaigrette and a pencil-case.

It ran as follows :

MOUNT STREET.

MY OWN DEARLY LOVED MARY,

The little perfume-box and pencil-case belonged to my sainted mother, she died with them in her hand. When she was a schoolgirl it was my father's first gift to her. Granny has given the watch and locket to me again. Your coronet is finished, my love. Granny said you had answered my last letter but forgotten to send it. I forgot yesterday was Ash Wednesday. Let old Granny arrange the time as we have too little to spare. My adored one, what is the matter with the old woman ? She seems out of sorts. We must keep her in good temper for our own sakes. She has to manage all for us and I should not have had the joy of your love had it not been for her, darling love. Mary, my sweet one, all will be well in a few hours. The dispatches have arrived. I will let you know all when I hear from my heart's life. Bear up, my fond one, and I shall be at your feet, those pretty feet that I love, and you may kick your old donkey. Two letters, you naughty little pet, and you have not answered one. With fond and devoted love,

Yours till death,
WILLIAM.

Mrs. Borradaile received several other similar letters purporting to come from Lord Ranelagh which " Granny," as Madame Rachel was called, or her daughters, handed to her. These were written in different handwritings and some were signed " Edward." In many of them she was directed to buy lace or diamonds or to find money for Lord Ranelagh. These things were all sent to " Granny's " shop in Bond Street and were seen no more by Mrs. Borradaile. On one occasion Madame took her to a livery stable to select a carriage, which was to have Lord Ranelagh's arms painted upon it. On another occasion she tried on an old-fashioned coronet, which Madame said would have to be altered.

By these frivolous and absurd inducements the poor dupe was led to part with all her money. Mr. Haynes was employed to sell property at Streatham of the value of £1,600, and to realize other assets. An order was signed authorizing Madame to dispose of any property, silk, jewels, linen, etc., which she held for her, and a bond for £1,600 in favour of Madame Rachel was duly executed. In the end, and when she was penniless except for her pension, which, fortunately, she could not alienate, Madame had her arrested for debt. This brought her brother-in-law, Mr. Cope, to her rescue, and having obtained her release they visited New Bond Street together to see what Madame and Lord Ranelagh intended to do in the matter.

Mr. Cope could get no satisfactory account of the business from Madame, who denied having had any money from Mrs. Borradaile and would give him no information about Lord Ranelagh. She, however, produced an absurd letter that Mrs. Borradaile had to admit that she had written to " William," and when Mr. Cope put the matter in the hands of the lawyers, Madame set up the story that " William " was a paramour of Mrs. Borradaile, that she had constantly warned her against spending money on the man, and that all the large sums she had raised had been spent on Mrs. Borradaile's lover. Lord Ranelagh denied all knowledge of the absurd business.

Mrs. Borradaile's lawyers brought an action for the return of her money, but ultimately it was decided that the case was one for criminal rather than civil proceedings, and Madame Rachel was arrested and committed for trial for obtaining money by false pretences. At her trial in August, 1868, her counsel produced a large number of letters which Mrs. Borradaile had to admit that she wrote to " William." The issue of the case which the jury had to decide, was whether Madame had bewitched Mrs. Borradaile into a real belief that in some mysterious way she was to be married " by proxy " to a peer she had only seen once or twice in her life, and who could if he had wished have courted her in person, or whether the true state of the case was that Mrs. Borradaile was carrying on an intrigue with a real individual on whom she spent her money, and Madame was her willing go-between for valuable consideration.

To consider this alternative proposition it will be necessary to look at some of Mrs. Borradaile's own letters. These, you will remember, were produced by Madame's lawyers, who did not, I need hardly say, produce Mr. " William." But there is not so much point in that perhaps, since " William," if he had an existence, would have been very unwise to put himself within reach of the law. Mrs. Borradaile, when confronted with a long series of letters written with her own hand, admitted that she had penned the actual words, but declared that they were written at Madame Rachel's dictation and that she could not explain the references and statements in the letters as Madame had bewitched her and doped her with whisky at the time she wrote them.

Here, for instance, is a curious epistle for Mrs. Borradaile to be writing to Lord Ranelagh. It was written in September, 1866, at a time when her brother-in-law had heard rumours of her losses and had come up to town to look after her. She had, it appears, told him the same story she told to the Court.

MY OWN DEAR WILLIAM,

If you knew what I have suffered since Saturday night on your account, one unkind word would never have escaped your lips to me. My brother in-law went to The Carlton to see Lord Ranelagh. They told him he was out of town and they said he would not be back for a week. . . . You would have been amused at the frantic manner in which he was running about town looking for the invisible person who could not be found, thanks to our lucky star. Mr. Cope and my sister made me promise I would not see Rachel again as I led them to suppose she had been the promoter of His Lordship in intriguing with me.

Mrs. Borradaile swore that she thought she was writing the letter to Lord Ranelagh himself, but could give no sane explanation of the words of it, which she said were invented by Rachel. But we must remember that Rachel was illiterate, and to invent a long series of letters containing vivid details of an actual intrigue requires the capacity of a novelist.

In another letter she writes to William :

You know there are such things as talking birds. I feel better now since you told me we shall leave Charing Cross next morning. Will that morning ever come . . . ? But you seem to know the overland route to my heart.

The phraseology here seems more like the genuine language of an Indian colonel's widow than the invention of an illiterate rogue. It seems hardly possible that the writer had never met and conversed with the " William " to whom she was writing.

In another extraordinary letter she writes :

One of your kind friends and your bosom companions has informed me that you have been and now are keeping a woman. Not one member of my family will hold any intercourse with me for forming such a degraded connexion, as it is well known in Pembrokeshire that I have been living with you for some months.

It seems beyond belief that any woman would write that at the dictation of another, or that Mrs. Borradaile could speak of marriage with Lord Ranelagh as a " degraded connexion."

Here is a still more extraordinary epistle :

MY OWN DEAR WILLIAM,
          It is very kind of you to take care of my comb and frisette ; it is my own hair. The man who keeps the hairdresser's shop at the corner of High Street, Cheltenham, made it for me—the man who used to shave you when you were there.

All these intimate details seem to show that " William " had a corporeal existence, and we know that he was not Lord Ranelagh, who admittedly only saw Mrs. Borradaile on one occasion casually in the Bond Street shop. But still more intimate allusions are contained in the following :

MY OWN DEAR WILLIAM,
          If you look at the enclosed bill you will see I am not the extravagant person your sister says I am. I bought Florence, my daughter, a pair of boots and three pairs of stockings, but not before she wanted them. Your sister ought to see that your stockings are mended. I cannot see why she cannot mend them herself and put some buttons on your shirts. It would be better than gossiping with the woman next room to her. Send all your clothes that want mending

to me. As you want boots we shall go to a maker in Oxford Street and get a pair. I am surprised that your flannels should be worn out though you have not had them six weeks. It is the result of bad washing. There is a man living in a Court off Regent Street who mends coats cheaply and I think you might give him a job.

On this letter Mr. Digby Seymour, who was cross-examining Mrs. Borradaile, asks her : " On your solemn oath did you when you wrote that letter to this shirtless, buttonless, stockingless, bootless, flannelless, hatless individual think that you were writing to Lord Ranelagh ? "

The lady replied that she did.

It is impossible to believe her statement. The letters she wrote are, to my mind, conclusive that there was an actual " William " beloved by Mrs. Borradaile on whom she spent her money, but this does not exclude the other sugges-tion that at one time Madame Rachel dangled the idea of a marriage with Lord Ranelagh before her dupe's eyes, and at the same time assisted her with an intrigue with some out-at-elbows rogue and vagabond who had taken Mrs. Borradaile's fancy. Madame would stick at nothing to rob her dupe, and when Mrs. Borradaile was face to face with exposure she had the wit to tell the Ranelagh story and credit all her letters as written in relation to that adventure, knowing that the real " William " would never venture into the witness-box.

The fact seems to be that the Court never did arrive at the truth, the whole truth, and nothing but the truth, about what was called " the Bond Street mystery." In those days prisoners could not give evidence and, luckily for herself, Mrs. Rachel Leverson could not be cross-examined. If she had been a competent witness, and had tendered herself as a witness, Serjeant Ballantine could no doubt have obtained from her enough to have satisfied the world of her villainy. She certainly robbed Mrs. Borradaile of her money but not perhaps exactly in the way Mrs. Borradaile described.

J

What probably really happened was something of this sort. There was no doubt a live and attractive " William " who was a tool of Madame Rachel and conspired with her to plunder Mrs. Borradaile. The money raised by her was paid to " dear William " and shared by him with Rachel. The possibility of a marriage with Lord Ranelagh was also used as a pretence to get Mrs. Borradaile to spend money on the " Beautiful for Ever " treatment. This supposition is far more reasonable than the theory upon which the prosecution proceeded, that the illiterate prisoner dictated to her dupe a long series of graphic letters which, if invented, were the product of genius in the brilliant invention of incident and knowledge of character they display. It also disposes of the burden of believing that even Mrs. Borradaile was such a fool as to believe over the course of years that she was corresponding with a nobleman and was going to be married by proxy to a well-known peer who, if he desired her acquaintance, could have met her at any time he wished to do so.

Mr. Commissioner Kerr, who presided at the second trial, did not trouble the jury with many subtle criticisms on the evidence. He merely told them that if they thought Rachel had obtained money by false pretences she was guilty. This the jury unanimously decided without long demur. She was sentenced to five years' penal servitude.

The woman was a pest to society and, apart from the technical question of whether the evidence supported a conviction on the indictment before the Court, her sentence was well deserved, and the trial popularly approved, except by old-fashioned experts who considered that, however big a rogue a prisoner might be, he or she ought only to be found guilty of the actual offence charged in the indictment.

Madame served her time in jail and when she came out returned, as rogues and vagabonds invariably do, to her old courses. Bond Street knew her no more but in a lower grade of society she carried on her ancient trade with some success, until she once again came into collision with the law and was sent to prison, where she died.

A governor of a jail once told me that he never met with a prisoner who believed he was guilty of the crime of which he was convicted or, if he admitted the facts proved against him, had not an excuse for them which satisfied him that he was really no worse than anyone else only he had the ill-luck to be convicted.

From Madame Rachel's demeanour at the time of her conviction I gather that she did not at all concur in the universal detestation expressed by the public of her behaviour and her business. She was very proud of her Bond Street shop and the fashionable men and women who haunted it. The proceeds had enabled her to support and educate a large family, and one of her sons was at the date of her trial studying medicine in Paris. She was of Mrs. Warren's profession, no doubt, and she took a pride and interest in the success of her business. This modern Rachel of ours did not sit about mourning over her children ; she worked hard for them, and fed and clothed and educated them out of the proceeds of her wickedness.

Assuming for a moment the gown of the *advocatus diaboli*, let me remind you that if you regard her merely as a human beast of prey her conduct was elemental. When fools came to her Bond Street lair she rejoiced with the Psalmist, saying " He giveth to the beast his food and to the young ravens which cry." Rachel was a beast and a raven with seven young ravens to feed, and as a good mother she regarded Mary Borradaile and the other fools who fell to her talons as quails sent by Providence. What she did was merely ravenous, which I suppose Herbert Spencer would tell us is " right action " in ravens.

A knave, hunting or fishing for fools, enjoys his sport

with the same zest and self-excuse for cruelty or fraud as other sportsmen. No man who loves salmon-fishing would admit to himself that it is a low thing to make a lure fly gaudy and appetizing enough to disguise the hook which he casts upon the waters " to the intent," as lawyers would say, " to do grievous bodily harm to salmons to the jury unknown." But if such a one fell into a pool and was tried by a High Court judge, some *salmo ferox* of the Old Bailey of Salmon-land, what chance of an acquittal would he have on an indictment of compassing the death of a salmo-citizen by fraud and chicane ? And this was poor Rachel's case.

In the underworld of Falstaff and Doll Tearsheet, or in the Alsatian kingdom of Duke Hildebrod, she would be regarded as a worthy and successful practitioner of her ancient mystery. But dragged out of her muddy waters on to the dry banks of Victorian morality, the woman who had pandered to the vanity and vice of Victorian society was received with the execration her wrongdoing deserved.

But this at least should, I think, be remembered to her credit, that the money she made by crime she spent royally on law and legal advice. Her solicitor, Mr. Haynes, did very well out of her, and she employed five learned counsel, whom she lavishly refreshed through the weary days of two long trials. Even after that she was sporting enough to finance a hopeless writ of error. Never was a criminal followed to the portals of the jail by a more costly array of counsel, and it seems only chivalrous that I should not forget to record such a desirable trait in the unfortunate woman's otherwise despicable character.

CHAPTER VII

JAMES ALLAN, THE WANDERING MINSTREL

A NORTHUMBRIAN admirer hails James Allan as "the Orpheus of the dales of Tyne," a judgment from which I must respectfully dissent. Both were noble musicians, and both were vagabonds, but Orpheus was no rogue. Would that the same could be honestly written of Jamie Allan. And though Allan, like Orpheus, was a genius on his instrument, it must be remembered that he played the bagpipe whilst Orpheus was true to the lyre. If by now they have met in Elysian fields, doubtless they have quarrelled over the rival qualities of citharœdic and auletic music and after a fierce duet parted in anger and mutual contempt.

For this controversy divides musicians much as the more important contention between the devotees of Rugby and Association football rouses bitter argument among more serious citizens. I am still a child in these matters and a wayward one. Even in the nursery I was one day for the concertina and the next for the penny whistle. In my native land when the sun is rising, or as I have more often seen it, setting over Snowdon, by all means the harp ; but on a Highland steamer ploughing across the grey waters towards Strome Ferry, by all means the bagpipe. As an accompaniment to a banquet of haggis the bagpipe is the only instrument that can utter the just note of devout gratitude for what we are about to receive.

Who can decide whether it is nobler to strike a lyre or blow down a pipe ? I wonder which the angels will do.

Orpheus we know was all for strings, Jamie Allan relied on wind. There were other differences between them not to Allan's advantage. For in truth he was a very careless lover, whereas Orpheus, as we know, was a devoted husband. Allan sent many wives to Hades but he did not go and look for them afterwards. On the contrary, he kept out of their way.

But James Allan was a divine musician, and if he must be compared to one of the gods, then I fancy it must be to the great god Pan, who was his godfather both in music and morals. For had Pan wandered by that gentle river of Northumbria, the sparkling Coquet, and Echo been born in Rothbury forest, and had he met her upon the flowing bank of the stream, she would have done him homage on the bended knee, and taken the road with him for life until he tired of her and stole away leaving her sad and sinning.

And James Allan played the part of Pan to many humble Echoes. He stole their hearts with his music, and for a few short weeks was content to teach his latest light o' love to " run her voice in music after his " whilst the kids and lambkins sported in the heather. But in a few short months the careless Jamie tired of wedded bliss, packed up his bagpipe and stole out beneath the stars in search of riot and new adventures.

That Pan is the deity of the bagpipe, and that this noble instrument is a lineal descendant of Pan's own pipes, cannot be gainsaid. It is doubtless for this reason that to hear it and to love it you must listen for it on the banks of rapid rivers, or on the foothills of mountain lands. It is for this reason, too, that all great pipers have been men who loved the outdoor life.

The Allans were such a people, being gipsies of ancient lineage, nor were they all such rogues as James, the wandering musician. In his favour it must be remembered, however, that he was the greatest piper they produced and out-rivalled all the pipers of Northumbria. But his father, William, was also a great piper in his day, though he is best remembered as a hunter and fisherman.

" Old Wull," as he was called by his patrons and familiars, was born in 1704 in Bellingham on the North Tyne, a parish of Simonburn in the west of Northumberland. He was not of the romantic gipsy type, being six feet tall, raw-boned, with a hardy weatherbeaten complexion. But he was a decent-living fellow and an expert player on the bagpipe. If there are any pipers left in Northumberland to-day and they still play " We'll a' to the Coquet and woo ! " or " Salmon tails up the Water ! " they will tell you that these once famous tunes were the music of old " Wull " Allan.

Why does not each county have its dictionary of topical biography ? How difficult it is to listen in to the happenings of even two hundred years ago. But for the chance meeting with Robert Roxby's poem *The Lay of the Reed-water Minstrel*, I could have had little certainty of the many excellent traits of William's character.

Scott had this poem in his library, and I cannot but link up the doings of the Allans with *Guy Mannering*. For James Lord Cranstoun, like the Laird of Ellangowan, was a patron of gipsies, tinkers, and vagrants, who built their shielings round his house at Elishaw, and provided him with smuggled brandy and hyson as the price of his protection.

Young Roxby, who was born at Needless Hall, was only a lad of twelve when Will Allan died. When he wrote his lay, in 1809, he wrote from memory and tradition, for the glory of Elishaw was departed. The failure of a trustee drove him to Newcastle and a city life of drudgery. He died in 1846 and lies in St. Paul's disused burial ground at the top of Westgate Hill. But in his lifetime he was a great fisher-man and true lover of his native land. He and young Thomas

Doubleday, a fellow bard, together wrote those Coquetdale fishing songs that some Northumbrians still cherish.

Elishaw was situated at the junction of the Durtre Burn and the Reed, and there Lord Cranstoun led a gay life of hunting and feasting, and Willow Wood, as some called the house, was another Osbaldistone Hall, where Mr. Andrew Henderson, " a gentleman remarkable for his convivial talents," and many other dalesmen of like character were hospitably entertained by my lord. The estate came to him through his wife, Sophia Brown, and in the end in 1756 my lord obtained an Act of Parliament to sell it and discharge his debts. Then he seems to have borrowed some money from the parish authorities, come to London, and died in poverty in Portman Square.

But the days that Roxby sang of were the great feasts that my lord gave to all and sundry, when Reedsdale ran ale and claret, and the gentry of the border and the Faas and the Allans all gathered together at his annual merrymakings. Robert Roxby is our last connecting link with these noble days, and very graphically does he describe his boyish memories of their rough jovial pleasures. There was hunting and fishing and feasting for a week on end, and one day was given up to racing and sports. After the races were over and the saddle and bridle were given to the prizewinners by my lady, and the shepherd who was adjudged the swiftest runner had received the new hat which he proudly wore for the rest of the night, then

> When a' the bets were lost and won
> An' when the rustic race was o'er
> The couples donned their dancing shoon
> An' Allan's drones began to roar.

Roxby describes the sweet, wild strains of his pipes, the merry lilts of his reels and jigs, and tells of the rapture of the village throng that delighted in his music. It is from him, too, that we learn that " Wull " was a stalwart tinkler wight who could mend a pot or a pan or weave the willow wands into baskets. Also he exults to recall how " deftly Wull could *thraw a flee*," or slay an otter with his barbed spear.

This " King of Tinklers," as Roxby calls him, was a welcome guest at all the great houses on the banks of Aln, Coquet and Reed, along which William wandered with his famous dogs, Charley, Phœbe and Peachem, and the rest of his pack. He loved his dogs. At one time Lord Ravensworth sent for him to kill some otters in the fishpond at Eslington Hall, and gave him a couple of guineas and a good feast for his trouble. As he was leaving, Mr. Bell, my lord's factor, offered for his lordship to buy Charley at his owner's own price. " By the wuns," said Old Wull with a contemptuous smile, " the hale estate canna buy Charley."

Peachem was perhaps his favourite. There was a reliability and accuracy about the hound that was super-canine. His note was a warranty, so that his owner used to say, " When my Peachem gives mouth I durst always sell the otter's skin." Peachem was stolen, and Allan left home and family on the trail of the thief, pursuing him to Stamfordhám across the Tyne at Newburn to Tanfield, through Witton-Gilbert, where all trace was lost, and so into Durham, jaded and forlorn. But here the fates were with him, for as he passed along a by-lane the good hound spied him from a window and leaped out to his feet.

When he was staying with Lord Ravensworth he turned up to the morning sport very languid and weary, and on his lordship asking him what was amiss said, " I likes thee living weel eneugh, but dinna like thee beds, on which I could na sleep a wink. They put me amang some things they ca' sheets, where I could get nae foot-haud but slid, and slid and tossed aboot, just iv a' the world as tho' I had been thrawn in to sleep amang salmon."

A rug and some straw were laid down for him in the hall the following nights, on which he slept, as he said, " as sound and as comfortable as at hame."

He married twice. His first wife, Betty, the mother of James, was a fine gipsy girl who had many suitors, and though she favoured Will, was in no hurry to leave her home. The hunter could not be fashed hanging about at the skirts of a lass who did not know her own mind and was not content with her good fortune. One night he strolled down with his pipes to her father's house and serenaded her with his favourite tune " Dorington Lads." She opened her casement and asked him what he was about.

" This bees the last trial," said Will grimly. " Tell me ance for a' if ye'll be my wife."

The maiden was conquered and won. The parents came out to offer joyful congratulations and the wedding-day was fixed forthwith.

These were James Allan's parents. From his father James inherited his love of, and skill with, the pipes. The old man was seventy-five when he died at Whitton, and was buried in Rothbury churchyard on February 18, 1779. They say his last breath was spent in a vain endeavour to pipe the tune with which he had wooed and won the fair Betty. " Dorington Lads " was a favourite air with both father and son. If Roxby be accurate they buried him with his favourite hounds, and the behaviour of the denizens of the Coquet was scarcely decent on the occasion. But these statements seem to exceed the license even of a poet and a fisherman.

> Now trouts exulting cut the wave,
> Triumphant see the otter glide ;
> Their deadly foe lies in the grave,
> Charley and Phœbe by his side.

Young James was at this time a man of middle age, for he had been baptized by the Rev. Daniel Salkeld in the parish church of Rothbury on April 21, 1734.

Where James was at the time of his father's death is more than doubtful. Chronology is not a hobby of his biographers. The date of his birth, for instance, is differently given as 1719, 1729 and 1734. The last seems the most probable. The early life of the boy was nomadic, but his stepmother, a daughter of the manse, gave him reading and writing and an outward veneer of manners. He is described as a splendid lad, carrying all before him in contests of jumping, running, and wrestling. " As hardy as the Highland heather, as swift as the mountain roe," says one of his admirers.

But he was vain, quarrelsome and deceitful, vexing his old father with his thievish propensities. Nevertheless, all was forgiven him for his divine gift of music. He and his father played the Northumbrian bagpipe which is blown with a bellows. When Jamie put the bag under his left arm, and the bellows under his right arm, and began to finger the chanter and sing some sly ditty to his own accompaniment, or started a reel and beat the time with his feet, the memory of his transgressions vanished like a dream.

Before he was twenty his father had recognized him as his musical successor. He called together the heads of the gipsy tribes, and all the best known wandering minstrels and pipers, who pitched their tents round Allan's cottage, and the next evening young James was called upon to play to this strange college who had power to grant or withhold his musical degree. The lad played his father's favourite " Dorington Lads " and many a well-known reel and pibroch, the elders listening critically. At the end of the ordeal each musician present gave him his hand and, the elders proclaiming their verdict, he was received into the fraternity as an Approved Piper.

He now seems to have joined the Faa gang of gipsies and lived independently of his father, but Willie and Jamie often played together at Lord Cranstoun's revels at Elishaw and on other public occasions. There was never a wedding in all the dales but the Allans were sent for. They headed the procession to church, they brought the bride home, and played joyous music when her friends lifted her over the threshold, and they played at the feast and the dancing afterwards. In accordance with custom they were the leaders at the great Donkin wedding, the fame of which reached the metropolis, for is it not chronicled in the *Gentleman's Magazine* ?

It was on June 7, 1750, that William Donkin of Great Tosson married Miss Eleanor Shotton of that parish. It was a proud day for Coquetdale and no fewer than 505 guests were invited to the wedding feast. It is recorded that the viands prepared for them were 120 quarters of lamb, 44 quarters of veal, 20 quarters of mutton, and 12 hams, without prejudice to poultry and sausages. The punch alone required 4 ankers of brandy, and the beer was brewed from 90 bushels of malt. There were also twelve dozen of cider and many gallons of wine. And during the feast there were twenty-five pipers skirling away to cheer the appetite to new adventures.

It was on this occasion that young James had the ill-manners to sneer at his father, who was the acknowledged leader of the orchestra, for playing out of tune. But the old man set him down fairly.

" Wha the deil learnt ye ? " he shouted more in anger than in sorrow. " Wha the deil learnt ye ? I'll shiver the back lill with you or so'er a piper in Breaton ! "

Now I am told that the " back lill " on the small pipes of Northumberland is the thumb note, or B in alt, the highest of the nine notes, to trill which effectively requires the acme of skill in the executant. Those who heard both gave the palm to Jamie. But William was great in his day and Donkin's wedding guests approved of the old man's rebuke, the more so as there was no love among them for " Breaton " as they called North Britain over the border.

And, as we have said, James had thrown in his lot with the Faas whose head-quarters were at Kirk Yetholm, north of the Cheviots in Roxburghshire. Jean Gordon—Scott's Meg Merrilies—had been head of that dangerous tribe of Faas, Youngs, and Gordons, which was a terror to the Border. Their present king was William Faa, a noted pugilist, smuggler and rascal and a patron of young James. Madge Gordon, Jean's daughter, claimed to be their queen and dominated the lad with her beauty and strength. James was too tricky and selfish to be a useful subject of the tribe. William Faa, like a wise general, though he planned and connived at robberies and raids, did not himself go into action, but kept on the windy side of the law, living to a great age and ending his life a respectable publican and fisherman in the Vale of Beaumont.

About 1750, or shortly afterwards, the authorities began to set the law in motion against the Faas, and several gangs were arrested, prosecuted, and the men and women transported. This frightened young James who began to hanker after the safety of civilization. Here the goddess of music came to his aid, for to the lad's intense surprise and delight, he received a message from the Countess of Northumberland to visit Alnwick Castle and play to her.

Lady Betty Percy and the Earl her husband had come to Alnwick Castle amidst the rejoicing of the people of Northumbria in the summer of 1750, bringing with them a splendid retinue of servants. The castle had fallen to ruin, and the Earl immediately started those repairs and new buildings over which he spent twenty years and great sums of money.

Indeed, as Walpole writes to Sir Horace Mann, they were all for ostentation and spending and pomp and pride. In London seven footmen preceded my lady's chair to the discontent of the Queen herself. In Northumberland my lady played the part of queen, lived according to the etiquette of the old peerage, and flouted her Swiss porters and her pipers in the face of an outraged aristocracy.

When she arrived at Alnwick Castle, Lady Betty found no piper to greet her. She made inquiries into the matter, and a local connoisseur of pipe music who had seen and heard Jamie " shiver the back lill," recommended the lad to the Countess, who sent for him to present himself at the castle.

James was in the seventh heaven of joy at the receipt of the Countess's commands, but he looked down at his rags with dismay. How could he present himself before her ladyship in such garments ? There was a rich farmer near by whose daughter had often cast longing glances towards the young piper, and to her the rascal went with words of love on his lips and vain boasting of his great future if he could but reach Alnwick Castle in worthy attire. He dwelt upon his golden prospects and the honours and wealth the Countess would shower upon him, and how he could then return and claim his bride. The girl encouraged him with smiles and words of hope, but young Jamie was silent and melancholy. At length he hinted at his trouble and the delighted girl rushed to her purse and poured the coins into his lap. James, swearing eternal constancy, dressed himself in gay attire and set out at once for Alnwick. The poor girl waited patiently for news of her lover, but none came. Her secret reached her father's ears, who, angered by his girl's folly and imprudence, hastened her wedding to a rich stock farmer of the west of the county, who carried her off to a safe home, where doubtless she soon forgot her faithless Jamie.

He, arrayed in the spoils of his flirtation, appeared before the Countess and shivered the back lill so skilfully that he won her heart at once. She appointed him her own piper, and from that day onward he was privileged to wear the crescent in silver on his arm, which was the trophy that the Percies had worn since the days of the Crusades. In the portraits attached to James Thompson's *Life* and the earlier Blyth biography this decoration is not omitted.

For two years he lived in peace and plenty at the castle and improved his style and education, and then his fatal fascination for women caused him to throw up his post, at all events for the moment. In this incident he was not blameworthy. He had at that time a real affection for a worthless girl he had left in his old home at Rothbury, and intended to return with his savings to his native village to see her again. His resolution to do this was hastened by the discovery that his lady's favourite maid had fallen in love with him. Not only did he learn the young lady's secret but everyone in the castle knew it, and in due course it came to the ears of the Countess.

The housekeeper was ordered to investigate and report on the matter, and she announced to her mistress that the girl's passion was alleged by its victim to be incurable, but that the young man absolutely refused to attempt its cure by a proposal of marriage, as his heart was in the keeping of another. Allan now behaved with great sense, if not with sincerity. He thought a temporary absence from the castle to continue his education would result in further advancement and release him from the temptation of carrying on any illicit amour with the maid. He therefore told the housekeeper that he wished to leave.

The Countess was more than pleased with Allan's generosity. She made him a handsome present of cash on his departure, and procured from Edinburgh a pair of small pipes handsomely made of ivory and decorated with silver chains. These remained his companions throughout his long and adventurous life. His fellow-musicians and the chief domestics, with whom he was on excellent terms, gave him many handsome gifts, and everyone from the Countess downwards expressed the hope that he would return again before long.

James's intention on going back to his father's house at Rothbury, was to have placed himself under the tuition of the local schoolmaster to improve his education, but he found that the good man was too ill to take pupils, and he naturally fell into his old practices of fishing, gambling, poaching and carousing at the alehouse, where he and his pipes were always welcome.

His sweetheart, Fanny, had been a servant at an inn at Rothbury but was now at Morpeth with her sister. Hearing that Allan had returned dressed like a gentleman with his pockets full of money, she hastened back to Rothbury. She was a sly, witty girl, forward with strangers, but well able to hold her own. She had returned with intent to capture Jamie, and her methods of securing him were worthy of the oldest tradition of the sport. She upbraided him for his neglect of her and charged him with strange amours, the stories of which had reached her, and wept over the mental agonies she had endured in his absence and refused his embraces. Poor Allan was driven to despair, and despair turned to madness when he heard that she intended to marry a rival. By these old-time and honoured methods did Mistress Fanny acquire a husband and James Allan a worthless wife.

For the woman was a drunken, quarrelsome, licentious creature and cunning in planning deceits. Had he not been infatuated with her and entered upon this unhappy marriage his story might have made a far more reputable and happier narrative. James seems at first to have made an effort

JAMES ALLAN

NORTHUMBERLAND PIPER.

From a contemporary engraving in "The Life of James Allan," 1818.

towards an honest and, hard-working career. His gains as a piper were considerable, but his wife was a spendthrift, and no matter what he gave her she spent more.

During his absence in the winter months when he was hired for feasts and dances, the woman used to invite her lovers to James's cottage and make merry with them at his cost. Her chief favourite was an ugly little bow-legged tailor with enormous bushy black whiskers, named James Hill. This Caliban was a man of great strength with very long muscular arms and seems to have dominated Fanny, for no sooner was Allan's back turned than the fellow would sneak into his house every night and be entertained by his wife until the husband's return.

Everyone in the village learned what was going on, except of course the poor dupe of a husband, who was still enamoured of his bride and made the best of her wild ways and drunken habits. But the end was bound to come. One winter evening James returned from a long tramp of some thirty miles and, meeting his father, the two turned into the inn for a draught. Here they found Hill who was more or less " fou," and started bantering James and winking at the company, who chuckled coarsely at his allusions to the loneliness of Mrs. James during her husband's absence.

James was too dull and tired to follow his drunken haverings, but at length he used an expression about his wife that called for an angry protest, and Hill retorted by an open boast of the favours he had received. Old Will Allan, who had his snuff-horn in his hand, dashed it in fury in the fellow's face and would have flung himself upon him had not the company restrained him. Others pushed the beastly drunken tailor out of the house, and when quiet was in some sort restored they found James lying motionless with his head on the table. Nor could they rouse him to speech. They carried him to bed and sent for a surgeon who diagnosed

K

a fever, and it was some days before he was out of bed or could use his legs. He sent to his wife for money, but she neither came near him nor sent him aid, but loaded his messengers with abuse.

A farmer friend carried the poor fellow away from the inn to his own farmhouse, and there he remained until he gradually recovered from his illness. He had no home, and no wife to call him back to it. The romance of his marriage had soon turned to very Dead-Sea fruit and the world before him looked drear and bitter. A wiser youth than Jamie Allan might have felt that fate was against him and made no further struggle towards honesty and industry. But he made one effort towards reinstating himself and, tramping to Alnwick Castle, asked to be allowed to take up his old duties.

He was made welcome and reinstated in his office. But the memory of his wrongs could only be drowned in drink or replaced by the excitement of cards and dice, and when he was wanted to attend her ladyship he was often found in such a condition that he could not master his pipes. He felt the disgrace of his situation and resolved to bring it to an end when opportunity arrived. This came with the embodying of the Northumberland Militia at Alnwick. The glory of uniform, the gust of marching at the head of a regiment with his pipes, were real lures to the despondent youth at the moment ; and here he thought he had found a career of music and adventure which would restore his self-respect.

He was welcomed by the regiment. He could give expression to the wild, melancholy, warlike notes of the pibroch as few pipers could. Mr. Richardson, the North Shields notary, who heard him play a post pibroch at Elsdon Court Baron on the regimental Northumberland bagpipe, records that his music not only created astonishment, but in some cases active terror among the audience. But, like other young men who have looked to find a soldier's life a romance, James soon discovered that a piper had other duties than to march proudly in handsome garb at the head of the regiment pouring his soul into the chanter and calling on his fellow men to " drive back the Scot on the border." There were drills, and parades, and inspection of kit, and cleanliness, punctuality, and other unpleasing details of a soldier's life, that Jamie had not counted on. Moreover, there was a sergeant with a coarse tongue and a foul manner whom it was death to punish as he deserved. James Allan's gipsy soul revolted against these things. The army was no place for a genius and a free man. Not staying to say farewell, he took leave of his comrades without lament. James and his pipes deserted. Henceforth he was a " wanted " man and a fugitive and vagabond on earth.

He dared not return to Rothbury, but made for Newcastle, exchanged his soldier's coat for an old one, bought an old hat and a leathern apron, and in this disguise went about of nights but kept house during the day for fear of detection. Strolling one evening along the quayside he met his wife stepping off a ship with a sailor. Joy filled his heart and making her a bow he turned on his heel and walked blithely along. For now he knew he could return home as his one enemy was not there to betray him. That very night he started north glad to be freed from skulking in the mean streets of the city, and the rising sun shone on the hills of Simonside and welcomed him to his home.

Old Will and his stepmother received him according to the precedent of the prodigal son. As the old man told his neighbours, had his son deserted from the regulars he would have played the Roman father and haled him back, but the militia was another pair of shoes. This patriotic reasoning was well received. Jamie and his beloved pipes were home again, his wife had run off with a sailor, and the lad and his music were welcome in the dale.

But he dared not visit the farmers and gentry, and for a while was cautious of moving about in the daytime. During his night rambles he had acquired a dog, and had discovered that the hound was as keen and knowledgeable as himself in the pursuit of the otter. For returning home along the river in the early dawn, they had on several occasions had what semblance of a hunt one man and one dog can put up against an otter. So that when his father was called for to lead an otter hunt the young fool must needs go with him, if only to give his dog a taste of the real sport in good company.

And for old Will's sake I doubt if any would have noticed him, but his quarrelsome nature was his undoing, for in the course of the hunt he disparaged the efforts of the constable's son, who cursed him roundly, and Jamie, to stop his foul tongue, threw him into a pool in the Coquet and left him there whilst he followed the hounds.

The soused youth dragged himself out with difficulty, and ran shivering home to his father with his tale of the ill-doing of Jamie the Piper. A council of war was called. The constable pointed out that if they harboured Jamie the militia might raid them and ballot another youth from their midst in his stead ; this reasoning satisfied all that he had better be taken and handed over to military justice.

But James, like the otter, was not to be caught in his holt without a struggle for freedom. The constable and posse came to old Allan's cottage and surrounded it. James's stepmother saw them coming and bolted the door. A friendly old Rothbury publican, one of the constables, knocked at the door and asked for James.

" We cannot give up what we have not," said Mrs. Allan, " poor Jamie has gone to Shields where he means to take shipping for London."

" I'm glad to hear that," whispered the constable, " for I would be sorry to see the son of an old neighbour punished, but I must do my duty so let me look in for the fox and that will satisfy all parties."

Whilst they were talking James made a noise as though he were getting out of the back window, and the party rushed round to catch him. At this moment old Will drew back the wooden bolt and ran off up the lane at top speed, his wife standing on the threshold screaming out : " Run, Jamie, run ! " The ruse succeeded. Will had a fair start and the constables joined in the pursuit with great spirit. After about a mile of it the old man sank on the ground and waited for his pursuers, when he sat up with a sarcastic grin and said he feared they would not find Jamie at home on their return.

Nor did they, for Jamie was away to Bewcastle in Cumberland, where he stayed with a friend and enjoyed a gay holiday with plenty of drink, gambling, running and wrestling, he repaying the hospitality of the jolly Cumbrians with the best pipe music they had ever heard.

But at Hexham fair, which he was fool enough to attend, a sergeant arrested him in the market-place and he was sent off with an escort of three soldiers, hearty fellows of Tweedside, to join his regiment. They stopped the night, at the end of the first day's journey, at an inn, and went into the yard to amuse themselves. Allan, who had still the remains of a guinea to spend, bet a gallon of ale that he could beat them all at quoits, and the corporal, seeing the yard wall was high, took off his prisoner's handcuffs and the game began. Allan allowed his friends to win, and one gallon of ale followed another.

Then a dispute arose as to who was the best shot, and a contest was decided upon. Jamie was appointed umpire and a mark was set up. After they had fired some time, with little effect on the mark, they laid down their firelocks and began wrangling over the result. Allan asked why they had ceased firing.

" Because all our shot is done."

" But you have surely one charge left, that I may show my skill," said Allan with a grieved look.

" No, none of us has a particle left."

" Ho, my friends," cried Jamie briskly, " it is time then for me to quit you."

As he spoke he sprang nimbly on to the wall and, wishing them a pleasant journey, disappeared from their sight.

The fellows were too dazed at their folly and his audacity to attempt a pursuit, nor would it have been of much avail, and whilst they remained concocting a story for the sergeant, Allan sped away south towards Durham.

After many similar adventures he was run to earth at last on Hedgely Moor, a sprained ankle having been the cause of his arrest. He was carried into Alnwick in a cart and handed over to a sergeant of the Northumberland Militia. In his misery he sent for an old domestic at the castle who had been a good friend to him, and he told the Countess a tale of sorrow and ill-fortune which Jamie had rehearsed for his benefit. The benevolent lady was grieved to hear of his distress. She sent money for his present needs and wrote urgent letters to the colonel of his regiment, begging for his discharge. So powerful a patroness could not be denied, and the Countess once again received into the castle her penitent piper, who humbly thanked her on his knees for his delivery from punishment, and promised to retrieve his lost character by future good behaviour.

For a few months he behaved with decorum, but he soon found the discipline of the household unbearable. He commenced to gamble and drink. The house-steward complained of his misconduct. Even his music suffered from his evil habits, and the Countess, wroth at his ingratitude, ordered him to leave the castle at an hour's notice. Even in his disgrace he had friends among the women servants, who hastily met and subscribed a purse of six guineas for the poor wretch, who was known to have but a shilling or two in his pocket.

James Allan had made England too hot to hold him and now he determined to cross the border, and with his purse and his pipes and his freedom he soon forgot his sorrows and journeyed towards Berwick with a light heart.

At Kelso, Allan put up at an inn and charmed the company with his music, his songs and droll stories, so that he won the heart of a hussy who carried him to her lodgings, but when he woke in the morning his mistress and his money were gone. Nothing daunted, he took the road again and at Jedburgh his music provided him with a collection that put him in funds. That night staying at an inn with a young farmer who loved the pipes, they sat up and made a night of it, ending with cards at which James won £30.

At Moffat he fell in with a gipsy girl named Jean, a pretty brunette, with sparkling black eyes. She was a clever fortune-teller, and they agreed to join forces. In a few hours they came up with a camp of gipsies where the marriage ceremony was duly performed and, Allan being in funds, the rejoicings and feasts were prolonged.

Jean was allied by blood to Will Marshall, a noted gipsy chief, and she insisted on carrying her husband across to Ayrshire to introduce him to Will. When they arrived Will received her very heartily and, looking at Allan, asked : " But wha's that wi' you, Jean ? "

" My husband," said the blushing bride, bringing him forward. " We were lawfully pledged in the presence of the Kennedy tribe."

" Weel, weel, lass, what can the callan' do ? " asked the chief.

" He can play fu' weel on the sma' pipes."

" Gi'en that be leel, ye hae made a braw bargain," said the chief, " but let's hae a swatch o' his skill."

James played Jean's favourite air " Felton Lonen," and knowing he was in the presence of royalty, played his best. Will's stern gaze melted at the tunes and, ere the piece was ended, he rose and took the young man by the hand saying, " Ye're weel worth your room ; nae music pleases me but the pipes."

And this was James's way throughout life. He could capture the hearts of men and women with the music of his pipes, but his own life was a tangle of broken discords.

He was now " royal piper to King Will." Marshall's gang made their walk through Wigtowshire and Kirkcud-brightshire, as the Faas patrolled Roxburghshire and the Allans the Northumberland dales. Allan's game was to pipe among the farmers and gentry and learn their secrets, and Jean did the fortune-telling afterwards. Jean of course was gifted with second sight. Jamie Allan was her second sight. She was the divining cup into which Allan poured his infor-mation overnight. They were never seen together, and the girl, being a witty, clever baggage, made plenty of money which she shared with James, and for a while he was as happy as a king.

But as ill-luck would have it he did not please Will Marshall, who feared that he had discovered the story of a foul and secret murder he had committed. James did not dare to discuss this matter with Jean, but a friend of his in the gang admitted to him that his life was in danger and he had better fly without delay. That night he took his pipes and his own savings, robbing his poor wife of every penny, and made away towards Ayr, where he found a sloop bound for Greenock. After some pleasant adventures on board, he disembarked at Dumbarton and made across country to Edinburgh where, having plenty of money in his purse, he took very genteel lodgings and appeared for the first time in his life in the character of an independent gentleman.

He attended the gaming tables and having a run of luck at the end of six weeks was £160 in pocket. He also frequented the billiard rooms and here, too, he found himself a match for most of the players. A young Irish nobleman played and lost several games with him for small sums, yet the habitués of the room used to persuade the young nobleman that he was really the better player. At length his lordship was goaded into playing a match with Jamie for £200, and all his friends offered good odds on Allan, who chuckled at the thought of rooking the young fool. The game was played, but the nobleman, who had played so indifferently before, ran ahead of James from the first and finished an easy winner. Allan had tumbled headlong into a new world of which he knew nothing, for the Irishman and his friends were a notorious gang of sharpers who had laid out for Jamie from the first.

Going through the streets and cursing his evil fortune he nearly ran into the arms of his beloved Jean, who it seems was still on his track, but he escaped her, made his way to his lodgings, packed his traps and his bagpipe, dropped out of a back window and was away on the road again, a fugitive and wanderer.

After several adventures he came into Cumberland and picked up with another lively young fortune-teller who worked the Lake District in the summer and made a good harvest out of the fashionables. She taught him many new tricks of legerdemain and pocket-picking, and the two seemed so well suited that having acquired an ass they travelled the road together towards Northumberland with great content. Here he joined his old tribe, the Faas, and Will Faa and Madge Gordon received him and the girl graciously for the sake of the music he brought with him. After biding awhile with his friends, he and his partner made for Appleby on a business tour. But whilst the girl was away at the Lakes, Jean made her appearance again and the hunted James fled to Whitehaven and got away to Dublin, where his music was rapturously received and he is said to have made an income of more than £10 a week.

A fool and his money are soon parted, and a career of extravagance landed James in a debtors' prison from which he was glad to escape by enlisting with some other young men in the East India Company's service. The agent of the Company carried off his troop by sea to the Isle of Wight, and here Allan was drafted on to a vessel bound for China.

It was clear that there was no escape from this service, but James had a bagpipe with him and, as they dropped down the Channel, he tuned it up and gave the sailors the old Northumbrian air " I saw my Love come passing by," which set the men dancing on the deck. The officers at dinner, hearing the music, sent for Jamie, who charmed them with his skill. Mr. Hume, the first lieutenant, who was a Scot and passionately fond of pipe music, appointed him his servant so that he had none of the privations of a common sailor to undergo and made a pleasant journey to Madras.

How long he remained abroad, and how many of the yarns of adventure that Allan spun in his old age to Mr. James Thompson, his latest biographer, are " leel," as Will Marshall would say, it is hard to tell. According to his own story he rambled about China and India and finding himself at Delhi went across the mountains into Tartary. Everywhere the universal language of his pipes gained him food and lodging and kindly greeting. From Tartary some camel-drivers took him to Samarkand, and if he truly visited this famous city he was the first European who had reached it since Marco Polo, and forestalled M. Vambéry by more than a hundred years.

From there he travels by caravan to St. Petersburg, and thence he pipes his way through Europe until he falls in with the English army in Prussia and plays his part with the 25th Regiment in the battle of Minden. This brings us to August, 1759, and a date is a rare event in the life of James Allan. Also it brings our hero, according to the Thompson chronology, to twenty-five years of age.

The 25th Regiment was the King's Own Borderers, and Allan and his pipes would no doubt be welcome recruits. They remained at the front until 1763, when they landed in Kent in the first week of April. If James had really done four years' active service and been present at Minden, Campen, and the other battles where the 25th did distinguished service, I think the rogue would have had a lot more to say about it. But his memories were very vague, and to my mind it seems far more likely that he loafed about the Continent and picked up with the regiment when it was coming home.

On arriving in England the regiment was divided into nine companies, in each of which there seem to have been nine officers to forty-five men, so that Allan's story that he was sent with his pipes on a recruiting expedition to Stockport is not improbable. For, though no hand at fighting, the gipsy minstrel was worth a hundred sergeants when the job was to win the hearts of lads of adventure with martial music and inspire their souls with the spirit of war. But Allan had no love for the discipline of the army and his heart was with his tribe in the dales to whom he intended to make his way at the first opportunity. Moreover, he longed to recover the beautiful pipes that the Countess of Northumberland had presented to him. These he had placed in the hands of a gentleman of the county at some time before he left the country.

He was not long at Stockport, and deserting in the guise

of a miner, made his way to Liverpool. Here he was arrested but again escaped and, after many adventures, reached his native land, recovered his beautiful pipes from which he never afterwards parted, and received a grand ovation from the gipsies of the glens.

But a deserter is a marked man with a price on his head, and even among the borderers Allan felt far from safe. He tried his old friends at Alnwick Castle, but the story of his desertion had reached them, and though his fellow domestics gave his messenger clothes and money, they held out no hope that their misguided friend would be received again into the service of the Countess.

So for the present he wandered along the border with his pipes attending feasts and fairs, but keeping his weather eye open for any signs of military parties. It was at this time at a Cumberland fair that he and a pal won a stake over a cock-fight from a gambling country squire by means of a clever cheat and then took him on in a horse-race, the story of which is still county folk-lore.

Jamie had acquired a galloway of no great pretensions, and the squire owned a young gelding that had won several races, and after he had lost the cock-fight, was offering to back his horse against any within five miles for a £100. Allan intervened.

" I'll run my galloway," he shouted, " against your fine horse the distance of a mile for £20, but you must give us 50 yards' start as I am at least 2 stone heavier than you are and that will make the match even."

The company thought him mad. The squire at once threw his money on the table and Allan covered it with the winnings at the cock-fight. Now Allan's pal was the squire's groom, and had been in with him at the cheat over the cocking. He was very wroth with Jamie for throwing their money away on a fool bet of this kind.

But sly Jamie had a plan of his own, and bidding the groom saddle his master's horse that night and meet him on the narrow road along which they were to race, he went his way. That evening, arrived at the course, Allan measured 50 yards' start and mounted his galloway with his pipes and set off at a trot, playing " I'll make ye fain to follow me." The ostler jumped on the gelding and soon overtook Jamie, who, as they came up to him, gave the poor animal a smart blow on the face and continued his course piping as he went. Every time the groom tried to pass Allan the beast received another smack in the face, until at last he got so frightened that he would not approach within yards of his rival, and Allan piped triumphantly to the goal.

Next morning a merry crowd assembled to see the presumptuous piper lose his money. The ground was measured and Jamie started off at a gentle trot, the squire at full speed. As he and his horse approached, the piper struck up the tune of the night before, on which the squire's horse planted his forelegs firmly on the ground and refused in spite of whip and spur to make an effort to pass the leader. Allan trotted along piping as he went, and nothing the squire or his friends could do would induce the gelding to come within reach of Jamie who trotted by the door of the " Crown Inn " which was the winning-post, an easy leader amid the cheers and laughter of the mob.

As he dismounted James said with a chuckle to the angry squire : " That fine gelding seems to have a lug for music and does not like to pass it for fear of losing the sound."

With the money he won at the fair Allan bought some fine clothes and again travelled east and presented himself at Alnwick Castle, where the Countess allowed him an interview and, believing in his promises of amendment once more, offered him a home and the post of piper to the family.

It is often amazing how a rascal of this type receives

chances and offers of work and employment, that never come near an honest, hard-working man. But this seems the way of the world, and it is the way of the ne'er-do-weel that he can never make use of the opportunities offered to him, but seems drawn by invisible chains back to the bondage of his sins.

Jamie was no exception. He had stolen a watch in his wanderings from a farmer at Otterburn, and now he was in work, made no effort to make amends for his crime, which might, one thinks, have easily been done. The farmer hearing he was at the castle brought a complaint to the Earl. Jamie would have brazened it out but the evidence was overwhelming. The Earl settled the matter with the farmer, rather than a servant of his house should be hanged for theft, and ordered the house-steward to give Allan ten pounds and charge him strictly never to come within the curtilage of his castle again.

Once more the piper was a homeless vagabond, and he set his face toward Yetholm to visit the Faa gang, who were always ready to give him comfort and hospitality. But he could not remain there long, for the military authorities hearing of his dismissal from Alnwick were again on his track, and he resumed his wanderings.

One disgraceful story after another does Mr. Thompson set down to his hero's discredit. At Ulverston he fell in with a company of strolling players marching after a cart filled with their scenery, dresses and young children. At an ale-house he and the manager made friends. He had never seen such a gay, careless set of boon companions, and when he had played them dance music on his pipes and accompanied the manager's wife, who sang with spirit, on the hautboy, he was greeted as one of themselves without further ceremony. It was a sharing company and on the first night *King Lear* produced a share of one and fourpence a head. They were " living on clover to-day and counting the chimney pots for a dinner to-morrow." But Allan stayed with them for six months and then persuaded the manager's wife to rob her husband and take the road along with him.

They lived together at Lichfield for some time, Allan teaching music, and then another girl took his fancy and the infatuated actress returned to her husband. Debt drove him from Lichfield and Allan fled south to avoid the bailiffs, leaving his latest love behind him. On his journey to London he fell in with a large gathering of gipsies feasting at the road-side and was invited to the feast by a beautiful gipsy girl, who, when she had heard him play and found he knew their language, commanded him to join them and declared he should be her piper.

Allan at first was taken somewhat aback, but when Mary, for so the girl was named, told him she was the king's daughter and taking him by the hand, led him to her father's tent, he followed spellbound, for her beauty had touched his heart. The chief was a man of great dignity. He told him that his daughter's knowledge of music was superior to his own, and as it was his custom never to refuse the princess any reasonable request, he would admit him to membership of his people.

Mary was delighted. The monthly gathering of the clan was prolonged for another day in Jamie's honour, and then they scattered until their next rendezvous. The chief was reputed a man of riches and rode a fine horse, his tents and baggage following in a cart. He was devoted to his daughter. He ruled his tribe despotically and would allow no thieving or crime.

Mary, too, was an adept at fortune-telling and asked her father's leave to take Allan with her on her next venture as loiterer and spy to procure her local information. The old man was not wholly pleased at the notion but he was easily swayed by the girl, and in the end, ordering Jamie to dress himself as an ancient beggar, he sent him to join her. The girl had no doubt fallen deeply in love with James and his music, but she was a proud, honest girl and James, to his credit, treated her with courtesy and respect.

Three months' tour together made it clear to him that here at last he had met with a woman whom he could honour and to whom he could devote his life. As they returned to the next gathering of the tribe he asked her to be his bride, and Mary accepted him subject to her father's consent. Since his first unfortunate marriage this seems to have been the one honest partnership that James sought, and it was a misfortune that it ended so tragically.

They found the old chief feasting amidst a crowd of his people, and when he retired to his tent Allan made bold to follow him and ask his daughter in marriage. The chief displayed no emotion but said he would send for him and give his answer in a few hours.

The two lovers sat apart from the throng of roysterers waiting the royal verdict with trembling apprehension. At length the summons came and Allan once more entered the presence. The old man told him that he had closely watched his conduct from the moment he had entered the camp and had been pleased with his discretion. He did not approve of his daughter's marriage, but knowing her wild enthusiastic spirit he was not intending to oppose her wishes. He stipulated that the marriage should be solemnized according to the rites of the Church of Rome, and then dismissed him saying : " Prove to her a kind husband, and, should you continue to deserve my good opinion, your reward is certain : if not, your punishment will be equally certain."

Early the next morning the ceremony was performed in a neighbouring chapel by a Catholic priest, two respectable farmers being witnesses, and the young couple, with their father's approval, left without undergoing any of the riotous festivities that were the usual sequel to a gipsy wedding.

The happy pair toured the country together with great content, but from time to time visited the tribe, and the old man treated James with great kindness, promising to make him his heir and generously supplying all their wants. To James's expression of gratitude he had one constant reply : " Be kind to Mary and I am amply repaid."

The girl was a good girl and had a good influence on Allan. Whether it would have stood the test of time we shall never know. For in their wanderings she fell ill at Bakewell, and though her husband procured a surgeon and the best nurses available and was at her bedside day and night for ten terrible days, death claimed the victory and once again James Allan was a vagabond and fugitive upon earth.

That he honestly paid the surgeon and nurses and all the expenses of her funeral before he left Bakewell, is strong evidence of his deep affection for his companion, and when he once again took the road he was too disconsolate to finger his beloved pipes. Hearing the chief had pitched his tent at Newbury in Berkshire, he journeyed thither, and after several mournful and strange interviews with the old man, convinced him of his honourable behaviour to his poor wife and parted from him in friendship.

This was the last effort the man seems to have made towards a settled reputable life and, perhaps for the girl's sake, the ending was a happy one. He now wandered to London and played the hautboy in a respectable orchestra, earning good money, but the life was too regular for his tastes. He soon got into bad and congenial company and, having been concerned in a robbery, was glad to take refuge in a vessel bound for Gibraltar. Once again we read of strange foreign adventures, this time among the Moors, in which his mastery over the pipes and his attraction for the fair sex carried him through with no serious mishap to life or limb.

L

On his return to England he wandered about the south and the west and we hear of him at Winchester and Bristol, occasionally thieving, or enlisting and deserting, but winning through with wit and music and escaping to further cheats and crimes. The call of the dales was always tugging at his heart-strings and he reappeared in Durham making once again for his native Rothbury. Here he seems to have settled down again for a while and married a girl named Alice Taylor at Coldstream, with whom he lived, apparently, for three years, when he basely deserted her and her two children.

Again he resumes his wandering, licentious life from which no tie could reclaim him, and among other adventures was tried for horse-stealing at Newcastle Assizes. Much to his surprise when his trial came on he was represented by counsel who, it is said, raised some clever objections to the indictment. His advocate was, no doubt, employed by the good-natured Duchess of Northumberland who had heard of his peril, and the result of the trial was that he was only sentenced to be burnt on the hand with a cold iron.

After this escape he sailed for London and was admitted to Northumberland House, and his music and humour gained him the notice of many of the nobility. Ladies of fashion were particularly delighted with a sly ballad he piped and sang to the tune of " Come to Bed, Cicely, come, come, come," which for some time was a great favourite and earned him laughter and applause.

James Allan had many more strange adventures, the chronology of which is confusing, but at some time after the death of his patrons, the Duchess and Duke of Northumberland, which happened in 1776 and 1786, we find him again at Alnwick Castle where the steward allows him to remain awhile in the absence of the family. Again he wanders away, but hearing of a great piping contest at the Duke's baronial manor of Redesdale to be holden at Elsdon, where it was rumoured the piper for the new Duchess of Northumberland would be chosen, Jamie made up his mind to be there to show the new generation the music that genius could produce from the short pipes of Northumbria.

The judges listened to all the competitors and Jamie's efforts met with hearty and unstinted applause. But there was a young player of nineteen, William Lamshaw, one " whose self-taught strains Northumbria charm'd " as was written in his elegy, of whom James had never heard, and it was soon clear that the prize must fall to one or other of them. They were called upon to play again and once more the judges consulted and could come to no conclusion.

Seeing their trouble Jamie came forward and said he gave up all claims to victory. He told the judges that the youth's fingers were more " soople " than his and assured them that he bottomed the notes with admirable distinction and effect, and that he had the best bagpipe lug he had ever heard.

The act was the more gracious because Allan knew well that it meant that young Lamshaw would be made piper to Alnwick Castle. The crown was his to give and he gave it freely, for it was not possible for James to be dishonest in matters of music, any more than it was possible for him to be honest in matters of morals. It is good to read at the end that Jamie had still some of that sporting instinct latent in his soul that his good father " Old Wull " had been noted for throughout his career.

Would that the curtain could be lowered on this generous scene and Jamie Allan take his last call on the stage of the Elsdon heather surrounded by his cheering countrymen and honoured by his fellow pipers.

But truth must be chronicled and shortly after the meeting we hear that James Allan has stolen a bay horse, the property of Mr. Matthew Robinson of Gateshead, for which theft he was arrested at Jedburgh and lodged in Durham jail.

This was in May, 1803, and on August 2 of that year he is found guilty at Durham Assizes and sentenced to death. The judges reprieved him before they left the city and on October 17, 1804, his sentence was commuted to transportation for life. On account of his age and infirmity he was considered unfit to be taken to Botany Bay and was imprisoned in England during the rest of his life.

His last place of confinement was the House of Correction at Durham, and here he died on November 13, 1810, in the seventy-seventh year of his age. During his imprisonment one of his many wives, Ann Bennett, remained firmly attached to him and travelled the dales collecting money for his maintenance. He had many presents sent him from former patrons and was allowed the solace and companionship of the beautiful pipes that the kind countess had given him in his early days.

It is said that the Prince Regent signed a free pardon for James dated February 18, 1810, but by some accident it did not arrive in Durham until after his death. Seeing that the Regency Bill did not pass until February 5, 1811, it seems more probable that he signed it then, not knowing James was dead, especially as some chroniclers refer to it as his first official act. The new Duke of Northumberland was one of the Prince's circle and must have known James as a lad.

Rogue and blackguard as he was, James's world remembered him as a wandering minstrel, a man with music in his soul who could make men's hearts gay, rouse them to warlike ardour or set their feet twinkling on the turf.

When he died, a moan went up from the dales, and men and women as they met on the hill-side greeted each other with a sigh and the sad news " Allan's dead."

There are some humble verses in a chap-book written by some unknown native poet which tell of the sorrow of the country-side, and help one to realize what his music meant

to these kindly souls and why he was not forgotten by them
during his long years in jail. They seem a fitting *envoi* to
the story of his life.

All ye whom music's charms inspire,
Who skilful Minstrels do admire,
All ye whom bagpipes' lilts can fire
  'Tween Wear and Tweed,
Come strike with me the mournful lyre
  For Allan's dead.

No more where Coquet's stream doth glide,
Shall we view Jemmy in his pride,
With bagpipes buckled to his side,
  And nymphs and swains,
In groups collect at eventide
  To hear his strains.

When elbow moved and bellows blew,
On green or floor the dancers flew,
In mazy turns ran through and through,
  With cap'ring canter,
And aye their nimble feet beat time
  To his sweet chanter.

Attentive aye, and aye admiring,
I've listened to his pipe inspiring,
At feast and fair, at race and hiring,
  And then gat fou,
And never thought of home retiring
  While dune he blew.

CHAPTER VIII

SAMUEL FOOTE, THE PLAYER OF INTERLUDES

TO modern readers it may come with a shock to find the name of an actor among a company of vagrom men. Yet this must occur, if the words of the statutes are to be fulfilled, and we are to collect under one cover types of all the men and women whom our ancestors designated as rogues and vagabonds. From the earliest times you will find the " comon players of Enterludes " are subject to the same harsh penalties as beggars, gipsies, fortune-tellers, pedlars, bearwards and other vagrants. Indeed, it is not until 1824 that an actor was safe from apprehension as a rogue and vagabond.

It is, however, a providential arrangement of our social affairs that whilst for three hundred years Parliament kept passing different acts for the extinction of vagrants and the prohibition of the pleasures of the poor, no one troubled to enforce them to the full extent of their obvious absurdity, except a few tyrannical kill-joys in scattered places. The rich were always allowed to make holiday among the players. Even in Elizabethan days players who " belonged to any Baron of the Realm " were not accounted to be rogues and vagabonds, and by means of patent theatres and other devices the law enabled the well-to-do in the big towns to have what theatrical entertainment they liked. Even the barn-stormers in the winter were generally welcomed unless they came into a county where Mawworm and Stiggins had the consciences of the magistrates in their pockets.

The ministers of the Church of England by law established, who were generally of the magistracy, were not as a rule hostile to the vulgar amusements of their flocks. A Lancashire story tells of a bearward arriving in a country town on the wake's day before the evening church service was completed. Whereupon the beadle, who had been on the look-out, put his head in at the church door and called out to the preacher, " Mestur, th' bear's coom ; and what's more there's two on 'em." An adjournment was at once made to the village green, the dogs were brought out and the good rector and his party enjoyed the sport from the vantage ground of the churchyard which overlooked the arena.

Learned men who seek to reconstruct the social life of a nation from the statutes and ordinances passed by Parliaments and decreed by rulers and governors are the real writers of comic histories. The historian who goes into the highways and by-ways of letters and gossip, learns that in fact statutes that were not approved by the people were not enforced or were evaded. A place that is not " a place within the meaning of the Act " has always been found in our sensible country to screen the shorn lambs among the poorer citizens from the windiness of legislation. You find that in the eighteenth century, though the statutes broadcast their threats, the magistracy did not listen in overmuch. The law was used to protect the country-side from the robberies and assaults of dangerous rascals who travelled the country with evil intent. I gather from my desultory reading among letters and memoirs, that the village Hampdens made it very uncomfortable for those who tried to interfere with their common pleasures, and that the squires and parsons who ruled the country parishes were too sensible to maltreat every minstrel, pedlar or player, who came to bring some of the joy of the outer world into the drab lives of the toilers in the fields.

But Samuel Foote was not another Autolycus, though technically he comes under the same statute. If he was a rogue at all he was a very merry and amusing rogue ; if he was a vagabond it was only when he had money to put in his purse, and instinct impelled him to wander in search of enjoyment and squander his patrimony at the booths in Vanity Fair. In the normal business of theatrical management and as an actor and playwright he was a professional success As a wit and a social star in the houses of the great he was both feared and loved, but always welcomed wherever he deigned to make himself at home.

But " one Foote a player," as Walpole called him in contempt, had something of your true rogue and vagabond about him, and it is that which enabled him to do and say things with applause that from other men would have offended. It was the nature of the rogue to mimic mankind and jeer at their misfortunes, and sensible men of the world took it in good part and joined in the laugh against themselves. When you have recognized this you do not need to make apology for him as John Forster does in the *Quarterly*. Still less need you join in Dr. Doran's verdict that " the applause which he received helped to make Foote ultimately famous and infamous." This Victorian judgment must be varied by striking out the word infamous, unless indeed the good doctor, whose kindness of heart I can vouch for by personal recollection, was employing the word in the sense in which it is used among Pickwickians and the General Medical Council.

When Foote died, Dr. Johnson wrote to Mrs. Thrale that the world was impoverished by his loss, and that " he was a fine fellow in his way." There he was right. The doctor wanted Murphy to write his life or at least give the world a *Footeana*. That was an excellent idea. Then he went on to say, " I would really have his life written with diligence." This I think led Mr. Percy Fitzgerald astray. A literary portrait of Foote could only be attempted by collecting the material with diligence and then rejecting most of it. This is probably what the doctor meant.

The contemporary *Life* written by his comrade, William Cooke, is an uninspired biography, but it tells the story of his life. Cooke was an Irishman and a barrister and a member of the Essex Head Club. He was known in the coffee houses as " Conversation " Cooke and has the immortality of dishonourable mention in the *Dunciad.* He revolved around the outer circle of society that surrounded Dr. Johnson, Garrick, Sir Joshua Reynolds, Goldsmith, and the rest. But Foote, like an eccentric star, rushed across their horizon as and when he liked, his shining wit dazzling and subduing them for a moment, so that we find among their letters and biographies memories, not always complimentary, of this picturesque figure, that enable us to know the man more intimately than any of the others, except, perhaps, the great doctor himself.

Foote, as it were, had many Boswells, but they were not slavish admirers. His biting wit made him feared. Garrick, who flattered and befriended him, was said by some to have appeared openly afraid of him. Reynolds, who painted the splendid picture of him leaning over the chair in the club chaffing someone out of the picture, gravely disapproved of him. But our brave Dr. Johnson, though he shook his head at his rogueries and mimicry, was just in his verdict. For the man was a great wit, and when Boswell, who was never at ease with Foote and sought to belittle him, asked the doctor if Betterton and Foote were to walk into the room whether he would not " respect Betterton much more than Foote ? " he received the unexpected reply : " If Betterton were to walk into this room with Foote, Foote would soon drive him out of it. Foote, sir, *quatenus* Foote, has powers superior to them all."

Samuel Foote was born at Truro and baptized at St. Mary's Church in that city on January 27, 1720. His father was a commissioner of the prize office there and filled the office of mayor. His mother, Eleanor Goodere, inherited a considerable fortune through a terrible family tragedy. She was the daughter of Sir Edward Goodere, Bart., of Burhope in Herefordshire, and her mother was a granddaughter of Lord Rockingham.

On the death of Sir Edward in 1739 Sir John, his son, was left more money than Samuel, the younger brother, who was a captain in the Navy. This angered Samuel and a quarrel arose between the two of a very bitter character which ended in the brothers parting with a determination to hold no communication with each other. In January, 1741, Samuel, who was in command of the *Ruby* then lying in King's Road, Bristol, heard that Sir John was in the city at the house of an attorney named Smith. He visited him there and the two dined and smoked and drank together in great amity, having apparently made up their differences. As Sir John was walking home to his lodgings in the city he was kidnapped by some of the men of the *Ruby*, gagged and bound and carried on board, where he was flung into a disused cabin, Samuel himself standing guard over him with a drawn sword. The officers and the crew were put off with the story that he was out of his mind. The next morning, January 19, Captain Samuel persuaded three of his men, bribed with money and plied with brandy, to strangle his brother, his intention apparently being to put to sea at once and dispose of the body. Mr. Smith, the attorney, had, however, got wind of the story of a gentleman being kidnapped in the streets, no uncommon occurrence in the days of the press-gang, but making inquiries and finding Sir John was missing he acted with great promptitude and went at once to the mayor. To his credit the mayor had no hesitation in issuing a search warrant and sending his officers on board the *Ruby*. The officers and crew who had not dared at first to interfere with the action of their captain were no doubt overjoyed to be released from the rule of such a scoundrel. Goodere and his three accomplices were arrested and tried for murder and were all four hanged on April 15, 1741.

Foote was at this time about one-and-twenty and a student at the Inner Temple, and his first literary efforts seem to have been a memoir of his uncle, Sir John Dinely-Goodere and an account of the trial of his other uncle, Samuel. Mrs. Foote became heiress under her brother's will and it seems as if he left money to his two nephews, for Samuel who was studying for the Bar now relinquished the Temple for the more congenial occupation of a man about town. Edward, his younger brother, being a weakling, was destined for the Church, but he never obtained preferment and when he had dribbled his money away became a pensioner on his brother.

William Cooke was also living in the Temple and no doubt was very glad to scrape acquaintance with our lively young friend, Samuel Foote, who had just come into money. We hear of Cooke introducing him to a club as " the nephew of the gentleman who was lately hung in chains for murdering his brother," a coarse piece of wit that would not disconcert Foote in the least.

" Conversation " Cooke was something of a scholar and it is said he lived for twenty years by soliciting subscriptions for his translation of Plautus. Foote, too, was well educated and well read. He had been at school at Worcester and matriculated at Worcester College, Oxford, in July 1737, but he was too indolent to read for a degree. His talent for mimicry made him both friends and enemies, but it was remarkable even in childhood, and at college enabled him to make fools of the dons in many new and ingenious ways.

Dr. Gower, the Provost of Worcester, was a pompous pedant, and when Foote was sent before him to be reprimanded he would take with him a large dictionary. When the provost uttered a surprisingly long word with conceited emphasis, Foote would immediately interrupt him and after begging pardon obsequiously would with great formality produce his dictionary and, pretending to find the word, would say, " Very well, sir ; now please to go on." One would have thought the most self-satisfied don might have smelt that the incense was mere smoke, but Foote was an imperturbable tickler of this kind of trout and the victim is said to have enjoyed the treatment.

Young Foote had fine chambers in the Temple and a good library, not exclusively a law library, and ate his dinners with the rest and then sauntered across to the " Grecian " or the " Bedford." The former was in Devereux Court and was a favourite resort of the Irish and Lancashire Templars. This was Goldsmith's favourite haunt. The Bedford Coffee House was on the Piazza of Covent Garden and it was the rendezvous of the dramatic critics. Here, as an old memorist quaintly observes, " the noxious effluvia of St. Bride's is corrected by the genuine eau-de-luce from Pall Mall, and the predominance of ambergris at St. James's is qualified by the wholesome tar of Thames Street." Henry Fielding, who had just been called to the Bar and was writing *Joseph Andrews*, was often to be found at this house, and young Foote was not unwelcome in a congregation where jests and bons mots were echoed from box to box, and the beaux were glad to recognize one of their own set who could hold his own with the wits of Fleet Street.

Dr. Barrowby, a wit, a theatrical critic, and a " monster

of lewdness and prophaneness," whose famous desire to be a Jew, so that he 'could sin and eat pork chops at one and the same time has been plagiarized by many a modern humorist, was one of the frequenters of the " Bedford " in these days.   He pictures for us young Foote's triumphant entrance into that select company when he saw

a young man extravagantly dressed out in a frock suit of green and silver lace, bag-wig, sword, bouquet and point ruffles, enter the room and immediately join the critical circles at the upper end. Nobody recognized him, but such was the ease of his bearing, and the point and humour of remark with which he at once took part in the conversation, that his presence seemed to disconcert no one ; and a sort of pleased buzz of " *Who is he ?* " was still going round the room unanswered, when a handsome carriage stopped at the door, he rose and quitted the room, and the servants announced that his name was Foote, that he was a young gentleman of family and fortune, a student of the Inner Temple and that the carriage had called for him on its way to the assembly of a lady of fashion.

In this style, in the true way of your vagrom men, did young Foote capture the London of wit and fashion, and through the rest of his life he held unrivalled sway in the citadel, feared and loved by the rest of the inhabitants through the power of his wit.

For three years after his uncle's death, and his coming into his fortune, Foote lived the life of a man about town, squandering his money freely.   At the " Bedford " he made the acquaintance of a lively little vintner who, as he said, " lived in Durham Yard with three quarts of vinegar in the cellar and called himself a wine merchant."   Whilst Foote was wasting his fortune Garrick was learning the wine business, and laying the foundation of his great career by playing in pantomime in Goodman's Fields. The two remained friends to the last, though Garrick perhaps winced occasionally at Foote's sarcasms and certainly the latter never spared his colleague.

Both were delightful company, but the vintner was a greater gentleman than the man of family. As Dr. Johnson put it :

Garrick has some delicacy of feeling ; it is possible to put him out ; you may get the better of him : but Foote is the most incompressible fellow that I ever knew ; when you have driven him into a corner, and think you are sure of him, he runs through between your legs, or jumps over your head and makes his escape.

For the sturdy doctor had not been ready to accept the young fellow as worthy of his notice on the recommendation of his dear friend David and others who sang the young man's praises. That was not Dr. Johnson's way. It was not for him to receive a youngster as a wit at the hands of fashionable godfathers and godmothers. He was the sole arbiter in such matters. When he agreed to meet Foote at dinner, he frankly admits that he had no good opinion of the fellow, and was resolved not to be pleased and, as he sagely added, " it is very difficult to please a man against his will." The party took place at William Fitzherbert's, a pleasant Derbyshire gentleman who loved to entertain Burke and Garrick and the rest, having, as Johnson remarked, when Fitzherbert put an end to himself, " a multitude of acquaintance and ne'er a friend." But at this time the host was in all his glory, and in spite of Johnson's fixed determination not to enjoy himself, the party was, through Foote's genius, a great success. For, as the doctor told Boswell in later years, " I went on eating my dinner pretty sullenly, affecting not to mind him. But the dog was so very comical, that I was obliged to lay down my knife and fork, throw myself back upon my chair, and fairly laugh it out. No, sir, he was irresistible."

Reading that description calls to my mind similar scenes, where grave men have been reduced to laying down their

knives and forks by the delightful raillery of our own Seymour
Hicks, and by analogy I find it hard to believe that a man
who had the gracious gift of wit that could dissolve Dr.
Johnson into genial laughter was not really a lovable human
personality. I gather from the mere records of Foote's sayings that it was the certainty and rapidity with which he
caught up the words of others and threw back incongruous
replies that surprised the grave into laughter.

The wit of Samuel Foote and Seymour Hicks is like
the fielding at cover point of Johnny Briggs, who once threw
his heels in the air and darted at a low one only to discover
he had fielded a swallow. They catch the jest in the air
where you and I would miss it. It is the spontaneity of the
wit that you admire. But, as in spiritual séances, so in social
gatherings where the spirit of wit is in the company, there
must be receivers as well as the transmitter, else the sitting
may be a failure. And that Foote understood this is clear
from his complaint to Garrick after a weary party:
" Why does Lord Loughborough come among us? He
is not only dull but the cause of dullness in others."
Wedderburn was too recently a recruit from the Assembly
of the Kirk of Scotland to enjoy the sallies of Foote and his
friends.

But to return to the early life of young Foote. Three
years of pleasure and dissipation were sufficient for him to
get rid of his money. It seems to have run in the family.
Foote's brother ran through his money, so did his mother who
lived to a good old age, and Samuel was a good son to her.
On one occasion she wrote to him :

DEAR SAM,
       I am in prison for debt : come and assist your loving Mother,
                                                             E. FOOTE.

To which he replied :

DEAR MOTHER,
    So am I ; which prevents his duty being paid to his loving
mother by her affectionate son,

                                        SAM FOOTE.

P.S.—I have sent my attorney to assist you : in the meantime
let us hope for better days.

Foote now returned to the " Bedford " stripped of most of
his fine feathers, and turned his attention to the ancient art
of living on his wits. His grand air of assurance never
forsook him. We see him in the coffee-house handling a
gold repeater, a remnant of the days of his vanity, and pouting
with annoyance, " Damme ! My watch does not go ! "
    Dr. Barrowby looks at him with a smile of amusement
and says in a tone of consolation, " Never mind, Sam ; it
soon will go."
    Dr. Barrowby was an influence among the actors and
was ready to help Foote to make a start to earn his living.
The famous quarrel between Macklin and Garrick was
now raging. Garrick drove Macklin from Drury Lane.
Macklin's friends, headed by Dr. Barrowby, tried to deprive
Garrick of the fruits of his victory by means of rotten eggs
and apples. The riots were put down and Dr. Barrowby
drew off his forces. Macklin decided to open a rival show
and here the doctor befriended Foote. In those days an
anonymous " gentleman " with a following of fashion was
often a good draw. So we find Macklin opening the Haymarket in February, 1744, with *Othello* played by " a gentleman " to his Iago. The " gentleman " was Samuel Foote,
and though he was not a success in the part, he had now
definitely joined the players, and as actor and dramatist
remained in the profession to the end of his days. He was
more successful as Lord Foppington in Vanbrugh's *Relapse*,
and in the winter of 1744 had a successful season at the
Smock-Alley theatre at Dublin with Thomas Sheridan.

SAMUEL FOOTE

From the portrait by Sir J. Reynolds, P.R.A., in the possession of the Garrick Club.
By the kind permission of the Committee.

It was on his return from Ireland, full of the praises of the hospitality of Dublin at a southern Irishman's table, that he was interrupted by his host, who said: "But you've never seen Cork, my boy!"

"No, sir," said Foote quickly, "but I've seen a great many *drawings* of it."

Actors quarrel readily, but with equal readiness they kiss again with tears of joy. Though Foote had sided with Macklin, Garrick was ready to welcome him to Drury Lane in the winter of 1745, and he played with Mistress Woffington and Mistress Clive. But though not a failure as a comedian, he was not a popular success, and he was wondering what the goddess Fortune intended to do about his future when he was cast for Bayes in the Duke of Buckingham's *Rehearsal*. The traditional business of Bayes was to introduce mimicry of contemporary actors. Garrick had done this, but Foote heaped Ossa upon Pelion and made a new mountain of mimicry which the stage had never witnessed before. He not only took off his comrades, but made fun of affairs of State, debates in Parliament, the failure of the Jacobite rebellion, the follies of politicians, wits, playwrights and leaders of fashion. Nothing was sacred from the scourge of his sarcasm and the house rose at him. Foote had found himself. He had come into his world as a mimic, a droll and a public entertainer. In the words of the statute in that case made and provided he determined to start a new form of entertainment as "a player of interludes."

Had he lived in this age the music-halls and revues would have competed for his services, but at that period it did not seem easy to see how he could turn this wonderful gift into money. But Foote was as daring in business as he was in wit. He determined to open the Haymarket with a concert, an entertainment and a farce. On April 22, 1747, he started his first matinée to a crowded house. The whole

M

show was a continuous " taking off " of actors and other public characters, and a scene which displayed the personnel and the amenities of the " Bedford " was enormously enjoyed. The success was undoubted and the delighted habitués of the theatre came away buzzing with delight and singing the praises of Foote as the English Aristophanes.

But the entertainment was strictly against the law, which did not technically permit rogues and vagabonds and players of interludes to perform except at patent theatres. The Shallows of Westminster were up in arms. Public dignitaries had been made fun of, which was " most tolerable and not to be endured." An information was sworn and the show was stopped.

Here Foote was in his element and rejoiced at the advertisement given to his speculation. On April 28 he invited his friends to take a " dish of tea " with him at noon at the Haymarket, tickets for which would be obtained at George's Coffee-house, Temple Bar. There was no law against tea-parties.

The entertainment was of course much the same thing as before. The magistrates felt they were outwitted. The populace delighted in the show and Foote's " dish of tea " was the laugh of London. But Johnson strongly objected to this kind of mimicry and would not allow that Foote deserved the praise he received.

" Sir," he said to Boswell, " it is not a talent ; it is a vice ; it is what others abstain from."

" Did not he think of exhibiting you, sir ? " asked Boswell.

" Sir, fear restrained him," replied the valiant doctor; " he knew I would have broken his bones."

And it seems to be true that when Foote was doing a similar interlude called *The Orators* he had prepared a scene in which he was going to imitate Dr. Johnson. The doctor, having got wind of it, sent a message to Foote that he would plant himself in the front row of the stage box carrying a stout oak cudgel, and if anything of the kind was attempted, he would knock him down in the face of the audience and appeal to them for protection.

But not everyone had the same weight of authority as Dr. Johnson. Poor Macklin, who had introduced Foote to the stage and taught him his business, was a familiar butt to Foote's audiences. He determined to go and see his pupil's mimicry for himself and find out what the people laughed at, and one afternoon he placed himself in a back seat in the boxes. Foote wound up his imitation with a pompous lecture to an imaginary pupil which ran in this way :

" Now, sir, remember I, Charles Macklin, tell you there are no good plays among the ancients, and only one among the moderns and that is the *Merchant of Venice*, and there is only one part in that and one man that can play it. Now, sir, as you have been very attentive, I'll tell you an anecdote of that play. When a royal personage who shall be name-less (but who doesn't live a hundred miles from Buckingham House) witnessed my performance of the Jew, he sent for me to his box and remarked : ' Sir, if I were not the Prince—ha—hum, you understand—I should wish to be Mr. Macklin.'

" Upon which I answered, ' Royal Sir, being Mr. Macklin I do not desire to be——' "

Macklin could no longer restrain his indignation and, starting up, he stretched his body forward and shouted at the top of his voice, " No, I'll be damned if I did."

The audience yelled with pleasure, and turning on the old man like a pack of hounds, hunted him out of the boxes, and he escaped down the stairs followed by derisive applause.

Such were the amenities of the Haymarket in those days, and the town flocked there to see who was to be the latest victim of the rogue, and in hope that some such scene as this would crown the artist's successful mockery.

Macklin, with his serious, earnest, single-minded love of his profession and conceited belief in his own somewhat narrow learning, was a temptation to Foote, and he could not leave the old man alone. In his later years, when Macklin was lecturing on " Memory," Foote sat in the front row, and when the old man informed the audience that he himself could learn anything by heart on once hearing it, so perfectly had he trained his memory, Foote rose respectfully and asked to be allowed to test him. Permission being granted, Foote read out that wonderful jingle of words which is perhaps the best piece of nonsense prose in the English tongue :

" So she went into the garden to cut a cabbage leaf, to make an apple-pie ; and at the same time a great she-bear coming up the street, pops its head into the shop. ' What ! no soap ? ' So he died, and she very imprudently married the barber ; and there were present the Picninnies and the Joblillies, and the Garyulies, and the Grand Panjandrum himself, with the little round button at top ; and they all fell to playing the game of catch-as-catch-can, till the gunpowder ran out at the heels of their boots."

When Foote was about thirty he had a second fortune left to him. He now rejoined the world of fashion, left the stage, and wandered away to Paris, where he enjoyed the best society of the gay city and incidentally planned out in his mind some excellent farces. When he had run through his money he brought back with him several plays and once again took up his theatrical career. Nearly every piece he wrote contained a caricature of someone whom he had met in society, and these caricatures on the stage were often resented by his victims, and trouble ensued. Boswell once suggested to Johnson that a miserly acquaintance of theirs, whose conduct had disgusted the doctor, ought to be introduced into one of Foote's farces, and that the best way to do it would be to bring Foote to be entertained at his house. But Johnson felt that this would not be playing the game.

" Sir," he said, " I wish Foote had him. I who have eaten his bread will not give him to him ; but I should be glad if he came honestly by him."

When he returned to the London stage Foote played with Garrick, and the friendship of these two geniuses was a curious one. Garrick was very generous to Foote and in 1759, when Foote was in straits, lent him £100 to take his show to Edinburgh, where his mimicries fell rather flat. If you read his farces, which are cleverly written and constructed, you can see what added flavour they must have had for a London audience, many of whom recognized on the stage some eccentric habitué of the " Grecian " or the " Bedford." This atmosphere of personality could not be carried to Edinburgh.

In spite of the outward and indeed the real friendship between Garrick and Foote, the latter never tired of jesting about Garrick's little failings, and Garrick laughed it off, partly because he liked the rogue and partly perhaps because he did not care to anger him. Garrick was not a mean or greedy man in important affairs, but he had that curious trait of petty economy, the display of which in society is as distressing as ostentation. Foote loved to invent stories about this.

At the Chapter-house coffee-house one afternoon Foote and his friends were making a contribution for the relief of a decayed actor who held out his hat to the company. As Foote dropped a coin into it he said, " Don't let Garrick hear of this or he will certainly send in his hat."

Foote had a small bust of Garrick which stood on his bureau, and when a friend was admiring it said, " You may be surprised that I will allow him so near my gold—but you will observe that he has no hands."

Nor did he only jest of his friend in his absence, but
at his own table, when Garrick's servants were announced
as having arrived to escort their master home, Foote said,
" Oh, let them wait," and then added in a stage whisper :
" but, James, be sure you lock up the pantry."

This kind of badinage among friends gives no offence
when it is spoken, as when Comyns Carr on a festal occasion
started his speech, " Gentlemen—among whom I of course
include my friend Mr. Tree." A jest of this sort sets the
table on a roar at the moment because of its absurdity, and
no man of sense resents it. But reproduced in print, and
read by those who cannot visualize the scene in which it was
said, it is apt to appear wanting in charity.

Nor can it honestly be said that Foote did not overstep
even the wide limits which society allowed to the wits of
the coffee-houses of his own time. Garrick, as many short
men are, was very touchy about any allusion to his stature,
but Foote found a mine of amusement in the subject. When
he was bringing out his *Primitive Puppet Show* at the Haymarket a lady of fashion asked him : " And pray, Mr. Foote,
are your puppets to be as large as life ? "

" Oh, dear no, madam, certainly not ; not much above
the size of Garrick."

As Pope has pointed out, the life of one who ridicules
his fellow-men is " a warfare upon earth." No doubt
Foote made many enemies, but fear checked them from
attacking him. On more than one occasion cruel reprisals
were made upon him by those he offended, as when late in
life wicked accusations were made upon his moral character
and a disgraceful prosecution upon perjured evidence came
to a proper conclusion to the satisfaction of all right-minded
men.

Much of Foote's wit, even taken from the cold store of
the memorists, has not lost all its savour. When a fashion-

able doctor consulted Foote about the decoration of his new chariot and explained to him at some length that he intended to have his crest on the door-panel and wanted an appropriate motto :

" And what is your crest, Doctor ? " asked Foote.

" Three mallards *volant*," replied the doctor proudly.

" Why there you have it," said Foote on the instant, " Quack ! quack ! quack ! "

What a pretty wit is there too in his famous saying that " Woman's age must be counted like a game of piquet : twenty-five, twenty-six, twenty-seven, twenty-eight, twenty-nine—sixty ! "

Dr. Johnson himself could not have cast a stone at his jest against Scotland, when in reply to a lady who asked him whether there was any truth in the report that there were no trees in Scotland, he replied with much indignation :

" A most malicious report, my lady, and not a word of truth in it, for I assure you as I was riding from Edinburgh to Berwick I saw two blackbirds perched on as fine a thistle as ever I saw in my life."

Like many men who delight in making fun of their neighbours he was very sensitive if anyone was witty at his expense. Old Quin, who had no use for a young gentleman who came butting into the profession without any proper training, and was disgusted with the success of Foote's tea-parties at the Haymarket, was reported to have said at the " Bedford " : " Well anyhow now, poor devil, we may expect to see him with a clean shirt on."

Foote of course had this sneer repeated to him, and went up to the old actor in the coffee-house and asked him if he had taken such a liberty with him as to say " he should now wear clean shirts."

" No, sir," says Quin very gravely, " I did not say shirts ; I said shirt."

The laugh was against Foote, and for once the older generation scored. Macklin was especially delighted with the story.

Foote's career as a dramatist was long and successful, but his habit of caricaturing living people was constantly bringing him into trouble. On one occasion Mr. Faulkner, the Dublin printer, who had lost a leg, was ridiculed in a character of Peter Paragraph in *The Orators*, and brought an action against him in Dublin and obtained nominal damages. Then when he appeared as Cadwallader in *The Author*, he made himself up like a certain Mr. Ap-Rice, a Welshman of large fortune whom he met in society. The first night he was received with enormous enthusiasm, and Mr. Ap-Rice himself joined in the general merriment. But the piece ran through the rest of Garrick's season and the victim of the joke began to tire of it. He consulted his friends about sending a challenge to Foote, but was wisely dissuaded from doing anything so absurd. He had, however, influence in high places, and on the morning of Foote's benefit in which he was to have played at Drury Lane in *The Author*, a missive was received from the Duke of Devonshire, then Lord Chamberlain, that the piece was suppressed. Foote made a spirited address to his audience against the edict of the Lord Chamberlain, but the skit was seen no more.

These things in no way diminished his circle of friends, and perhaps gave his dramas greater popularity. He had now received and spent three fortunes and his profession had brought him another, and in 1766 he was one of the best known men in London. Although he entertained lavishly and drove as good horses as any in the Mall and had the *entrée* to nearly every house of fashion in town and country, he never lost his character of independence. He did not seek the society of the great ; they sought him. When the Duke of York returned from the Continent it was said that

" he went first to his mother, then to His Majesty, and directly from them to Mr. Foote." The Eton boys showed him round their college with respect and were rewarded for their hospitality with some bons mots. The very night that he was turning noblemen of fashion away from the theatre during the run of *The Minor* he personally took the trouble to squeeze Gray and Mason into a side box. And it was the same at his famous dinner-parties. Lord Mansfield, Garrick, Reynolds, or the Duke of York himself, received no more respect or attention from the fellow than some poor player or author for whom he had taken a liking. He had the true vagabond's immunity from snobbery. If he liked a man he would make a pal of him, chaff him, give him meat and drink, the best he had in his house, be he peer or pauper. Society could offer him nothing, and finding he cared for none of their vanities they poured them at his feet.

In the winter of 1766, in the prime of life, when he was at the zenith of his fame, he had a terrible accident, from the effects of which he never really recovered. He had been invited down to Lord Mexborough's to a merry house-party to meet the Duke of York and others of his set. John Savile, Lord Mexborough, was a man of Foote's own age, connected by marriage with Sir Francis Delaval, a boon companion of Foote, who with his friends had once staged a society performance of *Othello* with Sir Francis in the title part. The story goes that Foote, after the manner of Mr. Winkle, boasted of his horsemanship overnight, and being asked to join the hunt the next morning was ashamed to refuse. At the very first burst the boaster was thrown, and his left leg broken in two places. I confess that there seems no evidence which satisfies me that Foote was a boaster. As a lad he had been brought up in the country, and there was no reason why he should not have been a good rider. The story was spread about London at the time, and I think it is alluded to by Garrick in his very kindly letter to his friend when he says, " I have sent a paragraph to the papers to contradict the false reports about you."

Poor Foote was terribly injured, and to save his life his leg had to be amputated. This was skilfully done by William Bromfield, the surgeon, himself an amateur dramatist and lover of the theatre. Two letters preserved in Garrick's correspondence go far, I think, to negative the idea which is accentuated by some writers of stage history that Foote bullied Garrick with his jests, and that Garrick toadied to him and suffered his companionship out of fear. Those who understand the freedom of friendship know that many wild and whirling jests are permitted that are never intended to be repeated, or remembered, or set down in print ; and if they are published the true meaning of them can only really be understood by those who have had the advantage of living in a society where pompousness and dullness are more offensive than badinage. Garrick speaks from the heart when he says, writing on February 13 : " It gives me infinite pleasure to hear by Mr. Bromfield that you have passed all danger, are in the best way and in the highest spirits." Very likely Bromfield had brought to town Foote's saying after the operation about his old enemy, the one-legged Dublin publisher, " Now I can take off old Faulkner to the life ! "

Garrick continues with an offer that could only be made by one real friend to another : " All I shall say at present is, that should you be prevented from pursuing any plan for the theatre, I am wholly at your service, and will labour in your vineyard for you in any capacity till you are able to do it so much better for yourself."

It is nearly a fortnight before the doctors will allow Foote to reply. He is still lying at Canons Park, near Edgware, and expresses his deep gratitude for Garrick's offer of help. " Nothing," he says, " can be more generous and obliging nor, I am sure, at the same time would be more beneficial for me than your offers of assistance for my hovel in the Haymarket."

He writes, poor fellow, in great pain, being very weak and unable to sleep without opiates, and his sufferings must have indeed been terrible, but through the letter runs a thread of real gratitude and affection to his " dear Mr. Garrick " which is as sincere as his friend's generous offer of assistance. Letters of this kind throw a far surer light on the relationship between the two men than the gossip of memorists. After all, are not our childhood's canine friends, " Dignity and Impudence," typical of human friendships such as theirs ?

It was through this unhappy accident that Foote came into his kingdom, and the " hovel " which was the home of farce and interludes became the Haymarket Theatre, whose great traditions are part of the history of the stage and continue to our own day. The Duke of York, who had been of the party when the sad accident happened, used his influence with his brother, and Foote obtained a royal patent for performances at the Haymarket from May 14 to September 14 in every year.

Since 1762 Foote had leased it as a summer theatre, but now it became a " patent theatre," like Drury Lane, and Foote purchased the freehold and rebuilt the theatre, giving it a handsome new frontage. Foote, just before his death, sold his interest in the theatre to George Colman, and when he in turn sold it in 1820, the new theatre was built by John Nash, whose work in Regent Street has so recently disappeared. Thus in the short space of a hundred years does the latest new thing of our grandfathers become to their grandchildren either a temple of historic interest or a nuisance that cumbers the earth.

Foote was able to open his new theatre in May, 1767,

with a witty *Prelude*, in which he played with the assistance of a cork leg with shoe and stocking attached. He hobbled on to the stage and gave his audiences their fill of laughter and delight, and continued his mimicry to the joy of the town and the agitation of his victims. " There is hardly a public man in England," says good Mr. Davies, the bookseller, with some exaggeration, " who has not entered Mr. Foote's theatre with an aching heart, under the apprehension of seeing himself laughed at."

I fancy that is a shopkeeper's heresy. Foote was, as Walpole said, a Merry Andrew but not a fool, and though he overdid it on occasion, such of his victims as were not fools enjoyed his jokes well enough and the advertisement and fame that they brought them, much as a politician to-day enjoys the cartoon which is the evidence—and often the only evidence—of his importance in the political world.

That this view of the matter is correct receives support from the behaviour of Sir William Browne, an eccentric but able physician of the day and at that time President of the Royal College. Foote made a great hit in his mimicry of this well-known doctor and took him off with his identical wig and coat, his angular figure, his glass stiffly applied to his eye, and his volume of the classics under his arm.

Sir William did not threaten him with oaken cudgels, but sent him a little parcel with his card and compliments, pointing out that his portrait was inexact in one particular, since he omitted to carry a muff, which was always the President's custom, and therefore he begged to send him his own.

What the lawyers thought of Serjeant Circuit and the arguments in Hobson & Nobson in Foote's *Lame Lover* we may readily guess, since no profession laughs so pleasantly over its own infirmities as the members of the Inns of Court. Foote, too, left a choice collection of stories about attorneys, who have been food for humour for all time. The best story perhaps is his serious conversation with a country farmer who had just buried a rich attorney relation with much pomp of mutes and scarves and carriages.

" Do you really bury your attorneys here ? " asked Foote in surprise.

" Yes, to be sure we do ; how else ? "

" Oh, we never do that in London," said Foote, shaking his head gravely.

" No ! " said the other, with open mouth, " how do you manage ? "

" Why when the patient happens to die, we lay him out in a room overnight by himself, lock the door, throw open the sash and in the morning he is gone."

" Indeed ! " says the other in amazement. " What becomes of him ? "

" Why," replied Foote mysteriously, " that we cannot exactly tell ; all we know is there's a strong smell of brimstone in the room next morning."

Dr. Doran, whose Victorian modesty was perhaps unnecessarily offended at Foote's license, scarcely does credit, as Mr. Forster did, to his kindness of heart. Like a good vagabond, he was certainly well liked by his fellow-vagabonds and did many kindnesses to those who worked with him. He encouraged and brought forward many debutants who made names for themselves in the profession : Shuter, Weston, Tate Wilkinson, Castello, Baddeley, Edwin and others owed their advancement to his early encouragement. Many old actors were with him when he sold the Haymarket to Colman, who had been with him when he first started with his " Afternoon Tea " entertainment. And some were still on the pay list, whose acting days were over ; but he used to justify this extravagance by telling the new-comers that " he kept them on purpose to show the superior gentlemanly manners of the old school."

With the stage hands, too, and the small-part men he was always a prime favourite, and that to my mind is a test of an actor's sense and humanity as well as a tribute to his art. During his last winter tour to Dublin he was taken so ill at rehearsal that he was obliged to announce on the stage that he could not play.

"Ah, sir," said a poor actor, who overheard him, "if you will not play we shall have no Christmas dinner."

Foote replied at once, "If my playing gives you a Christmas dinner, play I will," and ill as he was he kept his word.

The end of his life was embittered by a foul libel and attack upon his character in which his enemies endeavoured to make use of the perjuries of a discarded coachman to their own disgrace and condemnation. All his friends, Garrick, Sir Joshua Reynolds, Burke, Dunning (his counsel), and the best men of the profession, stood by him in his trouble, and Lord Mansfield presided over a trial where his assailants were demolished and a special jury, without turning round to consult, rose and gave a unanimous verdict in his favour.

But his sensitive nature had been deeply hurt, and when Murphy hastened to Suffolk Street to bring him news of the verdict he fell to the ground with some sort of seizure. Soon afterwards he appeared at the Queen's drawing-room, and was well received, and the King was present at a command performance at the Haymarket.

May, 1777, was his last performance. He appeared in the *Devil on Two Sticks*, and his lank and withered appearance was noted by his friends. He had handed over his theatre to Colman and was drawing from him an annuity of £1,600 a year. Although he was weak in body and tired beyond measure, he still imagined himself young enough to enjoy a well-earned holiday and turned his face towards his beloved Paris. Foote had not Johnson's dismal apprehensions of death, and the latter considered that he was probably an infidel, and " if he be an infidel, he is an infidel as a dog is an infidel ; that is to say, he has never thought upon the subject."

It is possible, however, that many men who talk little on these subjects think more deeply upon them than those who boom, like minute-guns at sea, warning sermons to their neighbours. We know from Foote's friend, William Jewell, the treasurer of his theatre, that, although the set in which he lived knew naught about it, there are certainly many entries of his silent charity in the ledgers of the Recording Angel, for which he will have credit in the last account. His holiday and the rest that he was yearning for came upon him suddenly and mercifully, saving him from a lingering illness. The morning after his arrival at Dover he was taken with a shivering fit and, before noon, passed suddenly away. A week afterwards he was buried by torchlight in the west cloisters of Westminster Abbey.

Thus at the age of fifty-six died Samuel Foote, who began his theatrical career as a rogue and vagabond and ended it as one of His Majesty's servants.

CHAPTER IX

JOHN NICHOLS TOM, THE ZEALOT

JOHN NICHOLS TOM—or as some write him John Nichols Thom—was certainly a rogue and vagabond of sorts, though in his time he played many parts. He was what Devonshire folk call a " whither-witted man," that is to say a man whose wits went no man knew whither. He was by turns a patriot, a teacher, a prosperous trader, and an inspired saint with devoted disciples ; also a perjurer and a murderer. Beyond doubt there were periods of insanity in his remarkable career, and this unfortunate condition increased with age.

The strange account of his wanderings in the East, which his anonymous biographer " Canterburiensis " sets down as coming from Tom's own lips, may be, as many suppose, pure fiction, but not, I think, the fiction of the biographer. Professor Raymond, the French psychologist, describes a type of vagabond who leaves his family and sets out on an hysterical spree from which he returns unable to give any connected account of his wanderings. Such vagrants seem to live in a dream, the details of which they cannot recall. In these unhappy subjects there is always an irresistible impulse to go on a voyage, the business is carried out with intelligence and outward sense, yet on returning to their friends they have no real memory of their wanderings.

It appears to me, from a study of the lives of vagabonds, that there is another type of wanderer who has the same vagrant impulses, who sets out with the same deliberation, and returns, not with a blank memory of what he has passed through, but with a detailed account of adventures and incidents that have never happened. The hysteria of these wanderers does not take the form of amnesia, but produces a condition of false or exaggerated memory, which leads them to narrate, as facts of travel, what are really only the kind of adventures they would have desired to experience.

Tom's account of his visit to Lady Hester Stanhope in Palestine may have been a mere dream related as a fact to a wondering disciple, or it may have been founded on some actual journey and dramatized by his diseased imagination. These are speculations for scientists, and no one but a trained alienist could decide with authority the scientific classification of John Nichols Tom in the catalogue of neurotics. That he deserves a place in the history of vagrom men will, I think, be allowed by those who read his story.

John Nichols Tom was born in the town of St. Columb Major, in Cornwall, in 1799. The date of his baptism is November 10. His father and mother were a worthy couple living at the "Joiners' Arms." They had also a small farm, where they grew barley for malting, and they brewed a genuine ale of malt and hops which had a good reputation in the neighbourhood. John was the Benjamin of the family, and from the first was considered by his parents, his uncle Nichols, a well-to-do farmer, and all the friends of the family to show wonderful precocity of talent.

Unfortunately, he had extraordinary outbursts of mischief, and his mother, who spoiled him, could do nothing with him. Uncle Nichols persuaded his unwilling parents to place him at a school kept by a learned dame who was a strict disciplinarian. For a few months the good lady administered admonitions accompanied by the application of the birch rod, a method of moral instruction which had never hitherto failed, but it had no satisfactory effect on John.

N

The lad, to revenge himself on his tyrannical mistress, cut off the long and beautiful whiskers of her pet cat, for which purpose he had brought his mother's scissors from home. Having satisfied her wrath and administered a lasting lesson against cruelty to animals by means of a farewell birching, the good dame expelled the young rascal from school and sent him home to his indignant parents.

After this unsuccessful experiment he was sent to a boarding-school at Launceston kept by Richard Cope, a well-known Nonconformist minister. Most unhappily for him he was allowed to return home at the week-end, and when at home was not under any control and spent the Sunday bird-nesting in the fields and prowling along the seashore looking for wreckage.

It is doubtful whether Cope was an ideal master for this clever, erratic boy, for the lad seems to have been attracted at an early age to hysterical manifestations of religious fervour, and Cope was a man of evangelical piety who did not discourage such adventures. Nor did Cope restrict his studies with any care, and the boy read with avidity in his master's library any books he could find about mythology and occult sciences. At twelve years old he was attracted by the pamphlets of Richard Brothers, a prophet and madman who had many followers. Young Tom declared that Brothers was a greater man than Luther, Calvin or Huss. It is interesting to note this, as we shall find in Tom's own claims to be an inspired leader of men a curious echo of the insane boasting of Richard Brothers about his own divine mission.

The lad's other great hero at this date was the demagogue, William Fitzosbert, the famous Longbeard who " died a shameful death for upholding the cause of truth and the poor." We shall find that in later years Tom modelled not only his actions, but in Longbeard's case his outward appearance, on that of the hero of his schoolboy reading.

For Tom in the end became a demagogue with an inspired message to deliver, and but for a lucky bullet he too would have died a shameful death on the scaffold.

When he left school he had already a gospel of his own and a rabid desire to preach it to the world. His unstable mind had picked up all the popular heresies of the day, and he was but too ready to jump on a tub and fling them into burning words. Yet in much that he said there was a sense of justice which rendered him an outcast from among the sectarians. He could wax eloquent on the iniquity of the clergy stewing in fat livings drawn from the distressed farmer and the sweat of poor men's labour. But he checked the enthusiasm of his dissenting hearers by reminding them that if the Methodist ministers could get a snack of these baked meats they would be as greedy over them as the parsons themselves. It must be remembered, therefore, in studying his career that he started life with what to him was a real faith. He believed his own ideas to be inspired, and from the first he thought he was set apart for some great and particular purpose, which in due course would be revealed to him by Providence.

When he left school his father put him into the management of his small farm, but he neglected the business and sat in the farmhouse studying Tom Paine's *Rights of Man* and William Godwin's *Political Justice*. He was greatly taken with Godwin's objections on principle to the status of marriage, and preached this among his other wild doctrines to his shocked but admiring disciples.

After he has been at the farm for some time his father comes up one summer's day on a visit of inspection, only to find the place deserted. No one is working in the fields. The farm kitchen is empty, the kettle boiling over on the fire. The horses are in the stable munching their fodder. The old man listens and hears a droning buzz in the great barn.

He peeps in at the door and finds his son, surrounded by all the workers on the farm, standing on a wheelbarrow preaching eloquently on the evils of compulsory worship on the Sabbath, a doctrine which the boys and girls receive with evident approval.

This was the end of his career as a farmer. Proud as both his father and mother were of the great abilities of their beloved son, it was clear that barley could not be grown in this fashion, and barley and ultimate beer were the mainstay of the family. Old Tom had an ignorant man's notion that a gift of the gab was a necessary part of a lawyer's equipment. Mrs. Tom was flattered at the idea of her dear boy becoming a lawyer, and as the young man made no objection he was taken from the farm and apprenticed to Mr. F. C. Paynter, attorney at St Colomb.

But he was no more fit for this business than William Cobbett himself, and his humanitarian principles, which manifested themselves by lenient methods with unhappy debtors and other bottom dogs, were not at all to the liking of his employer. However, he stayed out his time, working in the day at the office and talking politics to open-mouthed customers in his father's inn-parlour during the evening. He was a tall, handsome fellow, and his eloquence and jargon about liberty and equality pleased his hearers and was good to listen to. It was said of young John Nichols by his schoolmaster : " Like Naphtali he is a hind let loose : he giveth goodly words." This was his undoing. It was one of the misfortunes of his life that he had that strange gift of leading simple men and women to follow the sound of his speech and believe, whilst they were under the spell of it, that it was the voice of inspiration. Political and religious Pied Pipers are curious specimens of humanity, but no age of the world has been without them. The next generation, laughing at the absurd folly of their forefathers, goes trotting with childlike faith along the same street at the heels of the latest charlatan of their own time.

Whilst John Nichols was studying law, his poor mother fell into a melancholy and had to be removed to an asylum. Her name was Cherry, and her neighbours had for long called her " Cracked Cherry," and there can be no doubt that John Nichols inherited his mother's disposition. The poor woman died in the asylum.

John gave up the law and returned home to look after his father. Then he started schoolmastering, but this was a failure, and then when his father married again he determined to leave home. For some time John Nichols had been courting a girl, named Eliza, of good position at St. Columb. She was much in love with him, but her parents looked askance at his wild opinions and irregular ways, and she for her part could not bring herself to accept his views on the wickedness of matrimony.

A copy of Mary Wollstonecraft Godwin's *The Wrongs of Women* fell into her hands, and this, and the love she bore to the fascinating John Nichols, overcame her wise scruples. Tom was seized with a mad desire to go to London where he assured his beloved he would be received with joy by the great social reformers of the day. She believed in everything he said. It was arranged that she should accept an invitation to some relations at Falmouth, and that Tom should arrive there a few days afterwards.

He took passage for himself and his wife in a ship bound for London. The night the vessel sailed the foolish girl joined him on the quay. They were both young things, barely twenty, without knowledge of the world and its ways. He full of selfish half-insane enthusiasm, she worshipping her hero, thinking him all wise and all sustaining. So they fled from home. The tea-tables of St. Columb Major rattled joyfully with the scandal of it for a few weeks, and then the affair was forgotten.

John Nichols Tom knew not a soul in the great city. There was no welcome for them. They had a boisterous and distressing voyage up the Channel and arrived in the Thames, disembarked at Billingsgate and put up at the " Gun Inn ". A friendly fishmonger of Cornish origin let them some rooms at Somers Town. Tom had put money in his purse, perhaps his mother's legacy, and intended to buy a school. This he managed to do some miles out of London, but it was a failure and he re-sold it and came back to London, settling in Albemarle Street and living there above his means, spending what capital he had.

He had joined the Spencean Society, a hole-in-corner club with a room in Bouverie Street, whose members preached and discussed the doctrines of Thomas Spence relating to land nationalization. The enthusiast spent his time among these people and spoke eloquently at their meetings, and when at home wrote long letters to the papers which were generally rejected.

Meanwhile, poor Eliza, who had cut herself off from her family and friends, and had found that her wonderful husband was not received among the reformers of London as a leader and prophet in the way he had honestly foreshadowed to his beloved, felt her position very keenly. She heard that her father had sought her in London unavailingly. The Cornish fishmonger who had befriended them on their arrival had heard from him the story of their elopement and would no longer receive them. The girl had no friends. Her enthusiastic comrade left her very much alone in Albemarle Street, while he rushed about from meeting to meeting. Even when he returned he could only talk about his schemes for the regeneration of mankind. Tom had no eyes for the suffering of his faithful friend. She was fast falling into a decline, but never complained of her condition, and bravely hid from him her own knowledge that they were nearing the parting of the ways. She had neither nurse nor doctor to attend her. It was no difficult task, alas, to keep, from the man who should have cherished her, the secret of her pain and disease. The insanity and selfishness which is characteristic of prophets enables them to accept with cheerfulness the sacrifices of their followers—even unto death.

The end came suddenly. Tom had written one of his prophetic revolutionary letters to a cheap journal, and they had sent for him and handed him a proof of it—actually a proof, in print! His joy was boundless. At last the world of London would read his wisdom. He rushed back to Albemarle Street. Eliza should share his joy. The girl was lying on the bed. When Tom entered she opened her eyes and stared vaguely before her. Even the selfish madman saw that something was wrong. The wretched proof fluttered to the ground. Eliza raised herself and the man kissed her. She sank back with the word " forgive " on her pale lips. He sat beside the bed and took her hand. She drew it gently towards her and laid it on her heart. So they sat in silence, until the woman fell into the sleep of death and the man knew that the heart he had broken would never beat again.

This tragedy seems to have sobered Tom for a while. He gave up, at all events for the present, his insane crusades against the established order of things, and, leaving the Spenceans and their crazy followers, he returned to Cornwall and was lucky enough to obtain a situation with Messrs. Turner and Company, spirit merchants, at Truro.

Mr. Turner, whose business Tom ultimately managed with great success, describes him as generous, open-handed, and humane, and says that he served him honestly, zealously and intelligently. This is of great import as it shows that

in his right mind, as the phrase goes, he was capable of useful
social work, and that at all times, whether sane or mad, he was
actuated throughout life by a love of humanity.

John Nichols Tom, manager of Turner's spirit business
at Truro, was a good match from the worldly point of view
for any girl. But young Tom was also a fine manly, spirited
fellow with luxuriant curls and fascinating manners. His wild
oats were safely sown. Dear mamma might have heard the
story of Eliza ; rich Mr. Philpots certainly had, but their
two sweet daughters, Julia and Cattern, knew nothing of
such naughty doings, and the young man being invited to
the house, the spritely Cattern soon annexed him for her own.

The marriage, which took place in February, 1821, was
not a very happy one perhaps, but so far as John Nichols
Tom's business was concerned it was a useful alliance. When
Philpots died, his son-in-law rebuilt his house, and also
built at the rear a factory suitable for the business of a maltster,
which he carried on profitably. At this period of his career
Tom, like many another religionist, was a valuable and successful man of business, but on religious matters he continued
to exhibit unbalanced views and strange enthusiasms. He
had, too, at all times an overweening love of eccentric and
highly-decorated costumes. He would appear among the
farmers of Truro in the Corn Market, dressed in the height
of fashion, and even in the office he wore the clothes of a
London dandy. In spite of this he made money and business
prospered.

But politics were not by any means forgotten. He sent
out a prospectus for forming a society to abolish the Church,
which he considered the root of all evil, but by the Church he
explained that he meant what he called " the Church of
Mammon, not the Church of Christ."

All the time that he was dealing with large affairs and
complicated details of practical business he was still corre-

sponding with wild visionaries in London and elsewhere. Through all these epistles, many of them very sane in style, ran the fixed idea that the time was drawing near when the plans he had for the regeneration of mankind would be brought to maturity, and he would receive a call from above to place his " great commanding mind " at the service of the New Jerusalem.

In 1831 it must be remembered that Tom was only a little over thirty years old. The escapades of his youth were long behind him, and for the last ten years he had been outwardly living the normal citizen life of a successful tradesman. And now an event happened that seemed to turn his mind away from trade and business towards higher things. His business premises were burned down. Some of his enemies maliciously suggested he had fired them himself. The Fire Office did not take that view, but Tom indignantly insisted on a strict inquiry into the business, and this was held and he was acquitted of any blame in the matter.

He rebuilt his premises, but the worry of the affair, the want of sympathy of his wife, and the attacks of his enemies, seemed to give new force to the strange call that was always sounding in his brain, that there was a great work for him in the world which he alone could perform. The trials he had undergone affected his health, and especially the health of his mind. We hear of his suffering from an epileptic fit at this period. Then he worries himself with the idea that his trade is an immoral one, and that it is his duty to go out of it. His wife and her friends call in a doctor to see him, but he will not advise that his condition is really one of insanity, and then suddenly Tom tells his wife that he is taking all his stock by ship to Liverpool, where he proposes to sell it. He seems to be overpowered by an irresistible desire to wander away from home and friends. He hires a vessel, he puts his stock on board and sails from Falmouth early in 1832. On May 3 he writes to his wife from Liverpool that he has sold his malt and is well and in good spirits. From that moment John Nichols Tom disappeared off the face of the earth. His friends and relations never heard from him, and after making some inquiries gave him up for lost.

What he did during the next few months is wholly unknown, unless you like to accept the detailed story told by one of his biographers of a visit to the Holy Land to see Lady Hester Stanhope, a fanatic like himself. There is no corroboration of the story, and maybe all it amounts to is that he wandered away abroad intending to make some such voyage but never achieved his purpose.

That Tom should have a strong desire to visit that beautiful, eccentric woman, Lady Hester Stanhope, is easily understood. She, too, was a disciple of Richard Brothers. When that mad prophet was imprisoned, in the time of her dear uncle, William Pitt, Brothers sent for Lady Hester, who visited him in jail. Here he told her that she should " one day go to Jerusalem and lead back the chosen people ; that on her arrival in the Holy Land, mighty changes should take place in the world, and that she would pass seven years in the desert."

In 1832 she had long been settled in her mountain home at Joon with the wonderful mare, Lëila, who was foaled ready saddled, and was kept in accord with prophecy by " a woman from a far country " for the use of the Mahdi at his second coming. Tom would have read all about this delectable lady with faithful enthusiasm, and that he should have an intense desire to see her in her mountain palace in the Holy Land is obvious. But it seems difficult to believe that he had time to have visited all the places he described to the author of his life. His own story, given in much detail by his biographer, is that he visited Lady Hester but that she refused to see him, and he made his way to Constantinople, Damascus, Beyrout and Jerusalem and other places in the East.

So far as the man Tom himself is concerned he never did return to his friends and relations, and the second part of his story must be related under the designation of Sir William Courtenay. No doubt like many vagabonds he had fully intended when he left Liverpool to voyage in the East, and I think it very possible that he did travel from Liverpool to Havre and visited Malta, of which place he seems to have some knowledge, and that he then returned to England where he reappeared in or about September, 1832.

He had been in retreat for at least three months, and when he reappeared he must have been quite insane, and may indeed have wholly forgotten his own identity. We hear of him in lodgings at Pentonville as the Hon. Sidney Percy, at the Clarendon Hotel, London, where he is Squire Thompson, and he also assumes the name of Count Moses Rothschild. In these guises he is reported to have lived a lonely, quiet and respectable life. It is when leaving his Pentonville lodging that he seems first to have assumed the title of Sir William Courtenay, and promises to repay his landlord £5 which he owes him, when he receives the estates to which he lays claim.

For practical purposes his new incarnation may be said to occur in September, 1832, when he arrived at the " Rose Inn," Canterbury, from Herne Bay, having come down to that place by the steam packet from London.

Harrison Ainsworth reckoned him a conscious quack and in his ballad in *Rookwood* thus describes his descent upon Canterbury :

To execute my purpose, in the first place you must know, sirs,
My locks I let hang down my neck—my beard and whiskers grow,
    sirs ;

A purple cloak I next clapped on, a sword tagged to my side, sirs,
And mounted on a charger black, I to the town did ride, sirs.
With my coal black beard and purple cloak,
Jack boots and broad-brimmed caster,
Hey-ho ! for the Knight of Malta.

Impostor or madman, this seems an accurate description
of the strange figure that the men of Kent received and welcomed as Sir William Percy Honeywood Courtenay, Knight
of Malta, patriot and inspired prophet. It was not till many
years afterwards that his identity became known, and it was
proved that the unhappy madman was in fact John Nichols
Tom, late maltster of Truro.

The human following that anyone can gain by crazy
quackery is a real danger to the community, but it seems to
be a natural instinct in mankind to worship imposture, and
this forms a terrible temptation to the feeble-minded. Some
day science will explain the why and wherefore of these
strange manifestations of mob hysteria. Meanwhile the histories of these outbursts are worth recording as warnings to
new generations.

In so far as one can speak of an insane man as honest
or dishonest, I do not accept Ainsworth's view that Tom
gulled and bullied and diddled his disciples. It seems to
me that leader and followers were all madly in earnest, except
perhaps some few mischievous cynical citizens who supported Tom to annoy their betters. But how the poor wretch
was permitted to enter upon the series of adventures which
followed his arrival at Canterbury it is hard to understand.

How he was supplied with money, why he came to Canterbury, what attracted round him a considerable following,
and who were his backers in the business, is not known.
His claims to estates and titles were in themselves enough
to make him popular with the mob, and the rumours that
the cellars of the " Rose " were full of barrels of sovereigns,

and that the strange man with a flowing beard was in the habit of giving away to those who pleased him watches and jewels of value, were multiplied all over the city. The man of sense who craved leave to doubt these things was scoffed at as a sceptic.

But at the end of the year Tom had established himself at Canterbury as Sir William Courtenay, a popular political leader. Some say that his nominators entered him as a candidate at the General Election as a joke, but on December 10, 1832, Sir W. P. H. Courtenay, Knight of Malta, issued his election address to the free and independent voters of the City of Canterbury. There were two other candidates, the Hon. Richard Watson and Lord Fordwych, but no one seemed interested in their affairs. The popular excitement was all lavished on the splendid knight, his horses were taken from his carriage and he was drawn in triumph to the " Rose Inn ", from the balcony of which he made eloquent harangues on the rights of man.

At the end of the first day he had polled 177 votes. During the whole of the polling he issued wild appeals to the electors promising them everything they could desire, and every day he rushed about in his carriage dressed in velvet and gold making speeches at every corner. In the result he was at the bottom of the poll, the result being : Watson 834 ; Fordwych 802 ; Courtenay 375.

Though no one knew who the man was, no doubt many gathered that he was no Courtenay, and had a shrewd suspicion that all was not well with his wits. He remained at Canterbury and the neighbourhood, and issued from that city a weekly journal called *The Lion*. There is in his strange incoherent magazine, a fine flavouring of noble sentiments, and some basic sense in the man's social and religious ideals, but the wild attacks on any man or institution that he disliked, and the religious ravings and rambling arguments make it difficult to understand how anyone could receive it and read it even in that age.

Whilst the patriot was pouring forth from the Press noble sentiments of religion and reform, he seems to have busied himself with the affairs of some of the smuggling fraternity. Spirit merchants were not unknown in those days to have acquaintances among the smugglers, but it is only fair to Tom to say that, the only smuggling transaction he was mixed up with in Cornwall, was one in which he was the victim of the smugglers who, having sold him a consignment of smuggled spirits and got their money, afterwards waylaid him and re-took the goods from him.

Sir William Courtenay, on one occasion, appeared before the Rochester magistrates to assist some smugglers who were charged with attempting to run a cargo near the Goodwins in the month of February, 1833. Sir William desired as a matter of charity to appear as a kind of " next friend " to these poor men, but in the excitement of the proceedings he allowed himself to be lured into the box and gave evidence of facts that he could have known nothing about.

The story against the prisoners was that *The Lively* of the Preventive Service was cruising near the Goodwins on February 17 when she met the *Admiral Hood* and started in chase of her. During her flight the *Admiral Hood* was observed to be jettisoning her cargo of small tubs, and when in the end *The Lively* put a shot across her and she hove to, there was no contraband aboard.

The guilt or innocence of the prisoners depended upon whether it could be proved that the tubs were thrown out of the smugglers' vessel. For the defence Sir William Courtenay went into the witness box and swore that on the day in question he was in *The Active*, a fishing boat of Deal ; that he was a witness of the encounter, that there were a great many tubs floating about on the tideway, but that none of them came from the *Admiral Hood*. There was, however, abundant evidence that the tubs did come from the *Admiral Hood*, and it was also proved that no other vessel was about at the time, and that this was the only day on which *The Lively* had fired at any vessel in the month of February.

The matter was further investigated, and it was discovered that on Sunday February 17, so far from Sir William Courtenay being at sea, he was attending the church of Boughton-under-Blean, about six miles from Canterbury and more than twenty from the site of the smuggling affray. Sir William was therefore arrested on a charge of perjury and thrown into Canterbury jail to await his trial.

On July 26, 1833, Sir William Courtenay appeared at Maidstone in the Crown Court before Mr. Justice Parke to take his trial. In spite of the intense heat of the weather the court was packed, and a large number of ladies from Canterbury adorned the bench. The prisoner appeared in a less eccentric dress than usual and his clothes were of a puritanical cut, which suited better what the reporter calls "the wonted beauty of his beard," of which he seemed perfectly conscious by the manner in which he handled it, while his fine eyes looked complacently at the different classes around him.

Serjeant Spankie, for the Crown, made no effort to inquire into his identity. He was indicted by the name of Courtenay, and the story of the absurd perjury was placed in a businesslike way before the jury. The prisoner's Kentish friends had subscribed for a counsel, Mr. Wells, to be employed, but he was not instructed to raise the plea of insanity. He made a sensible speech, and called many respectable citizens of Canterbury who gave the prisoner a splendid character for morality and religion. One enthusiast said he was utterly incapable of committing the diabolical act he was charged with, and another, a doctor, said he had given up everything to follow him and would follow him still.

The jury consulted for about twenty minutes and returned a verdict of Guilty, coupled with a recommendation to mercy. No doubt they thought that the man was half-witted and had tried to help the smugglers out of crazy kindness rather than with criminal intent.

Mr. Justice Parke said he could see no ground for mercy, and the wretched prisoner by a wild, incoherent address to the mob in court, rather than to the judge, probably made matters worse. At the end of his speech poor Sir William made the very sensible observation that " politics are a whirl-pool of misery," and suggested that if he were given another chance he would adopt the politics of the *Standard* newspaper. With this strange attempt to make a bargain with the judge he came to an abrupt end. The judge immediately sentenced him to imprisonment for three months, and at the expiration of that time to be transported beyond the seas for seven years.

The wretched man was now imprisoned in Maidstone jail where he manifested the greatest resignation, reading his Bible and exhibiting an unrepining acquiescence in his fate. I have often thought that if he had been transported he might, in simpler surroundings, have recovered his mental balance and once again become a useful member of society. But it was not to be. A worse fate awaited him, and the surgeon of the jail having duly certified him to be insane he he was removed to the Kent County Asylum at Barming Heath.

Here he remained for four years, and that many believed that the man was inspired seems clear from the fact that, in 1835, when Municipal Corporations were first instituted, he issued an address recommending certain candidates for the Town Council of Maidstone which a doctor and two ministers adopted as their own. His father and his wife had about this time found out his whereabouts, and moved Lord John Russell, then Home Secretary, for pardon and release. His former employer, Mr. Edward Turner of Truro, now M.P. for that city, was very urgent on his behalf. Here again if he could have been placed in suitable surroundings all might have been well, but when in October 1837 he was granted a free pardon on condition that he was handed over to the custody of his father, this was never done. The authorities at Barming allowed him to be taken away by a fanatical disciple, one George Francis of Fairbrook, near Canterbury, who was the worst host that could have been found for a religious maniac, who for four years had been in close confinement, suffering under repressive discipline among unsympathetic custodians.

It seems remarkable that Tom's father and wife, who had taken steps to obtain his release, did nothing whatever to carry out their promises to the authorities that he should be taken care of. He remained in Kent surrounded by the congregation, who had from the first believed him to be inspired, and the poor man himself was lured into greater extravagances of religious mania than any that he had as yet exhibited. He rode about on a white horse in a strange garb carrying a sword and pistols, declaring himself to be the Saviour of Mankind and violently denouncing the ruling authorities for their treatment of the poor.

There was at that time great local excitement about the administration of the Poor Law, and much discontent in the country. Mr. Francis, who discovered that his guest had brought a new pair of pistols, got frightened of harbouring him and turned him away early in 1838, but other humbler and less wary disciples were honoured to entertain him. Not only did he live among his dupes, but he obtained considerable sums of money from them on the undertaking that

o

when he came into his estates he would return them a pound
for every shilling they lent to him.

Toward the end of May he was not satisfied with
haranguing the farmers and labourers in every village he
entered, but he called upon them to follow him in his progress through Kent to compel others to come in to their
cause. What exactly was to be done nowhere appears.
The poor had their grievances and they were to be redressed.
The religious were happy in wandering after a divine being
whose presence they adored, and whose ravings they heard
with devout attention. But the general public were frightened
to death at the antics and threats of the troop that had gathered
round their mad leader.

On Monday, May 28, Courtenay and his mob set out
from Boughton, headed by a white and blue banner decorated
with a rampant lion, the pole of which was crowned with a
loaf. They marched through Goodnestone, gathering followers by the way, until they reached Dargate Common,
where they went to prayers, and that night supped and rested
at Bossenden Farm, the home of a supporter named Culver.

The next morning he announced to his followers that
" this is the first day of the Millennium and on this day I
will put a crown on my head." Thus exhorted, the crowd
followed him in even greater numbers through the peaceful
villages. They started early and about 6.30 a.m. arrived at
Sittingbourne. More than sixty of his men marched in
military order and were armed with bludgeons and fire-arms.
Whatever the main body intended to do, there is no doubt
that a lot of the camp followers, who swarmed after this
mad leader, committed thefts and other excesses, and the
farmers and gentry of the county were not unnaturally
alarmed at what was going on. The Rev. John Poore, a
county magistrate, was approached by Colonel Groves to
issue a warrant for Courtenay's apprehension, and warrants

against the farm labourers who had left their work, and this he did.

On Wednesday, the 30th, Courtenay and his army wandered through Eastling, Throwley, Seldwich, Lees and Selling, arriving back at Bossenden Farm at night. On the Thursday morning Mr. Mears, a constable who knew Courtenay, went to the farm with a warrant to arrest some men who had been enticed from their work. Mears and his brother well knew that it was going to be a dangerous job, and Mears had volunteered for it because, as he grimly said to his brother who had a family, " I shall leave no children." They went together to the farm and walked towards Courtenay. Mears approached him with the warrant.

" Are you the constable ? " asked Courtenay.

" Yes ! " replied Mears.

And before another word could be said Courtenay drew a pistol and shot the poor fellow dead. Afterwards he wounded the body with his sword and kicked it as it lay on the ground.

The brother took to his heels. Courtenay ordered his men to throw the body into a ditch, which was done. Then he led his men off to a wood where he administered to his followers a sacrament of bread and water, and assured them that neither bullets nor weapons could injure him or them, and that if 10,000 soldiers came against them they would either turn to their side or fall dead at his command.

In spite of the brutal murder they had just witnessed, the scene that followed was typical of the usual revival service. One man sprang in the air crying " O ! be joyful ! O ! be joyful ! " Another fell down at Courtenay's feet and worshipped him, and many shouted in ecstasy their intentions to follow him whither he should lead.

It is to be wondered perhaps that others did not drift away from him, but those who were not filled with enthusiasm were terrified by fear. To scare would-be deserters Courtenay held forth the customary penalties of the professional soul-saver. If they would not follow him, Heaven would consume them in this world, and their lot in the next was eternal damnation.

It must have been a strange sight in civilized Kent, less than a hundred years ago, to have seen the handsome figure of the prophet, his long, reverend beard waving in the morning breeze, his handsome eyes gleaming like bright coals, as he uttered these horrible menaces to the simple peasants standing round him, who were all for the moment convinced that be he demon or god, he was certainly endowed with supernatural powers.

An old wood-cutter who was there went boldly up to him and asked if it was true he had killed Mears.

" Yes," replied Courtenay, taking him by the hand, " I have executed the justice of Heaven in virtue of the power which God has given me."

The old man dropped his hand but dared not leave him. He looked into his bloodthirsty eyes and felt if he had turned his back on him he too would have been shot. All these simple folk seemed mesmerized by the man. Their hearts quaked at his threats and leapt at his promises. As one said afterwards, " He could turn men which way he liked if they only once listened to him." This is the gift of the Devil that makes a man, sane or insane, a successful rogue and vagabond. Some day maybe the scientist will find a cure for those afflicted with this dangerous propensity, or at least some prophylactic to render their poor dupes immune from the deceit of their tongues and the poison of asps which is under their lips.

The morning after the tragedy of the constable's death Courtenay and his followers were at Mr. Francis's house. His followers were given beer, but Francis would not allow them to remain, since for some time he had parted from his guest and ceased to be his disciple, fearing lest he should be drawn into trouble by association with him. Courtenay led his men into some osier fields and later on took them away to Bossenden.

The whole county was now in a state of terror. A major and a hundred men of the 45th Foot were placed at the disposal of the county magistrates, and on the morning of the 31st, accompanied by the Rev. Dr. Poore and Sir N. Knatchbull, representing the magistrates, arrived from Canterbury and came up with the rioters at Bossenden Wood.

Lieutenant Bennett went boldly up to Courtenay and called upon him to surrender, but before anyone could interfere the madman drew out a pistol and shot him dead. A private soldier at once levelled his piece and Courtenay fell. Miss Sarah Culver, a daughter of his host, ran to him with a cup of water at the risk of her life, but the prophet was dead. Then a shocking scene of slaughter arose. The rioters, in no way intimidated, fell on the military, but the superior arms prevailed and after eight of them were killed, as well as a private individual who bravely came to the assistance of the magistrates, and an officer and several others had been wounded, and some prisoners taken, the rest fled into the woods and made away.

A writer who described the affray afterwards declared that all those who fell were believers in Courtenay's divine mission. The Elysium he promised them was to be obtained by getting all the fine seats in the country and dividing the land among the faithful. Not one of them, after Courtenay killed the lieutenant, endeavoured to take shelter from the bullets of the military, for they devoutly believed they were invulnerable, and the worst destruction took place within three minutes of the murder. It was common knowledge that had too small a force been sent against Courtenay, and had he attained a temporary success against the military, thousands of waverers were ready to have left their homes and followed his fortunes.

The bodies of Courtenay and his dead followers were carried to Boughton where they lay in the barn of the " Red Lion " awaiting the inquest. It is said that 20,000 persons came to see the corpse of this strange leader of men. The authorities were at first intending to carry away his body and bury it at night, but wiser counsels prevailed. Had they done so a myth would have rapidly filled the minds of the simple, for Courtenay had often prophesied that he would be caught up to heaven in a cloud and the living should see him depart from the earth.

He and the victims he had lured into the shadow of death were buried in the churchyard at Hernhill. No relatives or mourners followed him to the grave, but among the hundred and twenty peasants who thronged the church-yard, many expressed their pleasure at seeing the last of him, so fickle is the enthusiasm of the mob and so rapidly does a discredited cause vanish before a whiff of grape-shot. But there were some who remained true to his memory, and Charles Igglesden in his interesting *Saunters through Kent* tells us that Miss Sarah Culver, who died at Kennington at the age of eighty-two early in this century, kept his portrait hanging in her room to the day of her death, and never wavered in her belief that Courtenay was an inspired prophet.

There were loud complaints of the conduct of the Home Office in having turned this dangerous madman adrift on a peaceful country-side, but Lord John Russell indignantly repudiated any charge of negligence, or any case for inquiry. The great traditions of government had been maintained in everything that every official had done, and their conduct redounded greatly to their credit, and in spite of the unfortunate incidents that had occurred, all was really for the best in the best possible of worlds.

There was, however, much debate and grumbling and bickering and committee-mongering over the matter, but as always happens in these affairs the official world was held blameless, and after a considerable waste of public time the whole business was forgotten by all but the poor victims of the tragedy.

CHAPTER X

MARY BATEMAN, THE FORTUNE-TELLER

THE law against fortune-telling is of respectable antiquity. It is a proof of the wisdom of our ancestors, who understood the mischief that dishonest fortune-tellers could work among the more ignorant of mankind. The gipsies were the worst and cleverest offenders, and carried their art to a pitch of perfection not often achieved by the clumsy practitioners patronized to-day by West End idlers.

There was a good story told in Lancashire of two grave citizens who were on a holiday in the New Forest, where they were quite unknown, when they were accosted by a gipsy girl who trotted after them for some way, asking for her hand to be crossed with silver that she might tell their fortunes. One of them was inclined to amuse himself with the experiment, but the other sternly forbade it.

" These people are pestilent frauds," he said, " and I will not allow you to give them money."

The other, as many do nowadays, thought there might be something in it, and the gipsy assured them that she had the true gift of prophecy as her mother and grandmother had had before her.

" Very well, then," said the unbeliever, " here is half a sovereign. I do not want any fortunes told, but tell me my name and address and the money is yours."

The girl protested that this was too easy a task and his Honour would never give her the money for so small a service. The wise citizen laughed triumphantly at her and handing the coin to his friend, said : "He will give it you if you will tell me my name and address."

The girl saw that the men were honest, and smiling at their simplicity said, "You are Mr. John Heywood, of 'The Pike,' Bolton."

Mr. Heywood and his friend were greatly interested. The girl took her money and curtsied her thanks, and would have gone away but Mr. Heywood, with Lancashire thoroughness, determined to investigate the matter more nearly.

Drawing another half-sovereign from his pocket he said to the gipsy : "I have been cleverly tricked and now I will buy the method by which I have been fooled."

There was a lot of parleying and chaffering over this, the girl offering the usual cant explanations of second sight and magic powers, but Mr. Heywood was adamant. He would pay a second half-sovereign for the truth, but for nothing less. At length greed overcame her professional scruples and she said with a slight chuckle : "Well, it's on your umbrella."

"Of course it is, and you've earned the money very cleverly, my girl, but all the same you ought to be in jail for being a knave, and I ought to be there too for being a fool."

And they parted company with each other in a very friendly spirit.

All successful fortune-telling is based on this method. Like all branches of magic and mystery, it has an appearance of the supernatural about it until you know the machinery by which it is worked, and this, of course, is not often given away. Had Mr. Heywood grudged the second half-sovereign he would have gone home puzzled, and his friend would have been converted to the faith.

Of recent years there has been a recrudescence of the patronage of fortune-tellers and crystal-gazers, and last autumn the police put the law in motion in the West End

of London against some of these quacks. Actual victims
will never come forward to prosecute, but as the professors
of the mystery are generally dull-witted, greedy people, they
have not sufficient sense to discriminate between a policeman's
wife and a *bona fide* fool customer, and are easily caught-out
cheating and obtaining money by false pretences.

One of these prosecutions raised a small storm of disapproval from students of the occult who, like Mr. Bumble,
consider that the law is an ass for interfering with their
amusements. Sir Oliver Lodge wrote to *The Times* to explain
that as Bradshaw could foretell the times of future railway
trains, other predictions were possible, and fortune-tellers
should not be interfered with. He took occasion to say that
" the law against foretelling was passed in times of ignorance
and unscientific stupidity," and he felt aggrieved that fortune-
tellers " if they exercise their curious and ill-understood
faculty, provided their circumstances are such as to entitle
them to reasonable remuneration for the time expended, are
at present in danger of fine and imprisonment."

What a reasonable remuneration for a fortune-teller ought
to be was not discussed, but the police records show that it
is in practice the largest sum that the quack can squeeze
from the victim by means of appeals to his—or more often
her—terror or cupidity. Fortune-telling is in law and fact
a branch of the class of crime which is known as blackmail.
I am by no means satisfied that the common sense of our
ancestors, who passed laws against fortune-tellers, was not
sturdier than that of some of our contemporaries. To speak
of the age of Bacon and Shakespeare as an age of " unscientific
stupidity," because in that day laws were made against
fortune-telling, seems to me as much a " terminological
inexactitude " as if one were to speak of our own time as an
age of " scientific stupidity," because some of our men of
science have the same crude appetite for necromancy that

has been common to humanity since the days of King Saul. To compare the foretellings of *Bradshaw's Time-Table* with those of *Zadkiel's Almanac* seems to me fallacious; and to call the gift of a fortune-teller " curious and ill-understood " ignores the history of the craft and begs the question.

For anyone who is interested in these matters can make his own historical study of the methods of fortune-telling, in the same way that he can study the methods of the kindred quackeries of necromancy, and witchcraft, and demoniacal possession. These have been similar in all ages and prompted by the same motives as they are to-day. If you study the lives of the fortune-tellers you will find what dangerous people these quacks may be, and what real ruin and misery they bring into the homes of their victims. One does not choose the case of Mary Bateman on account of the horrible nature of her crimes, but because she is, as it were, the leading case in modern fortune-telling, and her methods are typical of fortune-tellers of all generations and are still used by members of the fraternity to-day.

Mary Bateman, known to her contemporaries as " the Yorkshire Witch," was born at Aisenby in the parish of Topcliffe, near Thirsk, in 1768. Her father, whose name was Harker, was a small farmer of respectable character. She manifested a thievish disposition at an early age and showed considerable cunning. As a child of five she was detected stealing a pair of Morocco shoes which she hid in a barn and presently brought them out with the story that she had found them. Nowadays she would have been classified as a feeble-minded child, and perhaps received a special education and training that would have saved her from a career of crime. There is in most fortune-tellers, mediums, and cunning impostors, an abnormal element, manifesting itself in youth, that should receive early discouragement; but as long as dupes are so plentiful, and the reward of evil-doing so lavish, the temptation to persevere in imposture is a very serious one to young persons of this character.

A child of this nature had very little chance of education or stimulating surroundings a hundred and fifty years ago. From the very outset one may admit that Mary Bateman was foredoomed to the gallows, and the society into which she was born did everything in its power to urge her along the path of her fate. She left home at the age of twelve and went into service at Thirsk. One can imagine the kind of life the poor little drudge would lead, when we remember the life of " the Marchioness " who did all the housework at the respectable establishment of Mr. Sampson Brass in Bevis Marks.

The clever little wretch seems to have survived by her innate fitness to cope with the conditions of life into which she had been called, and for seven years entered many services and quitted them under very suspicious circumstances. In those days no one wanted a child to be hanged or transported for theft, and the little criminal was passed on to a new employer. Mary found her way to York in 1787, and after detection of further thefts during the next year, fled from York to Leeds, leaving her clothes and wages behind her.

Here she obtained work with a mantua-maker, for like many thieves she was handy with her fingers at more honest crafts, and here she began to practise on the simple girl customers the arts of fortune-telling and witchcraft in relation to their love affairs and domestic troubles. Here, too, she met a decent, honest wheelwright named John Bateman, whom she married, after a courtship of three weeks, in 1792. She seems to have recognized, that as a married woman with an establishment of her own she would have a better opportunity of carrying on her remunerative frauds. At this time she had not mastered the command of the new decalogue—

> Thou shalt not steal ; an empty feat,
> When it's so lucrative to cheat.

We must remember that the poor girl was entirely self-taught, but we shall see in the evolution of her career that she gradually discovered for herself the great truth which that gentle scholar, Arthur Hugh Clough, put into rhyme for the education of the young some fifty years afterwards.

Her last effort at direct robbery occurred soon after her marriage, when she was detected robbing a fellow-lodger of a watch and some silver spoons and two guineas. Poor Bateman had to part with his savings to hush the matter up, though had his wife been really able to foretell his fortune, it had been better for both of them if he had handed her over to the police.

She now entered a higher branch of ill-doing and began obtaining goods by false pretences, and within a year of their marriage the happy pair took a house in Mr. Wells's yard and furnished it in a tolerably comfortable manner. But even false pretences, though not in those days an indictable offence, was a risky business and led to claims and reprisals and threats of police interference.

Mary was a woman of great resource and her methods of getting out of difficulties were often very praiseworthy. In order to meet the demands of some of those she had wronged, it is related that she went one morning to her husband's works with a letter, which she said had just arrived from Thirsk, saying that his father, who was sexton and town-crier at Thirsk, was at the point of death. Bateman laid down his tools, borrowed some journey money from his employer, and hurried off to his home. Here, to his surprise, he met the old man in the street lustily crying an auction. There was nothing wrong with him, and the angry son rode back to Leeds to find out by whom he had been tricked. On his return home there was no need for any elaborate investigation, for there was his wife sitting in an empty house, having sold every stick of furniture he possessed to hush up some crime she had committed. The story ought to be recorded, because it goes far to show that John Bateman, though a fool, as many loving husbands are, was not actor, art and part, in the crimes of his better half.

Mary seems during these years to have practised all the ordinary frauds of the minor long-firm craftsman. She posed as a nurse of the celebrated General Infirmary of Leeds, and when she could not collect subscriptions she begged linen, which she took to the pawnshop. She made quite a harvest in 1796 out of a terrible fire that broke out in a large factory in the town in which many lives were lost. For the victims of the disaster she collected money and stores, which she used for her own purposes. But frauds of this kind grow increasingly dangerous by repetition and are unpopular among the community, and these considerations were not lost upon Mary's mind. As she had rejected theft as a career, so she gradually weaned herself from the practice of simple and clumsy fraud and began to devote her undoubted talents to fortune-telling.

Fortune-telling, *pace* Sir Oliver Lodge, has for many a long year been a statutory crime and a police offence. But a fortune-teller is only a rogue and vagabond like a minstrel, a player, a bearward and the rest. The public have always had a soft spot in their hearts for fortune-tellers, and here Sir Oliver is in the majority and I am in a hopeless minority. To my mind, it is a pity that it should be so, since it leads a lot of ingenious but somewhat feeble-minded people into the toils of crime.

Although a woman of limited intelligence and entirely self-educated, Mary Bateman knew more about the practices of sorcery and magic than many a modern scientist; and that may well be true of many an ignorant woman of to-day.

For whilst the well-to-do are moithering themselves with spiritualism in the drawing-rooms, the country cottagers with sturdy conservatism still stand out for the ancient practices of witchcraft. Now and then it lands them in the police courts, but not often, for as we know dupes do not talk. Nevertheless, the " evil eye " has not winked its last in Merry England. The last witch suffered in Dornoch in 1722, and the laws against witchcraft were only repealed in 1736 ; but the belief in witchcraft in Mary's day was still very widespread, and it has not disappeared.

Fortune-telling based on witchcraft has always had its votaries, and Mary Bateman determined to make it her business in life. She had found herself through theft and fraud hovering dangerously on the edge of the dock, and she came to the very sensible conclusion that the profession of a fortune-teller and a witch would be a safe cloak for her undoubted talents. In this capacity she could rob her dupes thoroughly and deliberately without losing their friendship, support and gratitude. It is for this reason, I should imagine, that women, who are more dependent than men upon human sympathy, are attracted to this class of crime in which the pleasant friendship of impostor and dupe is an essential condition.

But before she could begin her new career she had to leave Leeds for a time, which in truth was becoming, as they say, too hot to hold her. John Bateman looked back on his three weeks' courtship and ruefully remembered that " short acquaintance makes long repentance," and to save what was left of his wife's reputation he joined the supplementary militia and took Mary with him on his campaigns. During the years she was away she seems to have graduated in her chosen profession. For in 1799, when the pair left the army and settled again in Leeds, in Marsh Lane, near Timble Bridge, Mary started a well-conducted and thriving trade, among love-sick girls and nervous women, in fortune-telling, charms and the usual quackeries of the business. Although judges no longer took judicial notice of witches, the common people believed in them, as indeed many do to-day, and those who were in danger of the evil eye or expectant of some dread calamity came to Mary Bateman for succour and advice.

There is a ritual common to all these deceptions. The great Dr. Torralva admitted that he had in his service an angel of the order of good spirits named Zequiel. The late Mr. Stead was directed by a spook called Julia. Often these things are, of course, mere self-deceptions. Sometimes they begin in self-deception but end in fraud. Sometimes they are undiluted fraud from beginning to end. But the ritual is common to all of the manifestations of ancient witchcraft and modern spiritualism. There are three parties to their proceedings. There is the dupe or faithful believer, the medium or witch, and the angel or devil with whom the intermediary alone can converse. Mary Bateman explained that a certain " Mrs. Moore " was able to do miracles for her if she was approached by Mrs. Bateman with money in her hand. Money has always been the essential motive power of prophecy or miracle. If the victim would bring " four pieces of gold, four pieces of blotting-paper, and four brass screws," these Mary would give to " Mrs. Moore," who had power to " screw down " the evil influences which were at work. Considerable sums came to her hands by this simple method of collection, and as the evils were mostly imaginary and did not happen, the dupes were secretly satisfied at the wisdom they had shown in seeking the witch's protection.

One does not cry out loudly against a knave for robbing willing fools, but Mary was a bad woman in the way she terrorized poor girls in trouble and simple mothers who were in nervous fear of evil befalling a beloved child. For foul

MARY BATEMAN
The Yorkshire Witch

From a contemporary engraving.

crime of this kind there is no excuse, but it is too often a resource of fortune-tellers even to-day. A certain Mrs. Stead was firmly persuaded by Mary Bateman that her child, a girl of fourteen, would be seduced and then commit suicide or be murdered by her seducer, unless her mother produced sufficient silver for " Mrs. Moore " to melt down and make a silver charm for her to wear until the danger was past. The poor woman scraped together seventeen shillings. This was melted down by " Mrs. Moore," and by some miracle of transmutation became a pewter charm which was worn, and the danger averted.

To give a certain sanctity to her misdeeds, Mary became one of the followers of Joanna Southcott. It is remarkable that when Joanna settled in Paddington in 1802 and began the practice of " sealing " the faithful, who were to be of the number of 144,000 certificated for the Millennium, Mary Bateman demanded and received the half-sheet of paper signed by Joanna and sealed with a red seal on the back. In 1809, when Mary Bateman was hanged at York, the " sealing" business came to an abrupt end. Some day, no doubt, the psychological nexus between imposture and religious mania and manifestations of religious excitement will be better understood. It is even possible that Mary in her distorted mind led herself to believe in Joanna as many reputable people did. I take it, however, that Mary Bateman had no authority from any leaders of Joanna's church to run miracles of her own, but doubtless she would have pleaded *vis major* for what occurred in her poultry-yard.

The Batemans had moved to a house in Black Dog Yard, at the Bank, and there they kept poultry. It became known that one of Mary's hens had laid a miraculous egg on which was inscribed " Christ is coming." Doubts were cast ; but some sort of watch was permitted, and two more eggs, similarly inscribed, were laid in the nest. There is a portrait

P

extant of Mary sitting in her cottage in cap and apron holding the holy egg in her hand. People flocked to see the relic and at a penny a head a good sum accrued. More important was it, that the sorceries of the witch seemed to receive in this way some sort of divine approval, silencing the sneers of unbelievers The interest, however, did not last long. The prophetic fowl was bought by a neighbour. It laid no more miraculous eggs and in due course its neck was wrung, and it suffered the common fate of other poultry.

If Mary had been content with reasonable remuneration for her frauds all might have been well; but this type of rogue knows no moderation in her greed, and that is one reason why I regard the profession of fortune-telling as a dangerous one. The prophetess may get swelled head and believe in her miraculous powers, and in the endeavour to keep up the pose she has assumed, resort to crime and wickeder deceit, rather than descend from her pedestal and acknowledge that she is in reality a common and very ordinary human being of a somewhat undesirable type.

" Mrs. Moore " had become rather blown upon in Leeds as a greedy and uncertain medium, and in 1806 or thereabouts, when Mary met the unhappy Perigo family, her new familiar who was able to cure all evils was " Miss Blythe " of Scarborough.

One may imagine that the Constable of Leeds had been watching the movements of Mary Bateman with professional interest. In 1808, the Batemans had removed to Campfield in Water Lane. Here a neighbour named James Snowden was afflicted with a presentiment that one of his children would be drowned. Mary Bateman, hearing of the trouble, was called in and at once agreed that the only person who could save the child from a watery grave was " Miss Blythe " of Scarborough. " Miss Blythe " was written to. Her directions were that James Snowden's silver watch was to be sewn up in the bed by Mary Bateman, which this good lady pretended to carry out. Then twelve guineas were to be supplied and sewn up in the bed, and this ritual was followed. By and by a new terror was announced to the family and the Snowdens were told that unless they left Leeds and removed to Bowling, near Bradford, their daughter would certainly become a prostitute. The terror-stricken family fled. They took with them the magic bed, but they left good Mrs. Bateman the key of their house which contained much valuable property.

Later on they asked Mary's permission to rip open the bed and take out the charms, but Mary said the time had not yet arrived and sent them a dose which she advised them to take. Fortunately for them they did not do so. At this juncture she was arrested by the police in relation to the Perigo case. Mr. Snowden returned to Leeds. He had ripped up the bed and found nothing in it but a lump of coal. He had opened his house and found it plundered of everything it contained. Some of the property was found in Bateman's home. He, too, good easy man, was arrested and committed for trial, but at the Sessions was honourably acquitted, perhaps reasonably. For my part, I think he had taken Mary for better or worse, and as an honest wheelwright working for one firm for over sixteen years he had attended to business, brought his wages home and was no more responsible for his wife's misdeeds than any other man who has the misfortune to marry a wilful lady who has a stronger character than his own.

There were no Courts of Law then (and indeed there are none now) which entitled a husband to apply to the Court for a separation or divorce, on the ground that he had strong suspicions that his good lady was about to commit a murder, or was carrying on an illegal business, when he had no evidence to support his thesis and was not a competent witness against her. I have the fullest sympathy with poor Bateman. He had drawn an unlucky number in the matrimonial lottery, and I am glad the jury acquitted him.

But the case against Mrs. Bateman was a much more serious affair, and her trial for the wilful murder of Rebecca Perigo of Bramley in the West Riding took place on Friday, March 17, 1809.

It is the details of this trial which I suggest in all humility the well-to-do patrons of modern fortune-tellers and crystal-gazers should ponder and consider, for though the guilt of the wretched woman was deep, the folly of her patrons was deeper and deeper still. And in an age when the semi-educated rush into the occult in a state of naked ignorance, it is no ill thing to set up before their leaders an object lesson of the actual results of the wicked rubbish to which they are lending their honoured names.

The trial took place before Mr. Justice Simon Le Blanc, a prim, precise, but learned lawyer. Mr. John Hardy, Recorder of Leeds, with him Mr. Williams, appeared for the Crown. The wretched prisoner had no counsel. It will be seen that although she was a very guilty woman, the actual murder with which she was charged is by no means clearly proved. The prosecuting counsel, seeing his difficulties, told the jury that

there may be doubts, as in a case of circumstances there must be, but the prisoner can expect to have the benefit of no doubts, but such as forcibly and powerfully resist the conclusions which go to establish her guilt. If, when the doubts are put into the scales with the probabilities of the case, the latter decidedly kick the beam, you will firmly and manfully discharge the awful duty that is imposed upon you. You are not called upon to say that you are certain of the prisoner's guilt, certainty is not attainable by the infirmity of human tribunals, but if at the conclusion of the evidence laying your hands upon your hearts you honestly and conscientiously believe her to be guilty you will so pronounce her, if not you will acquit her.

The events to which the witnesses spoke had commenced nearly three years ago. Mrs. Stead, William Perigo's niece, who herself was one of Mary's dupes, introduced the Perigos to the beneficent witch. At Whitsuntide, 1806, she was visiting her aunt, Mrs. Perigo, who told her that she was suffering from an "evil wish." She was also told that her uncle had consulted a country doctor about his wife's health, and that he had diagnosed that the poor lady was suffering from the effects of an " evil wish."

Mrs. Stead returned to Leeds and went off to consult the good witch at Black Dog Yard about her aunt, and Mary told her that her aunt must send a flannel petticoat or some other garment worn next her skin for her to send to the mysterious lady who could work the cure. This ritual is part of the machinery of modern spiritualism and fortune-telling to this day. William Perigo heard of what was going on with deep interest and came over to Leeds at the week-end, bringing with him a petticoat, to inquire from Mrs. Stead the whereabouts of this mistress of magic who was going to cure his wife.

He was a respectable clothier of forty-eight and had been married to his wife Rebecca for twenty years. Mary took the petticoat and said she would send it to Scarborough by that night's post to her familiar " Miss Blythe," and on Wednesday Perigo must return and she would tell him what " Miss Blythe " had prescribed.

On the Wednesday Mary read Perigo a letter which stated that " Miss Blythe " had sent her four guinea notes. These Mary Bateman was to carry with her to Bramley and sew them into the four corners of the bed upon which Perigo and his wife slept. It was essential that they should remain there for at least eighteen months or evil would ensue. William Perigo was to give Mary four other notes of the same value to be returned to " Miss Blythe." All this seemed very fair and hopeful, and it was duly carried out. On

August 4 Mary brought the notes.　William Perigo saw them
He saw they were genuine.　He saw Mary sew them into foui
small bags.　Man cannot help believing the insidious evidence
of his own eyes, whether he goes to see a conjurer, or attends
a séance in a darkened room ; and it is this pleasant conceit
of humanity in its limited power of observation that leads tc
all the trouble.　William and his wife were perfectly satisfied
that all was well and truly done, and they readily agreed not
to talk about it for fear the charm should be broken, a dangei
about which " Miss Blythe " was very emphatic.

" Miss Blythe " soon after this began to correspond personally with Mrs. Perigo.　The first letter arrived in October,
1806, and is typical of all the others.

MY DEAR FRIEND,
　　　　You must go down to Mary Bateman's at Leeds, on Tuesday
next, and carry two guinea notes with you and give her them, and she
will give you another two pounds, you must buy me a small cheese
about six or eight pound weight, and it must be of your buying for it
is for a particular use, and it is to be carried down to Mary Bateman's,
and she will send it to me by the coach.　This letter is to be burnt
when you have done reading it.

Unfortunately for Mary Bateman, though the letters seem
to have been burned, Perigo kept copies of some of them.
Some of these, however, he was not allowed to give in
evidence as the destruction of the originals was not proved,
and no notice to produce the letters had been given to the
prisoner.　The copies of these letters are all printed in the
report of the trial, but many did not come before the jury.
Perigo, on some occasions when the destruction of both letter
and copy was proved, was allowed to recite the contents of
the letters from memory.

" Miss Blythe " seemed to be undergoing great distress in
order to help Mrs. Perigo.　On one occasion it appeared that
she must have a new tea service as she " durst not drink out
of my own china."　Another letter in April, 1807, bearing

the Scarborough postmark, said that " Miss Blythe " must have " a camp bedstead, bed and bedding, a blanket ; a pair of sheets and a long bolster," for it appeared " Miss Blythe " had slept on the floor for three nights as " I cannot lay on my own bed owing to the planets being so bad concerning your wife." William Perigo, thinking no doubt that such a labourer was well worthy of her hire, handed all these things to Mary Bateman.

When it was money that was to be dealt with, then the ritual was always observed of Mary sewing it up in silk bags and giving these to Perigo, who solemnly sewed them into his bed, he himself having given in exchange his own money to the deserving witch. From December, 1806, to April, 1807, Mary Bateman received in this way from the Perigos £70 in money and a large quantity of good furniture, wearing apparel and food, including a goose, 100 lb. of butter, several hundred eggs, meat, malt, tea, sugar and three bottles of spirits.

In April, 1807, letters began to arrive advising the Perigos to take stuff which " Miss Blythe " would send to Mary Bateman in honey, pudding or other food. Perigo was permitted to give his memory of the following letter which arrived early in May.

MY DEAR FRIENDS,

You must begin to eat pudding on the 11th of May and you must put one of the powders in every day, as they are marked for six days, and you must see it put in yourself or it will not do. If you find yourself sickly at any time you must not have no doctor, for it will not do, and you must not let the boy that used to eat with you eat of that pudding for six days, and you must make only just as much as you can eat yourselves, and if there is any left it will not do. You must keep the door fast as much as possible or you will be overcome by some enemy. Now think on and take my directions or else it will kill us all. About the 25th of May I will come to Leeds and send for your wife to Mary Bateman's ; your wife will take me by the hand and say, " God bless you that I ever found you out." It has pleased God to send me into the world that I might destroy the works of darkness ; I call them the works of darkness because they are dark to you. Now mind what I say whatever you do. This letter must be burnt in straw on the hearth by your wife.

In consequence of these directions on May 11 the treatment began. Perigo says he tried some of the pudding but it was so nauseous that he could eat no more of it. His wife told him this was the illness predicted by " Miss Blythe " and they must now take the honey. Perigo took two spoonfuls and his wife six and they were both worse than ever. both of them vomiting incessantly for twenty-four hours. He declared that his wife would not hear of a doctor being sent for, and he described the incidents of his own illness and that of his poor wife who died on Sunday, May 24. Mr. Chorley, a surgeon of Leeds, was sent for, but as the woman died before he came, a message was sent to him to countermand his attendance.

However, the next day Perigo went to see Mr. Chorley, He seemed to think that his wife must have been poisoned, and suggested making a paste of the flour with which the pudding was made and giving it to a fowl. This was done, but the fowl was none the worse. A neighbour gave evidence that part of the pudding which Perigo and his wife had eaten was given to a cat, and the animal died soon afterwards.

All this evidence was given two years after the event. Although Perigo went to Mr. Chorley at the time, and it is said a cat died of the pudding, no analysis was made and no inquest was held, nor does Perigo seem to have told Mr. Chorley about the powders put into the pudding, nor was the honey mentioned to him. Another neighbour, Rose Howgate, gave evidence of the illness of Perigo and his wife, and the doctors, who listened to the accounts given, declared that in their opinions the woman did not die a natural death but was probably poisoned by corrosive sublimate of mercury.

There was evidence that when on October 20, 1808,

Mary Bateman was arrested, she had in her possession a square glass bottle full of a liquid which Mr. Chorley the surgeon said contained arsenic. Perigo brought the jar in which the honey had been put, and that contained corrosive sublimate of mercury. There was no evidence where Mary Bateman had bought these chemicals.

The only really important witness against Mary Bateman was Perigo, and his conduct at the time of his wife's death was very reprehensible even for a man under the influence of witchcraft. He had himself seen the poison put into the pudding and, if he had told Mr. Chorley that, no doubt a proper investigation would have been made. It would have been interesting to hear what explanation he would have given of his extraordinary conduct if he had been cross-examined.

Mr. Chorley seems to have sent Mr. Perigo, after the death of his wife, to Buxton, and he continued to receive extraordinary epistles from " Miss Blythe " asking him to send her his wife's clothes, and this he did, for the lady upbraids him for sending " such a shabby gown as this " and insists on " one of your wife's best gowns and a petticoat or a skirt." In spite of what had happened, Perigo's faith in " Miss Blythe " was unshaken.

Two of the last letters of " Miss Blythe " sent to him in August, 1808, were actually produced, and these were proved to be in the handwriting of Mary Bateman who was, of course, in possession of much of the Perigo property.

It was not until October 19, 1808, that William Perigo determined to open the bed and find his money, and the poor fool was naturally disturbed at finding waste paper in the bags instead of notes, and farthings instead of gold.

He went in to Leeds to upbraid Mary Bateman, who did not seem surprised and told him that he had " opened the bags too soon."

" I think it is too late," he replied, and told her he would bring some men down with him on the morrow and have things settled up. She, however, persuaded him to meet her on the bank of the Leeds and Liverpool Canal and he promised to do so the next morning. The loss of his wife was one thing, but the loss of his property was another matter, and at last it occurred to him that he ought to consult the police. He did so and they decided to accompany him to the canal bank and arrest Mrs. Bateman. Mary made no defence at the trial. She made a statement before the justices which was read. She denied that she had written all the letters. Some, she said, were written by a woman named Hannah Potts. She denied all knowledge of honey, puddings or poison and declared that the bottle found upon her had been given her by Perigo, which he stoutly denied.

The summing up left the main points fairly enough to the jury and the case was, of course, one of overwhelming suspicion, though the chief witness against the prisoner was, as the judge mildly said, a man " of uncommon want of judgment " with a very retentive memory. That the deceased actually died of poison was not proved in the way it would be to-day. But these things did not trouble the jury. They conferred for only a moment and found the prisoner guilty.

The judge who tried the case told her that there could not remain a particle of doubt of her guilt in the mind of anyone who had heard the case. As Mr. Justice Le Blanc had heard Perigo give his evidence he must have been satisfied that, fool as he was, he was a witness of truth, and most likely the judicial verdict was a right one. The judge also expressed his astonishment that the frauds of the prisoner could " in this age and nation have been practised with success." Could we get in touch with him to-day by modern methods of necromancy, he would be interested to know that fraudu- lent fortune-tellers still carry on the same old game with the same astonishing success. Fortunately, they do not all resort to murder to veil their frauds from the eye of justice.

The trial finished on Saturday night and the judge ordered that the woman in the dock before him should be executed on the Monday. During the few hours of life that remained to her she listened to the ministrations of the Reverend George Brown with attention and decorum, but nothing would induce her to confess that she had poisoned Mrs. Perigo. On the Sunday she wrote a farewell letter to her husband enclosing her wedding ring with a request that it should be given to her daughter.

She had the reputation among her neighbours of being a good wife and mother and an excellent housekeeper. Her manners were soft and insinuating with an affectation of sanctity. She readily admitted to the minister that she had been guilty of many frauds, but the charge of poisoning she denied strenuously. She approached her end with great calmness. There were, as was the usual case on a Monday morning in Assize week, several prisoners to be executed, and at five o'clock in the morning she received the Communion with her fellow-victims. Again she refused to acknowledge the justice of her sentence, and the time came for her to take her place on the scaffold.

Her infant child was sleeping in her cell and she took leave of it without waking the sleeper, when the jailer in charge of the ceremonies called her name. An immense assemblage had gathered together to see the execution and she was received with deep silence as she appeared on the platform with the Rev. Mr. Brown. Immediately before the drop fell, the good clergyman thought it his duty to make a last call on the woman to confess her crime ; but with her last breath she declared her innocence, the bolt was drawn and she died.

Assuming Perigo was not a liar there can be little doubt that she was guilty. But it is always more satisfactory before a criminal's life is taken to hear a confession and, as a rule, criminals, when all hope of reprieve is over, are very ready to confess. The exceptional conduct of Mary Bateman aroused considerable interest in her case. After her body was cut down it was carried to the Leeds Infirmary, for it was part of the sentence in those days that the convict's body was to " be given to the surgeons to be dissected and anatomized."

Immense crowds of people followed the hearse and so great was the desire of the populace to see her remains that the Infirmary Board, with characteristic zeal for the welfare of the institution they governed, arranged for her body to lie in state for awhile, so that the citizens of Leeds might pay her their last respects. Every person who visited the apartment in which the corpse of Mary Bateman was laid out was charged threepence for the privilege of visiting the shrine, and 2,400 people paid for admission. When we remember that Mary had in the days of her vanity fraudulently collected moneys intended for the Infirmary, there is a grim touch of comedy in the happy idea of the Infirmary Board.

Many strange stories of her frauds were current in Leeds after her death, and it was suggested that she had made away with some Quaker ladies who were deeply interested in her skill in divination and power of reading the stars. Gossip of this class is, however, not worthy of much attention. It seems probable in Perigo's case that she used poison in the endeavour to cover up all traces of her frauds. But it is not as a murderess that she will be remembered, because her methods were obviously clumsy and imperfect, even allowing for the unscientific ignorance of the age she lived in. But as a fortune-teller her practices were typical of the best that is done to-day in that occult craft, and her story is well worth the study of scientists, both those who are seriously interested in psychology and criminology, and those who patronize the modern manifestations of the ancient craft of fortune-telling.

CHAPTER XI

BAMPFYLDE-MOORE CAREW, THE MENDICANT

THE story of this strange rogue and vagabond is of especial interest to the student of history and sociology, because it illustrates the fallacy of the proceedings of many scientists in these departments, who compile their treatises on the past from statutes and departmental records rather than from humble biographical memoirs of real but obscure persons.

There have been laws in this country against vagrancy since Eadric reigned in Kent in the seventh century, and early in the eighteenth century they were peculiarly harsh. No poor man could leave his parish and wander in search of work or pleasure without a pass. If he was found begging, or fiddling, or play-acting, or doing any other forbidden act, or if he was a sailor or soldier going to or from ship or regiment and had no pass, he was a rogue and vagabond. As such the minister and the constable of the parish where he was found were to apprehend him, and it was their duty to see that such rogues " be stript naked from the middle upwards, and openly whipped till their body be bloody, and they forthwith to be sent away from Constable to Constable, the next straight way to the place of their birth." And the law was that this was to happen in each parish where they were found, if they exceeded the time given to them to reach their homes. So if you read the statutes you would imagine that for their own sakes these poor recurring human decimals would seek to recur as seldom as possible.

The Compleat Constable, a handbook of 1707, tells us in
detail that all persons over seven years old without lawful
passport are rogues liable to punishment, and that it is " felony
without clergy " for gipsies to remain above a month in
England and Wales.

These and similar laws having been promulgated for over
a thousand years before Carew came into the world, one
might suppose that the country was by his day rid of rogues
and vagabonds, and if the laws had been carried out this
might have been true. But humanity hates and always will
hate unjust prohibitions. The public were not wholly averse
to rogues and vagabonds ; indeed, they loved the fiddlers
and play-actors, they pitied the beggars and soldiers and
sailors, and delighted in the fortune-telling gipsies as people
of to-day enjoy the mysteries of mediums and crystal-gazers,
nor were they particularly annoyed when they were duped.
One of the most curious phenomena in the psychology of
quackery is that the majority of dupes are always full of pity
and excuse for the rascal that has taken them in, when the law
lays him by the heels. When Mr. Bottomley was sentenced,
the little people whose money he had taken were sorry for
him ; and when recently the police successfully prosecuted
a West End fortune-teller, quite respectable citizens wrote to
the newspapers deprecating their activity.

As it was in the beginning so it certainly is to-day, and
the reason that these cruel prohibitory laws did not, as the
Americans say, " cut much ice " was that the instinct of
humanity was against them. With the exception, perhaps,
of Home Secretaries, constables and the scrag-end of magisterial benches, the bulk of English people suffer rogues and
vagabonds very kindly.

All our great writers have a sympathy for them. Fielding,
Defoe, Smollett, Dickens, Thackeray, Borrow, and a hundred
others have brought joy to their readers with stories of rogues.

Two of our best beloved, Robert Burns and Charles Lamb, had each of them an especially soft place in his heart for your beggar. No real lover of Burns can reject what Carlyle has called " the most strictly poetical of all his poems, *The Jolly Beggars*." Every face in it is a portrait. One can see the very features of the crowd through the smoke in the dingy kitchen of Poosie Nancy's humble inn, and hear their choruses as they sit round the ruddy, flaming hearth, and feel the warmth and joy of it heightened by the sound of the hailstones driving outside " wi' bitter skyte."

And there you have Bampfylde-Moore Carew's friends and intimates. The " son of Mars " with his doxy within his arms, the " fairy fiddler " skirling out Encore! the " Merry Andrew in the neuk," the stout elderly " raucle carlin " with her moan for her braw John Highlandman, the " sturdy caird," the gipsy tinkler who soothes her woes with his welcome embraces; and, forgetting to murmur "without prejudice," we find ourselves chanting their creed as the curtain of night falls upon the scene.

> Life is all a variorum,
>   We regard not how it goes ;
> Let them cant about decorum
>   Who have characters to lose.
>
> A fig for those by law protected !
>   Liberty's a glorious feast.
> Courts for cowards were erected,
>   Churches built to please the priest.

In a calmer and more reasoning humour Charles Lamb takes up the praise of beggars and analyses his sympathy, almost his envy, for the members of that old and honoured profession and laments the passing of the picturesque tribe with their scrips, wallets, bags, staves, dogs and crutches. " Pauperism, pauper, poor man, are expressions of pity, but pity alloyed with contempt. No one properly contemns a beggar." The essayist points out, very justly I think, that it is the freedom of the beggar from the greater inconveniences of civilization, that in moments of contemplation makes us forgetful of the commandment and covetous of that liberty and independence which we ourselves have sold for lucre. Nor will he admit that there is anything detrimental about his favoured Beggar, for Charles Lamb with that deep insight of his can even find a cheerful symbolism in his very rags.

Rags, which are the reproach of poverty, are the Beggar's robes, and graceful *insignia* of his profession, his tenure, his full dress, the suit in which he is expected to show himself in public. He is never out of the fashion or limpeth awkwardly behind it. He is not required to put on court mourning. He weareth all colours, fearing none. His costume hath undergone less change than the Quaker's. He is the only man in the universe who is not obliged to study appearances. The ups and downs of the world concern him no longer. He alone continueth in one stay. The price of stock or land affecteth him not. The fluctuations of agricultural or commercial prosperity touch him not, or at worst but change his customers. He is not expected to become bail or surety for anyone. No man troubleth him with questioning his religion or politics. He is the only free man in the universe.

Lawyer-like, I fall back on these precedents of thoughts about beggars when I confess to a certain delight and sympathy with that rogue and vagabond, Mr. Bampfylde-Moore Carew, commonly called " The King of the Beggars." If his story had come down to us like the story of Robin Hood from an age of missals and manuscripts, he doubtless would have been disembodied by the learned and placed among the variants of a sun-myth. But he lived in the eighteenth century and told his tale to Mrs. Rachel Goadby, who—lucky woman—being the wife of Robert Goadby, the printer and publisher of Sherborne, had no difficulty in getting it published and it ran through several editions. Among the histories of vagrom men I know of none that bears out

Rich. Phelps pinx.   J. Faber fecit 1730.

Bampfylde Moore Carew

King of the Beggars

From the Original Picture in the Possession of Thos Carew Esqr of Crowcombe in Somersetshire

so completely the line of the cantata : " Life is all a variorum."

Bampfylde-Moore Carew was born in Devonshire at Bickleigh, near Tiverton, in July, 1690, and christened on September 23 at Bickleigh Church, where his father, the Rev. Theodore Carew, was rector. There was, and maybe still is, an ivied farmhouse called Bickleigh Court, where tradition says our hero was born. The Carew family were famous throughout the West, and at his christening there was a great gathering of gentlemen and ladies of rank and quality to welcome this new recruit. The Hon. Hugh Bampfylde, Esquire, and the Hon. Major Moore were his illustrious godfathers. These two gentlemen had a merry contest as to whose name should appear first on the register, and this was amicably settled by the throw of a coin. Mr. Bampfylde winning, he presented the infant with a piece of plate whereon was engraved Bampfylde-Moore Carew. This concession of a hyphen to his colleague godfather was highly appreciated.

The Rev. Theodore had other children but they scarcely come into our hero's story. At the age of twelve the boy was sent to the famous Blundell's School at Tiverton under the Rev. W. Rayner, where he associated with young gentlemen, sons of the squires and gentry of the West of England. Old Peter Blundell's " fair school," which that worthy merchant had founded a hundred years ago for the poor lads of his native town, had been already captured by the descendants of his wealthier neighbours.

From 1705 to 1710 when young Carew was nearly seventeen he spent his schooldays, as other boys of his age, in acquiring a reasonable knowledge of the classics and enjoying the outdoor sports of the country-side, fishing, shooting and hunting, for which the neighbourhood is still famous.

At an early age Carew was a noted huntsman. He was

Q

a tall, strong, well-built young fellow and possessed peculiar control over dogs, for he could entice any dog to follow him and he had " a remarkable Chearing Halloo to the dogs " which was of great service in the hunting-field. When he was at Blundell's the scholars had " command of a fine Cry of Hounds" and he and his school-fellows enjoyed much good sport. Three of his dearest companions were Thomas Coleman, son of William Coleman, barrister-at-law, of Gornhay, and John Martin and John Escott, all lads of good family. In view of their extraordinary careers it is interesting to know that he and his companions lived in their youth the normal life of the sons of country gentlemen of the time.

In the summer of 1710 a neighbouring farmer who was a great sportsman, and often joined the boys when their hounds were out, came into Tiverton with the news that he had seen a fine deer with a collar about its neck in the fields near his farm which he supposed to be a pet deer of some neighbouring landowner. Carew and his companions, followed by the bulk of their school-fellows, set off with their hounds to the chase. All this happened a short time before harvest. The day was very hot, the hunt lasted several hours, and they ran their quarry through fields of ripening corn, until they brought him down at last many miles from home. Upon examination of the collar the deer was found to belong to Colonel Nutcombe of Clayhanger, and within a few days this gentleman, and the farmers whose crops had been damaged, laid a heavy complaint of the huntsmen before the headmaster, Mr. Rayner. An inquiry was held and Carew and his particular friends were found to be the ring-leaders and remanded for severe punishment.

That evening Carew and his three especial chums absented themselves from school and, passing by an ale-house half a mile out of Tiverton known as " Brick House " or

" Red Hill," they found that it was occupied by a troupe of seventeen or eighteen gipsies, for the place was a noted resort of these wanderers and from time to time they gathered there for merry-making or business conference. The young men determined to stay the night there, and the gipsies received the " gentry coves " very hospitably. There was a banquet of fowl and duck and other country food, cider and good October ale flowed freely, and the night was spent in song and dance. So pleased were the youngsters with their entertainment that they announced their determination of joining the gipsy community.

Nothing was settled that night, but next morning, the four friends insisting on their resolution, a court was formed, the senior gipsy administered the oaths, and they were admitted members of the community. At that time the whole body of gipsies, vagrants and professional mendicants were joined in a society that held meetings, elected elders and a king who exercised some sort of sway over his subjects.

To understand the position of the mendicants and vagrants of the eighteenth century it is necessary to bear in mind that the criminal laws of our country were very severe against stealing, punishing that offence with transportation and death, yet cheating was not necessarily a crime. There was at that date no crime in obtaining money by false pretences, the law then considering that if people had not the common prudence to guard themselves against impostors it was not a bad thing that they should learn from experience. The body which Carew joined was a sort of trade union or craft guild of cheats. They taught an apprentice all the old tricks, and if he was apt he soon added new ones which he disclosed to his comrades.

The society of the time seems to have been charitably disposed on the whole towards vagrants. Many of them were skilled horse and cattle doctors or good tinkers and tailors and therefore welcome visitors, and some beggars were genuine and worthy of charity. If a man was taken in by an impostor it was regarded by his neighbours as an excellent jest, and if he had any good sense he joined in the laugh against himself.

As for dog-stealing, that also was not a crime, and though there was a limited property recognized in certain dogs, your only remedy if your faithless hound went off with a stranger was to bring an action against him for the return of the animal. This must be especially remembered in relation to Bampfylde-Moore Carew, for he had an illicit love for other people's dogs, who were strangely attracted by his personality. As a cheat, too, he gloried in his deceits which, to his mind and those of many of his contemporaries, were not only not criminal but were highly entertaining and humorous incidents worthy of applause and reward.

Among the oldest deceptions in the world are fortune-telling and divination, forms of quackery that have many devotees in high places to-day, and quite serious people resent the punishment of cheats who practise them. Carew took up this branch of art in his earliest years and became such a noted success that Mrs. Musgrove of Monkton, near Taunton, sent for him to assist her in finding a buried treasure that was said to lie near her house. Our hero lived with his patroness for some time, and after long toil and study informed the good lady that the treasure was under the roots of an ancient laurel tree in her garden but that her planet of good fortune did not reign until a certain day and hour some weeks ahead. Mrs. Musgrove was so overjoyed at Carew's news that she gave him twenty guineas, and he went his way rejoicing, but whether he miscalculated the orbit of the planet or the good lady blundered over the day we cannot now know—but it is certain that no treasure was ever found.

For a year and a half Carew continued to enjoy his roving

life, whilst his unhappy parents sent messengers far and wide
to find him. Our hero, learning of their sorrow and trouble,
now determined to visit them. After an absence of a year
and a half he returned to his home. The whole neighbourhood rejoiced to see him again. The church bells of Bickleigh and Cadleigh, a neighbouring village, rang merrily.
The parable of the prodigal son was a twice-told tale and all
the friends of the family vied with each other in doing honour
to the wanderer returned to the bosom of his family.

The Carews and their friends seem to have done everything that was possible to keep the young man at home, but
the call of the wild was too strong for him. Bampfylde-
Moore fretted for adventure. He missed the freedom and
simplicity of his vagrant pals, the constant change of habita-
tion, the mirth and good humour of their warfare against
respectability. Without a word to his parents he once more
set out for " Brick House," and finding some of the community at the inn he returned to his comrades and the work
of his life.

Carew now took up the business of the Shipwrecked
Seaman and, having imitated the necessary passes and certificates, made a successful tour of Devonshire. At Kings-
bridge he met Coleman again and the two joined forces and
went by Totnes to Exeter, gaining considerable booty by
begging as unfortunate sailors. It was about this time that
he underwent a training in the art of rat-catching, giving a
handsome gratuity to an expert known as " the Royal rat-
catcher," a rascal who had given himself a patent to that
effect. He also studied the gipsy lore of horse-coping and
cattle-curing, at which he became skilled. As a dog-stealer
he had from the first, as we have noted, shown great natural
ability.

In his predatory tours we find that he never retained the
same character for long. To-day he was a wounded soldier,

the next day a country farmer whose cattle had been drowned on the Rye marshes, returning to his family in Kent ; and at a town a mile or so farther on he would be " Mad Tom " offering to eat coals of fire, tearing his rags and beating his head against a wall. So great was his success in all these characters that it seems as if the opportunity for play-acting was one of the lures that drew him into vagrancy.

Indeed, like all great artists, he thought no trouble too great to arrive at perfection, and having parted with Coleman and picked up young Escott at Dartmouth he proposed to him a trip to Newfoundland. His friend agreed, the two approached Captain Holdsworth of the *Mansail* and joined his crew. They made the voyage to arrive in the fishing season, and Carew, having made careful observations of the industry, returned to Dartmouth with a " surprising fierce and large dog," full of a desire to make use of his acquired knowledge as a sailor and a traveller.

His fellow-gipsies, when they heard of his energy and courage, received him with joy and were loud in their praises when they realized that he had undertaken this voyage to enable him to deceive their common enemy, the public. His next tour as a shipwrecked sailor from Newfoundland was a real success, and not only did he gain much booty but no doubt taught the ignorant country-side some geographical knowledge in exchange for their pittances.

That he made considerable sums of money on these tours is beyond doubt, for we often find him leaving his work for a well-earned holiday. On one occasion he appears at Newcastle-on-Tyne as a gentleman of means on a visit of curiosity to the famous coal works of the city. It was here he met his fate and wooed and won Mary Gray, the daughter of an eminent apothecary and surgeon. Love overcame his scruples and he did not inform her that he belonged to the community of gipsies, but passed himself off as a mate of a ship, having found a friendly captain from Dartmouth in the harbour who was readily pleased to do a service to young Mr. Carew.

That he could have satisfied the girl's father with his position in the world was, of course, impossible and as the calls of love were paramount an elopement was determined upon. The young lady, under the protection of the captain, sailed with her lover for the south and, arriving at Dartmouth, the happy pair posted to Bath where they were married in great splendour. For three weeks they were the talk of the gay city, and no one could ascertain their names, though wild rumours of their identity haunted the rooms and the gardens.

What the paternal apothecary thought of it all history does not relate. He is left dispensing. Perhaps he had an ample margin of children without this errant daughter. The girl herself certainly gained a devoted husband and though he himself was at times cruelly parted from her, yet he always carried her image in his heart and returned to her as soon as fate allowed. It seems clear, too, that during his absences his family, and perhaps the community, looked after her and their only daughter.

Their early married life must have been a dream of delight to the obscure provincial girl, for here she was at Bath, which she had read of in romances, with a rich husband taking part in the gay life of the city. Tiring of Bath they visited the hot wells of Bristol and dazzled the staid citizens with their splendour. After that they made a tour of Somerset and Dorset into Hampshire where funds, as I surmise, running low, our hero condescended to visit an uncle of his who was a clergyman of position at Porchester, near Gosport.

The good man received the young couple very kindly and whilst they stayed with him tried to prevail upon

Bampfylde-Moore to give up his engagements with the gipsies and return to civilized life. But from preference as well as high principle Carew refused his uncle's offer of present hospitality and future support and, having explained his real position to his loving wife, the two bade a friendly farewell to their host and our hero carried off his beloved to live among his friends.

It was now necessary for him to put himself in funds again, and his next tour was a triumphant success. His stay with his uncle was not time wasted, for he had learned enough of the outward and visible appearance and conversation of a clergyman to appear in the world as a vicar of Aberystwyth, in Wales, who had given up his living on a change of government rather than take an oath against his principles, and had left behind him a wife and young family.

Like that excellent rogue, Ephraim Jenkinson, he garnished his talk with Greek and Latin sentences, and many a pious simple parson like Dr. Primrose took from his own poor purse to fill the pockets of the clever vagabond. The stratagem succeeded well, but hearing that a vessel bound to Philadelphia, on board which were many Quakers, had been cast away on the Irish coast, his quick brain thought of a new and even more hopeful speculation. Carew's genius as an impresario shows itself very clearly in the rapid way in which he sees the chances of a new situation. Quakers were no use to ordinary mumpers and turned a deaf ear on rogues and vagabonds, but among their own kind they were notoriously prodigal of charity. As a shipwrecked Quaker, Carew saw himself in for a long and successful run. He was right in his prognostication, and the sect made a substantial contribution to the relief of their ruined brother.

Soon after this he took up with the fire business and, whenever a house or mill was burned a few miles away, appeared as the ruined farmer or the ruined miller, with a testimonial from the parson and the squire of the village, begging his way to London to visit a charitable relation. And in all these disguises he was so successful that he would beg of his own friends and go through the same town in a new shape when the constable was searching after the rogue who had just defrauded the citizens. In this way Carew would levy a super-tax on his former dupes with a fresh disguise and some new and plausible tale.

His exploits became known far and wide, and his friends and family, though shaking their heads at his adventures, were secretly rather proud of him, in the same way as Victorian respectabilities would boast in whispers to their friends that some favourite actor of the town was a cousin of the family. Indeed, Carew seems to have been regarded by many of the country gentlemen of the West as a public entertainer.

Coming one day at Brinson, near Blandford, to Squire Portman's, to whom he was well known, he arrived in the guise of a rat-catcher with a hair cap on his head, a buff girdle about his waist and a tame rat in a little box by his side. Meeting with Mr. Portman, the Rev. Mr. Bryant and other gentlemen, to all of whom he was well known, in the court-yard of the house, he boldly asked the squire if he had any rats to kill. The squire asked his qualifications and, hearing from him that he had been employed in the royal shipyards, told him to go in to dinner and they would try his abilities afterwards. He was handsomely entertained at the second table and then called into the parlour among a large company of ladies and gentlemen.

" Well, honest rat-catcher," says the squire, " can you lay any scheme to kill the rats without hurting my dogs ? "

" Yes, yes," replies Carew, " I shall lay it where even the cats can't climb to reach it."

" And what countryman are you ? "

" A Devonshire man, please your honour."

"What is your name?" asked the squire.

At this there were smiles and whispering and Carew saw that he had been discovered, so he spelt his name out letter by letter amid the laughter of the company.

"What scabby sheep has infected the whole flock?" he asks, looking round indignantly.

Parson Bryant confessed that he alone had spotted him, and then the gentlemen came round to shake hands with the famous Mr. Carew.

There was a Mr. Pleydell among them, and the rat-catcher delighted the company by telling them how he tricked this gentleman as a shipwrecked sailor out of a guinea and a suit of clothes. At this the company and Pleydell himself laughed heartily and the latter wagered a guinea he could not do it again. Others of the company challenged our hero to attempt to deceive them and then discover himself, and he agreed to consider the matter. A generous subscription was then made for him and he went his way. As he passed through the hall the Rev. Mr. Bryant whispered to him that there was to be a gathering of all the party at Pleydell's a week hence, and Carew nodded his thanks.

The day arriving he went to the barber's and was carefully shaved and, returning to the head-quarters of his friends, he there dressed himself up in some petticoats, pinned a large "dowde" or night-cap under his chin and put a high-crowned hat on his head, making himself a very worthy old country woman. He borrowed a hump-backed child of a tinker and tied two more gipsy babies on his back, and was seen off by his colleagues who were full of admiration at his resource.

Arrived at Pleydell's he comes up to the door and, putting his hand behind him, pinches one of the children to set it in a roar. This sets the dogs a-barking and out runs the maid to whom the grandmother tells the tale of the Kirton fire and how her poor daughter was lost in the flames and she has to beg her way with the three poor children. Carew's tears mingle with the maid-servant's, and she carries the sad tale to the ladies who send her out with half a crown and some broth, which the servants give to the poor children as they listen to the old lady's tale.

At this moment the gentlemen come in from the stables, and Carew pinches the children as a cue to play their parts. Pleydell comes up to him saying, "Where did you come from, old woman ? "

Carew mumbles out the Kirton fire story with many tears.

" Damn you," says Pleydell, " there has been more money collected for Kirton than ever Kirton was worth."

However, he gave her a shilling and the rest of the gentlemen contributed, and then they went into the house and the old woman hobbled away.

The party had hardly reached the hall when their ears were saluted with a Tantivy ! Tantivy ! and a Halloo ! to the dogs. They rushed out, there was no one about and Pleydell swore that the old lady was none other than Carew, for that was his call. On this a servant was sent to fetch her back. The party examined his disguise with interest, congratulated him on his success and generously rewarded him for the mirth he had procured them.

This was the attitude of most of the gentry and clergy towards Carew's exploits. The idea that obtaining money by false pretences was a crime had not arrived. They regarded the whole business as a merry practical joke in which if the knave got the better of them he was worthy of his reward, which they did not grudge him since he had given them laughter and entertainment. All the picaresque novels and memoirs of rogues of the day are full of similar jests and practical jokes. It is difficult for moderns to enter into the spirit of the thing in an age when practical joking has, happily, gone out of fashion, and cheating is only permissible when it is done solemnly on a vast scale by highly respectable people. Even then, as in Carew's day, it must be successful or it will not be applauded.

But Carew, owing to his genius as an actor and his skill in choosing his scene and his story, was a continuous success. He was received by the Duke of Bolton, he drew contributions from the Mayor and the Bishop of Salisbury, and three times in one day in different disguises did he receive alms from his kind friend, Sir William Courtenay, who was delighted with the entertainment. These tales he told Rachel Goadby in his later years, but only on one occasion does he express to her any sorrow at his cheats. He was making his way to Totnes when he turned aside to visit the pretty little village of Stoke Gabriel where the friend of his youth, the Rev. Mr. Osborn, was minister of the parish. To him he appeared as a shipwrecked sailor, asking him for the thanksgiving of the Church for the preservation of himself and his comrades in a recent storm which had destroyed his ship. To his dismay Mr. Osborn readily granted his request. The reverend gentleman summoned the villagers together in the church, the shipwrecked sailor was put into a front pew and a handsome collection was made for him. Carew's professional pride forbade him from disclosing his identity and stopping the ardour of the good priest, but before he continued his journey he insisted on his retaining the bulk of the collection for the poor of his parish. Thirty years after when he is telling his reminiscences to Mrs. Goadby he speaks of the incident " with regret and compunction of mind," for though he was proud of it as an artist, he felt that in jesting with sacred subjects he had not acted in a gentlemanly way.

He was now nearly thirty years of age and was not only

a great favourite of the old King of the Mendicants, one Clause Patch, but was regarded by the whole community with great respect and affection. So that when King Patch passed away in London full of years and the members of the community met to celebrate his funeral and to elect a new king, Carew was regarded as the candidate with the best chance of office.

The method of election was by secret ballot presided over by the elders of the community, and though there were ten candidates for the position Carew received a considerable majority of white balls and was declared duly elected, a decision that was received with great enthusiasm and was the subject of a splendid carouse.

Carew, though proud of his advancement, did not intend, as some of the older monarchs had done, to retire from active work and live on the contributions of his subjects. On the contrary, as soon as the celebrations were over, he was once again on the road. Happening to be at Fleet, near Portland Race in Dorsetshire, he heard of a ship in imminent danger of being cast away. The next morning early he was down on the beach. No one was near. He stripped off his clothes and swam to the vessel. Only one half-drowned sailor was on the wreck, and he got from him the name of the master and some particulars of the voyage. He tried hard to persuade the poor wretch to swim back with him to the shore, but the fellow had not the spirit to make the attempt and, a large sea breaking over the wreck, both were washed off the ship. Carew, who was a splendid swimmer, reached the shore, though not ·without difficulty, being much spent and his arm being wounded by the shingle.

One need hardly say that so genuine a shipwrecked sailor as this was received by the kindly inhabitants with every favour. He was taken to the house of Madame Mohun and put to bed and restored to health. Justice Farwell gave him a guinea and a genuine pass to Bristol. A large collection was made. The justice lent him his horse to ride to Dorchester, and the parson's man rode with him to show him the way.

We now come to a turn in his affairs which at the time could only be regarded as tragic, though, in so far as the incidents introduced our hero to new and glorious and successful adventures, we cannot regard it as wholly unfortunate.

There was at Barnstaple one of those sour magistrates, one of those uncomfortable people out of harmony with the age he lived in, who did not appreciate the wit and humour of Carew's exploits, and at a date when false pretences were regarded as homely fun, presumed to set up his opinion that these merry cheats, if not actually criminal, were socially undesirable. Justice Lethbridge was a bitter enemy to the whole community of mendicants, and Carew, in the shape of a poor cripple with crutches, having got nothing out of the justice as he rode home across Pitton Bridge but a threat of arrest, had managed to frighten the justice or his horse, or both, so that the latter bolted and the cripple went his way.

Carew went to Barnstaple, to see his friends, having long forgotten the churlish justice. He went into the country to call upon Squire Basset and thought he would look in on his friend, Mr. Robert Incledon, as he passed through Barnstaple on his way home. His friend was out but his clerk asked him in, saying, " How do you do, Mr. Carew ? " He was no sooner in the parlour than Justice Lethbridge, who was in the house, and hearing his name had concealed himself behind the door, sprang upon him and arrested him and had him carried to his own house.

No sooner did it spread round Barnstaple that the great Carew had been seized by Justice Lethbridge, and was in his cellars a prisoner, than several captains of vessels and

other well-known citizens, and a large number of charming
ladies made their way to the justice to intercede for him.
But the fellow was not to be tampered with, a warrant was
made out against Carew and he was carried to Exeter Castle
where he was loaded with chains to await the holding of the
Quarter Sessions.

I confess that I was greatly puzzled with Carew's narrative
of what happened at Exeter Quarter Sessions. His account
to Mrs. Goadby was that Mr. Beavis, the Chairman, refused
to tell him under what law he was convicted, but merely
announced to him that he would be banished to Maryland
for seven years. He also asserted that " out of 35 prisoners
32 were ordered into the like punishment." This sounded
irregular and illegal.

It came to my knowledge, however, that Mr. Brian S.
Miller, the Clerk of the Peace for the County of Devon, had
in recent years arranged and indexed the records of the
Quarter Sessions of the County in Exeter Castle, and thanks
to his kind assistance I was enabled to see the actual entries
and documents connected with the case. These County
records date back to the sixteenth century and are indeed a
wonderful storehouse of local history, having been collected
and tabulated with the greatest skill and care. Would that
all public bodies dealt so worthily with their muniments.

It appears from the records that Carew's arrest took place
as late as 1739 when he was forty-six years of age. From this
it seems probable that many of the adventures narrated by
Mrs. Goadby as happening after his transportation really
took place before, when he was a younger man. From the
entries in the Sessions book we learn that Carew and a felon
named King were, prior to Easter 1739, in the custody of
Tobias Brown, the master of the workhouse. The Court
orders their transfer to the custody of John Laskey the
turnkey of the common jail. They then appear before the

Quarter Sessions on May 1, 1739, and King is ordered to be transported for seven years.

The order against Carew is a very curious one but evidently purports to be made under Sections 18–20 of 13 Anne c. 26, an Act of Parliament directed against rogues and vagabonds. It sets out that Richard Beavis, a magistrate, had already committed Carew to be an apprentice or servant of one Ethelred Davy for the space of seven years, and the Court of Quarter Sessions, of which Richard Beavis was Chairman, confirms this order. This the Court was entitled to do under Section 18, as it found that Carew had been a common beggar for two years, and adjudged him to be a dangerous and incorrigible rogue within the meaning of the statute.

The Court, however, made no transportation order against Carew but merely remitted him to jail to be delivered to Davy when he asked for him. Under Section 18 Davy was now entitled to detain, keep, employ, and set Carew to work either within the realm or in any of His Majesty's Plantations or any British Factory beyond Seas.

But this was a personal responsibility of Davy, and Section 19 enacted that no one should be sent beyond seas until his master entered into a recognizance of £40 to supply him with proper necessaries and discharge him in seven years. This does not seem to have been done.

At the Midsummer Sessions held on July 7, Carew is recorded to be still in jail. At this Court three vagabonds are sentenced to transportation for seven years. They had been wandering about the county, with their tongues doubled back in their mouths, pretending to be dumb sailors whose tongues had been cut off by Algerine pirates. There is also another transport order against other prisoners for felony.

As regards all these offenders the procedure is shown in the actual documents which are still in existence. Beavis and another magistrate, Caleb Inglett, are appointed by the Court to make a contract with Ethelred Davy to ship these prisoners to America. Davy was a merchant of position in Exeter. He had been sheriff and mayor of the city. He seems to have done a considerable trade with the magistrates in shipping convicts against whom actual transport orders had been made. Carew was not in this legal position.

There are two documents under seal and stamped, dated July 18, 1739, in which Beavis and Inglett carry out the arrangements about the various convicts with Davy, who enters into a bond to see the prisoners are duly transported. In neither of these documents as originally drafted does Carew's name appear among the list of convicts. But his name is written in, in another handwriting, in Davy's bond relating to the other prisoners. It could not, I think, be contended that this was a proper bond under Section 19, nor is it clear to me that Davy had any power to sell his apprentice abroad, but only to work him there if he had a plantation or factory of his own.

Be this as it may, the Court never ordered Carew to be transported, and maybe the magistrates friendly with his family would have objected to such a course. What seems to have happened was that some of the magistrates were desirous of getting rid of Carew and that Davy was willing to oblige them, as he was doing a large and remunerative trade in transporting men and women to the plantations. This is borne out by Carew's own story that when Captain Froade was trying to sell him to a planter as a schoolmaster he told him that Carew " was a great scholar and was only sent over on account of having disobliged some gentlemen ; that he had no Indenture with him but he should have him for seven years."

Carew lay in jail until after the Michaelmas Sessions, and although his friends visited him during his six months'

R

imprisonment at Exeter and were exceedingly liberal to him, no legal proceedings seem to have been taken on his behalf, and in due course he said farewell to his beloved wife and daughter and embarked at Falmouth for Maryland on the *Juliana* with the rest of Davy's convicts.

Arrived at Talbot County, Captain Froade, who had about a hundred prisoners on board, men and women, announced that a sale of his goods would take place the next morning.

The men were ordered to be shaved and the women to put on their best caps, the planters of the neighbourhood flocked on board and the sale took place, the joiners, black-smiths, weavers and tailors fetching good prices. One or two asked what Carew was by trade, to which he answered a rat-catcher, mendicant and dog-merchant, but the skipper intervened and assured them he was a man of humour and a great scholar, and would make an excellent schoolmaster. However, there were no bidders and he remained unsold. The captain then took him on shore to try and sell him privately, and whilst he was at a tavern, Carew made his escape. He was, however, soon arrested as a runaway and, refusing out of delicacy the generous offer of some Bideford captains named Hervey and Hopkins, who offered to purchase their countryman and set him free, he was returned to Captain Froade. The captain was very wroth with him, for Carew had boasted that he would find him back in England when he got there, and having handed him over to the boatswain for the discipline of the cat-of-nine tails he had a heavy iron collar or pot-hook riveted round his neck, such as they used for runaway slaves, and told him he would be taken to the mines.

The Bideford captains, coming on board when Captain Froade was away, made interest for him with the boatswain and mate, and told Carew his one chance of liberty was to get among the friendly Indians who would relieve him of his collar, and he might live among them until a chance of escape arrived. His escape was cleverly engineered by his friends, who, providing him with a compass, some biscuits and cheese and rum, saw him off into the bush, making for the mountains.

His reception by the Indians was very friendly, his collar was removed and he lived among them very happily, enjoying the hunting and open-air life. But after a while he took occasion to leave his friends and made his way, after many adventures, to Newcastle, Pennsylvania. Here he played the part of a kidnapped Quaker by the name of John Elworthy of Bristol, and, thanks to his skill in histrionic mendicancy, he travelled from place to place, first in one character and then in another, at the expense of the inhabitants, until he arrived at New London, where he agreed to take the run to England with one Captain Rogers for ten guineas, ten gallons of rum, ten pounds of sugar, ten pounds of tobacco and ten pipes.

They had a fair wind and a smooth run and the vessel was off Lundy Island in a month and three days. The sailors were now eagerly on the look-out for any man-of-war that might be about, for they knew that their chance of seeing their homes was very small if they met with a King's ship in want of men. Carew, who was taking no chances, determined to have the smallpox ; the appearance of which he skilfully simulated, pricking his arms and breast with a needle, and rubbing them with bay-salt and gunpowder.

A pilot came off to them from Clovelly to take them up the Channel, and Carew gazed lovingly at Appledore and Bideford and Barnstaple as they ran along the coast. Early in the morning they were anchored off Bristol, and, to their dismay, saw the *Ruby*, man-of-war, lying in the road with Jack ensign and pennant hoisted. The poor sailors were panic-stricken, but Carew, who had several times rushed on deck in delirium with only a blanket round him, had been taken back to his hammock where he now reposed in some hope. The *Ruby* was commanded by the famous Samuel Goodere, who was appointed to the command in November, 1740, and arrested in January, 1741, for the murder of his brother. This shows that Carew was only absent from England for about a year.

A man-of-war's boat with a lieutenant in command was soon alongside Captain Rogers's ship and the lieutenant insisted on taking all his men. When he found Carew in a terrible state of sickness, that worthy begged to be taken to the man-of-war to be blooded, and tried to persuade the lieutenant that he had not really got the smallpox. This clever ruse succeeded admirably. The lieutenant clapped his snuff-box to his nose and swore that he would not take him on board for five hundred pounds, and advised the captain to put him on shore at once. Carew begged hopelessly to be allowed to die on board, but the captain and the lieutenant insisted on his being lowered into a boat and taken on shore. Captain Rogers, honestly enough, gave him a draft on his Bristol agent for the money owing to him, though he never expected it to be presented, the lieutenant threw him half a guinea, and the poor sick man was huddled into his clothes with a blanket round his shoulders and put on shore with commands not to go into Bristol, where he might infect the whole city.

Caution and fear of the press-gang determined him not to be cured of smallpox until he reached Bristol. Once within the walls of the city he visited a barber and then repaired to the mumpers' head-quarters known as " Mendicants' Hall " on Mile Hill, where he received an enthusiastic reception from his subjects. Here he heard the joyful news that his dear wife and daughter were well, and the next day,

having cashed his draft, he made his way towards his native
county in search of his dear ones.

His progress through Devonshire was indeed a royal
progress. Squires, parsons, doctors and farmers, proud of
their countryman, turned out to give him welcome, and
though he had many offers of hospitality his perilous travels
had only whetted his appetite for a vagrant life. Having
enjoyed a few weeks' feasting and hunting among his equals
and found his dear wife and daughter, he once again took
the road in search of new and kingly adventures.

Among his schoolfellows at Blundell's of about his own
age, and with whom he was on intimate terms, was Richard
Annesley, sixth Earl of Anglesey, for some time governor of
Wexford. He had married a daughter of Captain Prust, of
Monckton, near Bideford, and had long ago deserted the lady
and was now living in Ireland. It occurred to Carew that
he had never seen that country and that he would make his
way there. He begged along the road to Holyhead and
begged a passage across, and finding my lord was not at
Dublin but had gone to Blessington, set out the next day in
search of him. Arrived at a tavern where my Lord and his
friends were staying, he told the host that he would speak
with him. The man demurred, looking at his ragged figure
with some contempt.

" Tell him I am an old schoolfellow of his and want to
see him," said Carew in commanding tones, and the innkeeper did as he was bid.

My Lord and two gentlemen who were with him came
out, and as soon as Carew mentioned his name my Lord
remembered him at once.

" Ha ! Mr. Carew. Is it you, man ? Walk in ! Walk in !"

" What," said one of the captains who was with him,
" is this old Carew ? " for his fame had spread over Ireland
though this was his first visit there.

He was now introduced to all the company, who listened with pleasure to the old schoolfellows' talk of their dog-stealing adventures at Tiverton. One of the party, putting in a word for himself, made the suggestion that Carew might " get him a good Pointer," which our hero promised to consider. Lord Annesley insisted on taking Mr. Carew home with him, and, having found him the necessary clothing and equipment, introduced him to the Irish gentry in Dublin and the neighbourhood, by whom he was received with true Irish hospitality.

And that was the way with our hero throughout life, and his strange method of living was by no means condemned by people of his own or of more exalted rank. They recognized that here was a man of breeding, education and genius, who, to entertain his love of adventure, had dedicated himself to the vagabond life, where his merits had been recognized by the community he served, and the community he preyed upon, so that wherever he went he was received with the respect and affection due to a man who had proved his worth in the profession of his adoption.

From time to time he made journeys to Russia, Sweden, Norway and Denmark, returning home at intervals to see his people and continue his depredations, and it is curious that though he was more likely to be discovered in the West of England where he was so well known, yet that was his chief hunting ground to the end. The reason probably being that in the West he had intimate local knowledge of places, people and affairs and, to the professional cheat, be he beggar, quack, medium or fortune-teller, knowledge of the affairs of others is a valuable stock-in-trade.

" What we are now going to relate will raise an honest indignation in the Breast of every true Lover of Liberty." Thus Mrs. Rachel Goadby, and for my part I concur and for the same reasons. What happened was this. Mr. Carew and his wife were on a visit to some old friends at Exeter. There is no evidence that he was there in a professional capacity or engaged in any of his merry cheats. On the contrary, he was staying with friends openly as any other citizen might do.

One summer evening strolling to Topsham he walked along the quay admiring the beauties of nature when he saw Merchant Davy approaching him with several captains of vessels that were lying in the river. The merchant had certainly been worsted in encounters with Carew, but that he should bear malice on that account was unthinkable.

As he reached the group Davy called out : " Ha ! Mr. Carew ; you are come in a right time, as you came home for your own pleasure you shall now go over for mine."

They then laid hands upon him and, overpowered by numbers, they forced him on a boat and carried him on board the *Philleroy*, Captain Simmons, bound for America with convicts. In vain he demanded to be taken before a magistrate and beseeched to be allowed to send a message to his wife. No mercy was shown to him, and he was chained in the hold with the convicts night and day and fell into a fever. For three weeks the boat lay in the river waiting for a favourable wind, and though his distracted wife sought him and inquired for him at all his houses of usual resort, so well did Merchant Davy and the captains keep their secret that his disappearance remained a mystery.

When he arrived for a second time in America and the planters came on deck some of them recognized him as " the man Captain Froade had brought over and put a pot-hook upon," and though they were interested in his adventures and civil enough to give him a glass on occasion they would not make a bid for him as he seemed a very doubtful security to invest in.

The skipper, however, kept a sharp eye on him and often told him with an oath that he would take care that he should not get home before his skipper on this occasion, as he had managed to do with Captain Froade. How he would have disposed of him we shall never know, for Carew, noticing many canoes and boats alongside the vessel, slipped over the side one dark night into one of them and made for the shore, where he took to the woods.

A hue-and-cry was raised at once and sailors and planters were on his track, but though they searched the woods they did not find Carew, who had climbed a high tree where he spent the night in safety. Early the next morning he went deeper into the bush. He knew that his only chance of ultimate escape was to get to Duck's Creek and steal a canoe and get across the Delaware River, but then his pursuers knew that too. For eight days he lived in the daytime hidden in a tree and often heard his hunters and their dogs crashing through the woods in his neighbourhood. In the early morning before it was light he would raid a planter's house for provisions, or milk a cow in the fields, and by short passages he made his way to Duck's Creek, arriving there on the eleventh day of his escape.

He ran down to the water-side that very night, but found every canoe had been securely chained, and by no means could he sever the chains or uproot the posts to which they were attached. Here was checkmate, and the poor fellow sank on the ground in despair. When the sun rose he saw in the fields down by the river several horses grazing, and as he watched them with weary, despairing eyes there came into his mind a memory of his boyhood when he stood on Shaldon Ness and saw his gallant cousin, Sir Henry Carew, win his glorious wager with my Lord Clifford. For this Carew, having little money, staked his royalty of Combworthy against my Lord's hundreds that he would swim his horse across Teignmouth Bar, to a lumber barrel moored five miles out at sea and back again to Shaldon beach. And this, as the world knows, he had done successfully to the surprise

and delight of his countrymen. What a Carew had done a
Carew could do, thought our hero, and he crept stealthily
down to the field where the horses were grazing. He had no
difficulty in making friends with a fine young horse well fit for his
purpose, and he fashioned a kind of bridle from his handkerchief
and, stripping off his clothes which he wrapped in a bundle, he
drew the animal gently to the bank of the river and, leaping on
to his back, urged him with his knees into the stream.

The good horse snorted and neighed to his companions,
but made for the opposite shore as though he guessed his
rider's will. Carew had no real hope of the horse making
the whole three miles' passage, but if he could get some of
the way across he would venture to swim the rest. Contrary
to his expectations, however, the animal carried him right
across the river and after coasting along the sandy mud of
the shore landed him in a little creek.

Our hero on dismounting fell upon his knees and uttered
a fervent prayer of thanks for his delivery and then, turning
to the brave horse to whom he owed his life and liberty,
took off his bridle, kissed him and so let him go into the woods.

How he dried his clothes, was befriended by a planter
at whose house he was sick of a fever, and obtaining a pass
as a sick man slowly journeyed to Boston, we need not detail.
Suffice it that once again he returned to Bristol before his
skipper, and made his way to Exeter to find his wife and
daughter. He put up at the " Oxford Inn," and all Exeter
came to visit him and hear of his adventures. His old enemy,
Merchant Davy, was among them, for he could not believe
the tale that was going round the city and must see the thing
with his own eyes.

When he saw Carew he was convinced and said, " So you
have found your way home again, Mr. Carew ? "

" Yes, yes," replied Carew pleasantly enough, " as you
sent me for your pleasure I am come home for my own."

This witty retort made all the gentlemen right merry, and Merchant Davy not only ordered a bowl of punch to celebrate his return but proposed a collection for the hero of the occasion, which he headed with half a crown. A very handsome collection was made and more might have been collected had Carew cared to linger in Exeter, but our hero was eager to be away in search of his wife and daughter.

He had news at Castle Lane that his wife was gone towards Newtown Bushel, and he was away after her as soon as might be. At Lord Clifford's, Mrs. Ratcliffe, the housekeeper, was overjoyed to see him and said his wife had been there in mourning sorrowing for his loss and was now at home at Newtown Bushel. Carew pushed on at once and late at night arrived at his usual quarters. Everyone was a-bed and all was in darkness, but as he was calling for the woman of the house his wife heard his voice and rushed to the door calling out that it was her poor Bampfylde. The landlady thought her guest had gone crazy, and putting on some clothes and lighting a lamp went to attend her when, to her delight and surprise, she found the poor thing crying for joy in her husband's arms.

The tale might well end there, and would that truth enabled us to say that Carew and his wife had now accepted the many invitations they received from friends and relations of hospitality and support. But they certainly did not do so at this period, and more adventures and stories of merry cheats are told of Carew and his followers, and it is recorded that he visited Scotland and was with the rebels in '45. So that if he retired it was not until after that date.

Perhaps it was his last encounter with the Statute of Anne that led him to thoughts of retirement. In Moore's *History of Devon* there is a piteous letter from him to a friend named Mr. Dolle of Thorverton. He appears to have insulted a magistrate named Lewis, being, as he writes, " a little aleified "

and accused him of sending him to America. " Whereupon,"
he says, " Lewis committed me to my old home St. Thomas's
Bridewell, had me whipped round the Castle Green and
confined for six months longer to be whipped 3 times more."
This he thinks " very hard on me," and he asks Mr. Dolle
to help him.

This sentence is duly recorded in the Midsummer Quarter
Sessions Book of 1747, the whipping taking place whilst the
Court was sitting, and the last of the further three being
ordained for Christmas Sessions week. As Carew was not
discharged until Epiphany Sessions 1747, the sentence, which
under Section 6 of the statute is the legal due of incorrigible
rogues, was no doubt carried out in full.

We find him on many of his wanderings visiting Sherborne, where he used to put up at the " Sign of the Boot,"
but how he became acquainted with Mr. and Mrs. Goadby
it is difficult to understand. But that the Goadbys liked the
man, and that in the year 1749 or thereabouts Rachel Goadby
took down his tales of adventures from his own lips seems
fairly clear. Goadby was the proprietor of the *Sherborne
Mercury* which had a good circulation, and most of his pub-
lications were of a religious nature. But when he published
Carew's *Memoirs* he was not thirty, and throughout life he
was a great lover of botany and natural history, so that he
may have sought the company of Carew when he stayed at
Sherborne to discuss with him the flora and fauna of Devonshire and Dorset, which in those days gipsies knew more
about than gentlemen. And though Goadby was a noted
Whig and a respectable citizen, an admirer of Richardson
and his Pamela, a despiser of Fielding and Tom Jones, and
was moreover a deeply religious man, yet one can understand
his being drawn to the real adventures of Bampfylde-Moore
Carew in the same way that Borrow, Watts-Dunton, and other
men of letters have been fascinated by the lure of the vagrant

life. For, like all who knew him, Goadby must have found Carew a pleasant personality, knowledgeable in the things of nature and, when he was not at his pranks, excellent company.

One of Goadby's bequests was an endowment to Sherborne Church, to provide for the preaching of a sermon on the first Sunday in May on the beauties of nature. I take the man who left money for such a purpose in that age to have been an honest tolerant Christian of broad sympathies, for Churchmen then were more interested in the ugliness of theology than the beauty of nature. That Bampfylde-Moore Carew was taken into his household and that Goadby and his wife busied themselves in making a book about him cannot have been entirely a business speculation, but was undertaken, I fancy, because they found in the vagabond traits of knowledge and character that appealed to their hearts.

There is no real knowledge of the last years of our hero, though some say he won £9,000 in a lottery and lived in comfort in the West of England. The date of his death is not, as some authorities suggest, uncertain. The Bickleigh parish registers say that his wife was buried on March 27, 1757, and he was buried on June 28, 1758. This seems to bear out the suggestion that in the last years of his life Carew and his family retired to Bickleigh and lived among their friends and relations. Whether he abdicated his position as King of the Mendicants is not known, but that he was not in actual practice in his profession for some years before his decease seems reasonably probable. The fact that there seems to be no account of any funeral gathering of his subjects on the occasion of his burial rather looks as though he had severed his connexion with the honourable Society of Mendicants, and returned to the path of life from which he had so unaccountably erred and strayed. This at least we know, that, at the end of his strange adventures and wanderings, he was laid to rest with his ancestors in the graveyard of his father's church.

INDEX